Blockchain and the Supply Chain

Blockchain and the Supply Chain

Concepts, strategies and practical applications

Nick Vyas, Aljosja Beije
and Bhaskar Krishnamachari

Publisher's note

Every possible effort has been made to ensure that the information contained in this book is accurate at the time of going to press, and the publishers and author cannot accept responsibility for any errors or omissions, however caused. No responsibility for loss or damage occasioned to any person acting, or refraining from action, as a result of the material in this publication can be accepted by the publisher or the authors.

First published in Great Britain and the United States in 2019 by Kogan Page Limited

2nd Floor, 45 Gee Street	122 W 27th St, 10th Floor	4737/23 Ansari Road
London	New York, NY 10001	Daryaganj
EC1V 3RS	USA	New Delhi 110002
United Kingdom		India

www.koganpage.com

© Nick Vyas, Aljosja Beije and Bhaskar Krishnamachari 2019

The right of Nick Vyas, Aljosja Beije and Bhaskar Krishnamachari to be identified as the authors of this work has been asserted by them in accordance with the Copyright, Designs and Patents Act 1988.

ISBNs

Hardback	978 0 7494 9845 0
Paperback	978 0 7494 8402 6
E-ISBN	978 0 7494 8403 3

British Library Cataloguing-in-Publication Data

A CIP record for this book is available from the British Library.

Library of Congress Cataloging-in-Publication Data

A CIP record for this book is available from the Library of Congress.

Typeset by Integra Software Services, Pondicherry
Print production managed by Jellyfish
Printed and bound by CPI Group (UK) Ltd, Croydon CR0 4YY

CONTENTS

LIST OF FIGURES

LIST OF TABLES

FOREWORD

Blockchain. For now, it is almost as mysterious as the universe itself. Fortunately, these terrific supply chain aficionados took it upon themselves to research and write a book that both helps us understand blockchain and provides a process for deciding whether it makes sense to use it.

I have had the pleasure of knowing the authors for a couple of decades now. It's no surprise to me that these inquisitive experts from the Walton College of Business decided to tackle this project. The Walton College for years has produced excellent supply chain thought, research and practical knowledge. And as president and CEO of the Council of Supply Chain Management Professionals, I've witnessed first hand how the authors have shaped, and continue to shape, our discipline with their wide array of experiences. They help ensure that we – CSCMP and the entire supply chain management field – innovates, evolves and remains relevant, which in many ways is the heartbeat of our industry.

Supply chain management is very much like the switch and the light. We flip the switch and the light comes on, but we don't call our power company and thank them. We don't spend time thinking about how the light came on. We give it very little thought, unless, of course, we flip the switch and nothing happens. And when do supply chain folks get called? When something goes wrong.

But that's changing, and in many ways has changed, largely because innovations in technology (such as blockchain) have helped supply chain professionals become more valued voices within their organizations and industries. We have seen our field grow from a cost to be managed to a powerful weapon in modern global business. Back in 1980, logistics costs in the United States were about 16 per cent of GDP; today, they are 7.7 percent (or about $1.5 trillion). We have got more productive, more efficient and more sophisticated with our technologies, allowing for the redeployment of people to more value-added positions.

I know I am biased about our discipline and its impact, but I'm confident supply chain management improves the financial position of companies and economies. Our stature and credibility are increasing, and innovations with technology is a huge reason why. We have benefited from decades of technologies and subsequent systems, with improved business processes built on top. Those processes have been successful because innovative and creative leaders took risks, experimented andused technology to develop new and better ways of working. New technology without changes in the way we do business only leaves us with more expensive technology. Modern supply chain leaders are perfectly positioned to prove (or disprove) that the technology is, in fact, worthy of implementing.

That will happen with blockchain, and this book will help make it happen.

Blockchain, as the authors note, is of high interest to leaders, yet with less understanding and even less activity at the moment. That undoubtedly will change if, as many suspect, this technology becomes a foundation for a better process that supply chain leaders can employ. For now, a variety of pioneers and early adopters are paving the way. The authors interviewed many of these individuals, from different industries and with a variety of understanding of blockchain, to provide a foundation of where we are, where we're going and how to best get there. Understandably, some of these practitioners remain sceptical, but others shifted their views substantially once they knew more. Several have bought into the idea that blockchain can introduce a change that creates, as Harvard professors Marco Iansiti and Karim Lakhani put it in the *Harvard Business Review*, 'new foundations for our economic and social systems'. All agree only time will tell and there's much to learn, experience and prove.

New technologies take time to implement, and they typically result in a better process than what existed before. Once installed and put into use, they become almost commonplace and we wonder how we accomplished these things in the past. Paul Lothian, a business solutions architect for Tyson Foods, put it this way when interviewed by the authors for this book: 'I believe it [blockchain] will be important, but the average Joe doesn't need to know it's affecting him until it's already affecting him.'

This book is for leaders, especially leaders in supply chain management, who want to be ahead of that knowledge curve. They want to understand blockchain's potential for the supply chain and, if it makes sense, use it to keep pace with (or move ahead of) their competition. They don't want to be caught off guard or left behind by the places this technology takes us.

If you go back in time, many of the technologies that are inherent in modern supply chains went through the same exploratory process. I recall the early days of RFID. There were sceptics, early adopters and those who really thought it would have major positive implications. What was then seemingly impossible is now a very functional part of our global supply chain experience. We are in a similar time with blockchain.

It is critical that the early stages of what can be a foundational change in supply chain management is supported by the diligence the authors have demonstrated. This book describes how blockchain applies and can apply to supply chain management. The notion of a "transparent" supply chain, where information is available to all key participants at the same time and cannot be altered, is very logical. The authors provide insight into why it's so difficult and what could be done about it.

They also provide a real road map to get going. This is often the most difficult step in any journey. They take us through definitions – and there are several – and into use cases and pilots. Importantly, they also explain how to evaluate pilots and provide insight into dealing with the plethora of opinions of value that will likely emerge.

No one has all the answers. But the authors' research and deep passion to find out all we can and anticipate future options is laid out in an easy-to-understand fashion. The most successful supply chain leaders by their very nature are inquisitive about new technologies. They'll absorb this content and make their own judgments, but they will certainly be better equipped as the blockchain future unfolds.

I had the pleasure of spending twenty-five years in the food industry, learning and leading supply chains and the organizations that made great strides by using new technologies. I vividly recall the leaders who took it upon themselves to research and advance difficult concepts, most of which became realities that we all benefit from today. This is what is happening with our authors and this book regarding blockchain. I love and I am passionate about this discipline. This book matters, and I know you will not only enjoy it, but that by reading it you will be so much better prepared for the journey.

Rick Blasgen
President and CEO, Council of Supply
Chain Management Professionals

PREFACE

Why this book?

Developments in information technology are rapidly changing the supply chain management rulebook. Thanks to the World Wide Web, we now have access to unprecedented amounts of data and computing power, providing the foundation needed for the development of artificial antelligence, the Internet of Things and blockchain applications that will allow us to automate as opposed to digitize supply chain operations. Of these technologies, blockchain is not only the newest, but probably conceptually and practically the most difficult to comprehend. And while there have been ample academic, trade and popular publications on blockchain, they are either too technical or lack the necessary depth to be of use for supply chain management practitioners and researchers.

Blockchain and the Supply Chain demystifies the subject, providing the reader with insight and awareness of blockchain technology and how to integrate it into a business plan as an effective supply chain tool.

Structure of the book

- Chapter 1 and 2 provide a contextual understanding of supply chain management. Beginning with a historical perspective, we look at the specific challenges of today's supply chain as well as introducing a number of concepts and the SCOR model that are used later on in the book.

- Chapter 3 and 4 provide an introduction into blockchain, AI and IoT, giving the reader the required technology background for the rest of the book. Complex concepts such as hashing algorithms and asymmetric cryptography are explained in an intuitive way.

- Chapters 5 and 6 are bridging chapters, integrating the supply chain management chapters with the technology chapters. Hence, these chapters focus on the discussion for what problems in the supply chain blockchain is an actual solution and what the expected impact is in terms of supply chain performance of the technology.

- Chapters 7 and 8 feature actual blockchain use-cases, offering an in-depth look at the opportunities and challenges blockchain and the other technologies have to offer. The last chapter of the book addresses the business case for innovation.

How to use this book

As each of the chapters can be read in isolation, instructors are free to mix and match the chapters, based on their specific needs. However, we do advise keeping the structure of the book in mind. Supplementary to the book, online resources have been created to further enhance your learning in this subject matter, including slides, discussion questions, case studies and research ideas. You can download the resources at **www.koganpage.com/bsc**.

The evolution of the supply chain

01

How we got here

The global supply chain is a worldwide technological phenomenon that can only be truly understood through examining its evolution over time. If we look at a historical timeline, technology does not simply begin when a tool or component is physically created. Instead, technology begins as a result of, and extension of, the catalyst of natural human instinct. Human instinct and technological evolution are interdependent, as each shapes the other in an endless feedback loop. If we look closely at the global supply chain, we can observe three unique dimensions of evolution: trade, technology and micro–macro patterns. Although trending technologies such as artificial intelligence (AI) and the Internet of Things (IoT) tend to dominate present-day discussions, the three unique dimensions identified above are foundational, and therefore play a unique role in the future of the global supply chain.

This book will examine the relationship between the global supply chain and emerging blockchain technology. Blockchain is an open, distributed ledger that can record peer-to-peer transactions efficiently and in a verifiable way. This kind of technology has the ability to radically disrupt each and every industry. It will certainly transform the supply chain, and the possibilities for supply chain integration are growing exponentially. This book will provide a historical context for these technological changes and trends, and will examine various use-cases. There are also some reflections on the ethics of technological evolution, potential abuses, as well as the limitations of energy usage and natural resources.

The power of unceasing curiosity

Ever since the dawn of civilization, people have been perpetually curious about everything around them. Within the natural course of evolution, a strong instinct to explore was instilled in early humans. Simply gathering information, which satisfies the most natural human instinct, has come to be one of the most rewarding endeavours. Today, information is one of the most significant assets any individual, firm or nation can possess.

The core ideas of the supply chain

The supply chain in its earliest form can be spoken of regarding our species migrating out of the African continent. The sole purpose of a person searching for food and shelter and striving for the continuity of its race can be seen from the perspective of their accessibility to the essential supplies needed to survive and thrive.

We can see a trend here (Figure 1.1) of the earliest forms of travel and deduce the most fundamental reasons for such explorations. Climatic changes, the uncertainty of what lies beyond, and the sheer intellectual curiosity along with information exchanges and the importance of mutual trust and collaboration are all attributes integral to the core supply chain ideas that we see today. Such exploration and settlements can be linked to the basic concepts of supply and demand. Even though these attributes couldn't be quantified at the time, discernment through senses and instinct was enough for meeting requirements and ensuring the existence of the race.

As importantly, climatic shifts played a significant role. The last Ice Age began about 110,000 years ago and lasted until about 11,700 years ago. It is believed that around that time the human population was reduced to a few million that survived only due to migration to habitable areas.

It is very likely that in such circumstances genetic drift and founder effects may have been maximized. When flying through continents today within a time span of hours, we tend to undermine the complexities that went into human migration at the time. Having more complicated needs than the animals around them, exploring unknown territories was a daunting feat, to say the least. The migrating humans didn't know what existed beyond the forests or the mountains. Moving along with groups of equally informed (or uninformed) people, they tested their mental boundaries by exploring real and imagined horizons through the process of migration.

Figure 1.1   The earliest humans left Africa through the Bab-el-Mandeb Strait on the Red Sea and the Nile Valley, heading to the Middle East

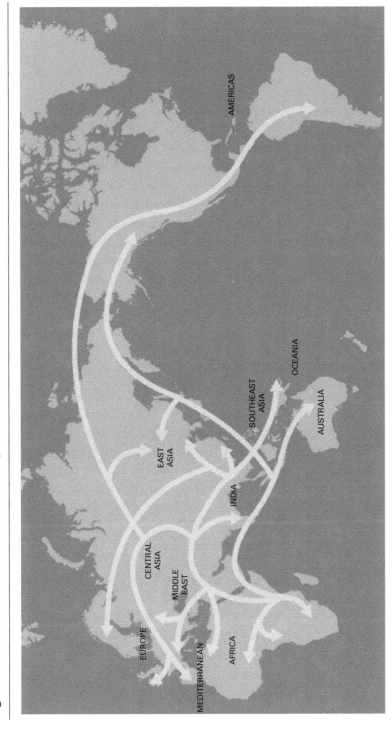

Information and innovation: the twin engines of evolution

The application of operations excellence in today's day and age and optimizing costs, errors, and factors that are critical to the customer (CTX), we tend to overlook the structure of thought humans developed a long time ago to overcome challenges through innovations. For example, the advent of tailoring and clothing oneself from the fur of animals and constructing shelters for storing meat and grains – overcoming difficulties through sheer improvisation and innovation is not new to humanity.

In today's supply chain, storage and obsolescence costs are meticulously monitored. Many take for granted the evolution of those concepts. It was because the brain developed and adapted to conditions to help the body survive by performing its most vital function – 'figuring it out'. We see adaptations regarding visible physical traits, but sometimes we fail to look at how we as a race are intellectually developing to achieve a state of utmost security.

The earliest supply chain network

It was about 8,000 BC when the Neolithic Revolution introduced agriculture as a way of life. Agriculture brought about a structured form of settlements, labour, trade and development of political, hierarchical ideologies. The supply chain in its most archaic form existed during this time.

In 5,500 BC the earliest known civilization came to exist in Sumer, Mesopotamia. An extensive network of canals, irrigation, and centralized labour came into being, creating one of the earliest forms of a supply chain network.

Due to a lack of historical records for most of human evolution, it is impossible to know what the humans 'felt' at early milestones of history. The need to record history and keep some written record came about much later – around the 6th millennium BC – when humans in certain parts of the world developed a sense of 'information', which would be of utmost importance for the survival of the human race.

Information sharing – one of the essential parts of supply chains today – came to exist in its earliest form during 3400–3200 BC in Mesopotamia, Egypt, China and Mesoamerica at different periods, but conveying the same concept. The idea of passing along information through written text was the beginning of the exchange of information and knowledge sharing.

Egypt: the cradle of supply-chain innovation

One of the most iconic moments in recorded history was the construction of the pyramids of Giza, built over 20 years around 2560 BC. One wonders about the advanced concepts of transport, carriage and development. Imagine how the Egyptians might have carried massive blocks of stone from one point to another, cut them to an exact appropriate shape and levelled the multiple layers of stone one on top of another to create the marvel that we see today. What is even more surprising is the materials used, as they have lasted in the dry climatic conditions of a desert for thousands of years.

The Egyptian civilization has birthed many concepts – including the creation of the solar calendar – that we take for granted today. The knowledge and exchange of information at that time were probably far more refined than people today realize.

Then there was knowledge

Education, being one of the keynotes for streamlining people's thoughts and recording the ideas in a manner so that one can continue to research further without trying to re-invent the wheel a hundred times over, was given a structured form in 385 BC. The Greek philosopher Plato, a disciple of Socrates, founded a philosophical school, the Academy, at Akademia in Athens, Greece.

The Academy is known to have produced many illustrious alumni. There, Plato taught many of the brilliant minds of the day, including the famous Greek philosopher Aristotle. Aristotle, in turn, mentored Alexander the Great and played a key role in one of the most inspired military enterprises the world has ever seen.

All this brought about the creation of institutions of learning where education was imparted in a structured and well-defined form. The birth of the discipline of philosophy itself provided a way to deal with existential dilemmas and brought about a different thought process that was acknowledged by many.

How great empires furthered the supply chain

Even though the concept of an urban centre was not developed until the founding of the city of Rome in 8th century BC, there were many fortifications that played the role of regional marketplaces. The first Greek colonies in Thrace were founded in the 8th century BC.

Darius III, the last king (336–330 BC) of the Achaemenid dynasty, was decisively defeated by Alexander the Great at the Battle of Issus (333 BC). The invincibility of Alexander the Great's Macedonian army is chiefly attributed to its logistics structure, which set it apart from other regiments of the time. It is well noted how he would gather intelligence about the marching route, the climate of the region, stocks and resources available along the way, and choose courses that ran along the rivers in order to have ready access to food and water (Bernard, 2017). We also read accounts of Alexander the Great storing wine and other food items in pre-modern, makeshift refrigerators, which were nothing but large pits dug in the ground to hold ice. Not only did these concepts introduce new ways of doing things, but they also inspired scholars to think on them deeply, resulting in them glorifying Alexander to a 'great' extent and justifiably so.

In 49 BC the massive conflict between Julius Caesar and Pompey the Great led to the Roman Civil War. These events were written down in the form of plays, poetry and literature for record keeping. A fascinating thing we see here is that people at that time recorded events by way of various forms of art so that the information appealed to the generations to follow. They had understood that the best way to keep the flow of information going was to make it as appealing to the senses as possible.

When we see such shifts and lands being conquered one after the other, and the consequent resettlement of populations, we always perceive it from the prisms of glory and who won or lost, who gained and who did not. One can look deeper into the fact that even though there was so much land around with abundant resources, all these wars were fought for particular pieces of land and for specific cities that were hubs of trade and commerce. People, kings and scholars alike understood the importance of conquering lands where trade and commerce were flourishing. They looked at architecture and culturally rich cities that housed people with diverse skills that would make a civilization flourish. Of course, military might was crucial for survival, but the progress and the prosperity of a society depended on the artisans, traders and providers of goods and services.

All these events regarding the advancement of civilizations suggest that the rise of the thriving urban centres that attracted conquerors and invaders could be attributed to early supply chain concepts which catered to commerce and utilization of resources in the best manner possible.

In another part of the world, in 268 BC, Ashoka the Great was crowned the emperor of the Mauryan Empire in ancient India. Historical records of this time were kept better than records of subsequent periods, due to advanced

Figure 1.2 The rise of the thriving urban centres led to early supply chain concepts which catered to commerce and utilization of resources

Figure 1.3   In 300 BC trading opened on routes of the Silk Road

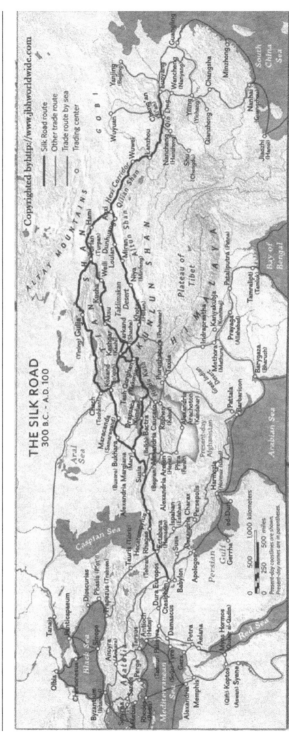

SOURCE Gandhi (2016)

record keeping. From trade and commerce to education, architecture, and art, this period saw a lot of progress. Ashoka the Great organized the digging of wells and large-scale planting of trees along roads across his kingdom. He founded public gardens, hospitals and institutions of learning for women.

A few decades later, a monumental construction project commenced in China. In 221 BC, the construction of the Great Wall of China began along China's historical northern borders to prevent the invasion of the nomadic tribes. Labour, procurement and transportation of material – all this involved supply chain planning and implementation methods that were far ahead of their time.

In 127 BC trading opened on routes of the Silk Road. This marked a great milestone in the development of trade, transportation, supply chain, logistics and commerce as a whole. Exchange of goods, the barter system, the price system, currencies, calculating surplus and scarcity concerning price, etc all come about in a very structured manner from this event.

The movement of people and goods: Faster. Higher. Further

Modes of transport

Land

The most critical historical invention, which revolutionized land transport concerning the exchange of goods over long distances, was the wheel (3500 BC). Initially, wheels were used to make wheel-thrown pottery, and were subsequently used in carts. From trucks wheeling to airplanes landing on their wheels, it is easy to see how wheels have created a platform for the rapid growth of the supply chain as an aspect of human evolution.

In 181–234 CE the wheelbarrow was invented in China by Chuko Liang to transfer supplies to wounded soldiers. This event signified a milestone regarding transport and shifting goods and supplies on a small scale.

Ground transportation witnessed a significant advancement in 1662 when Blaise Pascal designed the first horse-drawn public bus that ran on a regular route. In 1672 Ferdinand Verbiest built the first steam-powered car. Steam was being put to the test as a reliable power source at that time – many inventors were trying to develop prototypes of machines and systems that could be powered by steam. One of the most important inventions that revolutionized locomotion and movement is believed to be the steam engine. This transformed inter-country and inter-continental transport. In 1781 Scottish engineer James Watt patented a steam engine that produced continuous rotary motion.

The automobile industry exists in the form it does today due to the innovations that it went through back then. In 1883 Karl Benz invented the first car powered by an internal combustion engine. He called it the Benz Patent Motorwagen.

In 1908 Henry Ford developed the assembly line method of automobile manufacturing with the introduction of the Ford Model T. This defines a famous mark regarding production and trade that moulded the present-day perception of supply chains.

Water

Water transport is the most essential mode of movement of goods today, carrying 95 per cent of the world's transported tonnage by weight. Around 3500 BC people of the Egyptian Civilization were using riverboats as means of transport on the River Nile. The invention of the Compass Dial in 1350 CE by Ibn al-Shatir marked a milestone for both sea and land transport. Now ships and caravans could move along a predetermined line and reach destinations with proper voyage plans instead of being guided by the stars.

Figure 1.4 In 1908 Henry Ford developed the assembly line method of automobile manufacturing

SOURCE Hulton Archive, Getty Images

Sea transport made good progress regarding innovation, with the Portuguese, Spanish, Dutch and British continuously looking at avenues to enhance their fleets. In 1819 SS Savannah was the first vessel to cross the Atlantic Ocean partly under steam power. It arrived at Liverpool, England having started its voyage from Savannah, Georgia.

Travelling on water wasn't enough for human beings. One had to go under the water as well. So, in 1620 CE Cornelius Van Drebbel invented the first practical submarine. This could be manoeuvred 12–15 feet underwater for a couple of hours.

Air

Throughout history humans never stopped imagining better and faster ways to move goods and people. In addition to land and water, they had to be airborne. The first successful attempt was created when the Montgolfier brothers launched the first hot air balloons in 1783. This was a remarkable time during which the Montgolfier brothers were glorified for their creation and were depicted in many forms of art. There was flair, fashion, and style in the air now and it was well indicated by their designs of the hot air balloon itself.

Figure 1.5   In 1620 CE Cornelius Van Drebbel invented the first practical submarine

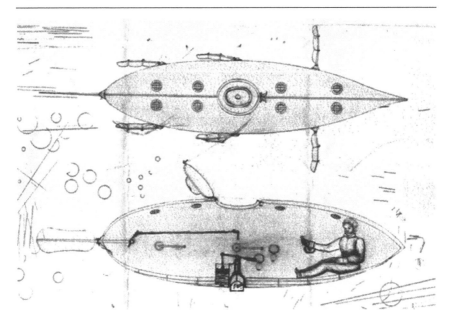

In 1903 Orville Wright and Wilbur Wright flew the first motor-driven airplane, sparking the potential for aviation movement of goods. Aviation is a big part of today's supply chain, with airplanes transporting valuable items all over the globe. FedEx, UPS, DHL and many others use planes with a fleet ranging from 20–75 jets to carry cargo.

Containerization

A significant landmark in the evolution of supply chain is the concept of 'containerization' – a system of freight transport using intermodal containers (also called shipping containers and ISO containers). All containers have standardized dimensions, with 40, 20 and 45 feet being most common. In 1955 a former trucking company owner Malcolm McLean worked with engineer Keith Tantlinger to develop the modern intermodal container. The challenge was to design a shipping container that could efficiently be loaded onto ships and would hold securely on long sea voyages.

Figure 1.6   A major landmark in the evolution of supply chain is the development of the concept of containerization

Modern waves of migration

The supply chain is greatly impacted during times of mass migration. Several major migration waves shaped the world as it is today. The Great Atlantic Migration from Europe to North America took place in the 1840s. From 1801 to 1914 about five million migrants, and between the First and Second World Wars approximately six million, moved from European to Asiatic Russia (Siberia).

Forced migrations for the slave trade and mass expulsions have been very controversial and sensitive topics of human history. Although they have had a significant impact on history and international relations, these events have been much less mentioned and recorded. The largest slave migrations were brought about by European slave traders operating in Africa from the 16th to the 19th century. There are debatable counts that nearly 20 million slaves were consigned to the Americas during this time. As they were transported by sea, countless died during these voyages across the Atlantic.

The most significant mass expulsions were done by Nazi Germany, which deported 7–8 million people during the Second World War (1939–45). Also, the Soviet Union expelled 9–10 million ethnic Germans from eastern Europe into Germany in the closing year of the war.

Since World War II the most significant migration involved groups from developing countries moving to industrialized nations. Some 13 million migrants became permanent residents of Western Europe from the 1960s through the 1980s, and more than 10 million permanent immigrants were admitted legally to the United States in that same period.

There was another massive expulsion count in South Asia. It is believed that nearly 14 million people migrated during the partition of British India into India and Pakistan in the late 1940s. Most of the migrations in the second half of the 20th century were refugees fleeing wars. In the 1980s, 3–4 million people fled Afghanistan.

Other than that, we see that the dominant trend in internal migration during the 20th century has been the movement from rural to urban areas. As a consequence of that, urban growth since World War II has naturally been very rapid in much of the world, particularly in developing countries.

Japan's reconstruction and the gift of TQM

Japan's rapid growth from the 1950s to the 1980s is credited to the adoption by the Japanese industry of Deming's quality management principles that produce unprecedented levels of productivity and quality.

Japanese industrialists took to Deming's teachings with religious fervour and helped transform Japan into an industrial superpower by the 1980s that began to outperform American and European industries. Even so, Deming and his work remained unrecognized in the country of his birth.

In 1980 an NBC TV documentary titled 'If Japan can, why can't we?' aired about how and why Japan's industry was beating that of the US. The TV documentary not only popularized Deming's work in the United States, but it also helped kick-start a quality control movement.

In 1982 Deming published his famed quality management philosophy based on 14 principles of management in the book *Quality, Productivity, and Competitive Position*.

In 1984 the United States Navy adopted the teachings of Deming to improve its operational effectiveness. The Navy termed the initiative 'total quality management' (TQM) a year later. Soon, the US Federal Government adopted the TQM principles, followed by the private sector in an attempt to regain its position as the world's most competitive industry from the Japanese manufacturers.

TQM also led to the augmented development in the USA of robotics and automation, which was initially invented in the US but taken for widespread use in Japan during the reconstruction period.

Cognitive computation: surpassing human capability

Humans have been using devices to compute since the Stone Age, and will continue to do so far into the future. Prayer beads and tally sticks made of wood and animal bones were the earliest counting devices found to be in use around 20,000 BC in the Upper Palaeolithic era. Abacus, a more compact form of a calculating tool, was being used to teach arithmetic in Babylonia around 2700 BC.

The idea of a mechanical device was possibly expressed for the first time by the Turkish polymath, Ismail al-Jazari, in his book *The Book of Knowledge of*

Ingenious Mechanical Devices in the 13th century. Jazari is also credited with inventing the first programmable analogue computer in 1206, the Castle Clock, which was a hydro-powered astronomical clock. The Castle Clock could be re-programmed to account for the changing lengths of day and night.

During the same period, a Spanish philosopher and logician Ramon Llull (1232–1315) conceptualized generative logic that many computer scientists believe to be the beginning of information science.

Llull's idea was adopted by Gottfried Wilhelm Leibniz, a German polymath, in the 16th century. Leibniz, regarded as the first computer scientist, was the one who introduced the binary numeral system for computing. In the mid-1670s Leibniz invented the machine 'stepped reckoner' that could execute all four arithmetic operations.

Meanwhile, the slide rule, invented in the 1620s, sped up the multiplication and division operations quite considerably. Calculating devices incorporating slide rules built by Edmund Gunter and William Oughtred in the mid-1630s continued to be used by engineers and scientists until the invention of the calculator.

Modern computers

An English mechanical engineer Charles Babbage is considered the 'father of the computer'. During the mid-1830s Babbage conceptualized the analytical engine, the forerunner of the modern digital computer. He envisioned the engine to have the capability of performing arithmetical operations using instructions from punched cards. The analytical engine, however, was not completed during his lifetime.

The American inventor Herman Hollerith used punched cards in the late 1880s by for data storage. His method was used in the 1890 United States Census. Hollerith's Tabulating Machine Company was renamed IBM in 1924.

When the United States instituted social security in 1935, IBM punched card systems were used to process records of 26 million workers. Punched cards became ubiquitous in industry and government for accounting and administration.

Commercial computers

Ferranti International Plc, a UK electrical engineering company, developed and delivered the first commercial computer, Ferranti Mark 1, to the University of Manchester in 1951.

A British catering company, J Lyons & Company, took up the commercial development of computers. Its LEO computer ran the world's first business application on a stored program in November 1951.

In the same year, an American business machines manufacturer Remington Rand (now Unisys) delivered the world's first mass-produced computer, the UNIVAC I (Universal Automatic Computer) to the US Census Bureau. Each of the 46 machines sold by Remington Rand was priced at more than $1 million ($9.43 million in today's value). UNIVAC used as primary storage serial-access mercury delay lines capable of storing 1,000 words of 11 decimal digits.

Three years later, IBM launched a smaller computer that cost $500,000 ($4.56 million in today's value), the IBM 650.

In 1958 Jack St Clair Kilby and Robert Noyce made the first integrated circuit (IC) while working at Texas Instruments. The integrated circuit ushered in the era of 'third-generation computers' during the late 1960s that used microprocessor ICs instead of transistors.

The use of microprocessors made possible the development of microcomputers that could be owned by individuals and small businesses. The first commercially available microcomputer kit was the Intel 8080-based Altair 8800 that was featured in the January 1975 edition of Popular Electronics. Soon, companies such as Cromemco and Processor Technology began to supply additional S-100 bus hardware for the Altair 8800.

The Altair 8800 is considered by many to be the first real personal computer (PC). Legend has it that the Altair was the inspiration behind the Apple computer circuit board that Steve Jobs and Steve Wozniak sold to the Byte Shop, Apple's first ever customer, in 1976.

PCs to supercomputers

For most of us, early PCs seem like tools from the Stone Age. While the Apple 1, comprising a single circuit board connected to a keyboard and television, was considered a marvel in 1976, the computer technology now available to any sixth grader can generate 3D designs, create high-quality music, and store up to 2.0 terabytes of data.

Meanwhile, China's Sunway TaihuLight supercomputer, the fastest supercomputer in the world, installed at the National Supercomputing Centre in Wuxi, uses 10.6 million CPU cores and is being used for climate research, earth systems modelling and data analytics. It is at least three times faster than the second fastest computer, the Tainhe-2, also built by China.

Such heightened computational capacity radically outstrips the human ability for calculation and efficient use of data. Supercomputers can perform tasks that formerly required large staffs of employees working at slower speeds and with less accuracy.

Research shows that computing technology allows humans to carry out about 60 per cent more computation every year than the volume of calculation that could possibly have been executed by all pre-existing general-purpose computers. The devices for a smartphone today can hold over 1,000 times more processing power than Apollo 13's total computing power.

It appears that newer technologies such as Neurocore and Quantum computing and the introduction of an alternative material such as graphene and indium gallium arsenide (InGaAs) could spell the end of Moore's law that states that the number of transistors that can be placed on a single integrated circuit will double every two years. So, human accomplishment on the technological front has really leaped forward and set the course that enables us to do what we are accomplishing today.

All that computing power is made possible through smart chips and supercomputing technology that generate speed, information storage, as well as adaptable cognition that imitates human learning.

Supply chain management may not need the power of the Sunway TaihuLight or the Tianhe-2 Titan just yet. However, as supercomputing technology has expanded in the past decade, computer scientists have adopted these tools to create more practical solutions, such as robots that are not only programmable but can perform complex functions within microseconds and develop new abilities through learning. These new developments in cognitive calculation and smart computing can reduce the need for human contributions that are at times erroneous and cause slowdowns and disruptions in manufacturing, order fulfilment and transportation. Just as technology developed for the military, like drones, is finding a home in the private sector, so too are technologies developed in the computer world.

Baxter, a robot developed by Rethink Robotics for collaborative industrial applications, and its smaller-footprint variant Sawyer, are good examples of the potential for applying these advances in cognitive calculation and AI in the supply chain. Using some of the most advanced AI on the current market, Baxter requires no traditional programming. Instead, the robot is 'manually trainable by in-house staff, reducing the time and cost of third-party programmers [and is] flexible for a range of applications and re-trainable across lines and tasks', according to its manufacturer. That means Baxter is capable of being taught to perform a multitude of tasks in the plant and distribution centre, unlike its human counterparts who typically specialize in a single field. One robot, for instance, can be trained to handle line loading, machine tending, packaging and materials handling. What's more, when it finishes a task at one station, it can be quickly moved to another station and taught the next job.

There is one other significant difference: most industrial robots are not only designed to replace workers, they also exist, typically in their own distinct work areas, for the protection of workers. Baxter, on the other hand, is designed to collaborate with human employees. In one warehousing application, a Baxter robot loads products into a machine that wraps and seals them for shipment while an associate at the same workstation unloads and visually inspects the products before putting them on a conveyor. Rather than replacing associates, the robot requires contact and monitoring of human behaviours to efficiently learn to process and replicate tasks.

Collaborating with these technologies within supply chains means that robots can perform monotonous tasks and free up skilled labour for higher level, value-added jobs. Beyond taking on tedious tasks, cognitive technologies can also tackle potentially dangerous functions in the fields of manufacturing and military operations, reducing injury or loss of life and allowing employees to put their skills to work more safely.

IDC's Worldwide Robotics 2018 study says that the advancement of robotics technology has entered a new era with embedded and/or cloud-based artificial intelligence. Dr Jing Bing Zhang, Research Director, Worldwide Robotics, said:

> In this new era of Robotics 3.0, intelligent robots are characterized by their
> ubiquitous sensing and connectivity, cyber-physical fusion, autonomous capabilities
> such as cognition, decision making, and learning and adaptation, and more
> human-friendly multimode interaction. This development will have a profound
> impact on industrial robots and service robots. Leading robotics technology
> vendors are already racing to develop and incorporate artificial intelligence
> capabilities into their product roadmap to stay ahead of the competition.

Disruptive forces

Artificial intelligence

The collaborative mobile robots that have made their way into modern fulfilment centres are able to autonomously navigate a facility because they have the onboard intelligence to identify an obstruction and make a decision about how to respond to that disruption.

Watson is an IBM supercomputer that combines AI and sophisticated analytical software for optimal performance as a 'question answering' machine. The supercomputer is named after IBM's founder, Thomas J Watson.

Applications for Watson's underlying cognitive computing technology are almost endless. Due to the device's ability to perform text mining and complex analytics on huge volumes of unstructured data, it can support a search engine or an expert system with capabilities far superior to any previously existing. In May 2016 Baker Hostetler, a century-old Ohio-based law firm, signed a contract for a legal expert system based on Watson to work with its 50-person bankruptcy team. Called ROSS, it can mine data from about a billion text documents, analyse the information and provide precise responses to complicated questions in less than three seconds. Natural language processing allows the system to translate legalese to respond to the lawyers' questions. ROSS's creators are adding more legal modules; similar expert systems are transforming medical research.

The Internet of Things

IoT provides a mechanism to communicate with and capture data about an operation in real time. Through such data capture, organizations can now capture data about previously manual business processes. It's more than just data capture; through IoT we have the capacity for a warehouse management system to deliver a pick list directly to a robot that then knows exactly where it needs to go as well as the most efficient way to get there. Finally, consider the inventory management capability: through connected robots, fulfilment centres have the opportunity to leverage connected robots to send inventory signals directly to the warehouse management system.

Omnichannel

Since the advent of e-commerce, omnichannel has replaced the traditional supply chain model of retail. Online platform facilitated banking payment transfer, creating web interfaces to enable market aggregation, making omnichannel distribution the new normal in retail.

3D printing

The promise of 3D printing is simplicity and speed: by producing products at the point of demand, supply chains become shorter, leaner and less complicated. While the technology is still emerging – and, like drones, still faces technical shortcomings and cost hurdles – a broad range of fields, from fashion to automotive to aeronautics to medicine, are utilizing advanced printing technology to create products on demand.

Industries that produce heavy equipment, such as commercial aviation, jet engines, and construction equipment, are utilizing 3D printing to create parts that are critical to the production process but with limited demand. Manufacturers like Boeing find that they can manufacture a single pieces on the factory floor more economically than they can purchase and warehouse a minimum order quantity that might not be consumed for months. As the technology is honed, it will produce a broader range of products, with improved endurance.

By locating local production centres closer to strategic markets, 3D printing will have a positive impact on:

- reducing carbon footprints by cutting back on delivery transportation, improving an organization's sustainability efforts;
- cutting back on warehousing costs by allowing quick, made-to-order production;
- speeding up turnaround by quickly and cheaply producing replacement parts; and
- meeting consumer demands for the swift delivery of personalized products.

High-speed networks will aid the entire supply chain in downloading, printing and distributing products with fewer steps in the supply chain and significantly less waste.

To see the potential effects of using 3D printing to cut back supply chain components in manufacturing, look at California-based SpaceX, which reduced the manufacturing lead time of NASA from three and a half years to 18 months. SpaceX 3D-prints the critical part of the rocket – the turbo engine component made of titanium – on demand.

Drones

For years – and in some instances centuries – products have moved across water, land and air by ships and barges, trains and trucks, and aeroplanes.

In some respects, very little has fundamentally changed in those technologies over time, except for gradually increasing fuel efficiency, incremental improvements in speed, and the addition of digital and computer tracking technologies.

Drones are emerging as a potentially game-changing alternative to traditional modes of delivery for some processes. Like so many disruptive technologies, drones have their roots in the military, where they are used to limit the loss of life while accomplishing their assigned tasks with fewer mistakes, in shorter periods of time, and with less risk to the safety of the operators.

In the last few years drones have caught the attention of the private sector. In the supply chain, drones could positively affect industries as varied as agriculture, medicine and retail by reducing the number of steps in the chain and speeding up delivery. The potential benefits are astounding, and, according to author Peter Sachs, the technology and associated laws around the usage of drones are evolving almost weekly. Corporations such as Google and Amazon were quick to realize that autonomous delivery could rapidly change how products make their way through the supply chain and on to the end customer.

Drones will improve the supply chain in several ways. For one, drones could be used in ports and in the air to make deliveries that require fewer individuals to handle materials. As an example, PINC Solutions, a provider of yard management systems, has deployed a solution that utilizes drones to identify the location of trailers, shipping containers, and other assets in hard to reach areas. Equipped to carry global positioning systems, radio-frequency identification, optical character recognition and barcode readers, the drones can fly overhead to quickly locate and identify assets that have been tagged in a yard or port. While drones will replace some traditional jobs, including some that are currently hard to fill like truck and delivery drivers, the operation of drones will create new jobs for employees with technical training and logistical knowledge.

Drones will undoubtedly alter how consumers order products, given that the lag time between ordering and arrival can be drastically reduced in some circumstances. They will also alter how retailers function, from how to where and whether they warehouse their products to whether they opt to maintain or move away from brick-and-mortar and omnichannel in favour of e-retail.

That future might be closer than we imagine. In a significant development that sent a wave of excitement through the tech world, the US Department of Transportation and the Federal Aviation Administration approved 10 commercial drone projects to test the integration of drones into the national airspace. The 10 tech (and aviation) companies chosen to participate in the Integration Pilot Program included FedEx, Alphabet and Uber.

Follow the future

Each of the technologies discussed here will be essential tools for supply chain managers as they follow the compass to address these new and rapidly evolving issues in our networks. Employing evolving and disruptive technologies such as drones, 3D printing, rapid networks and smart chips will be critical for us to meet the demands of consumers. Effective thought leaders will see the possibilities of harnessing these technologies to meet requirements, expand into desirable markets, and do so with heightened lean efficiency.

How blockchain will transform the supply chain

To provide some history on the evolution of blockchain in the supply chain, let us consider the idea of crypto-currencies as a preface. Long before industry experts and panellists, and data scientist with PhDs, sat in convention centres holding forth on blockchain, inhabitants of a small Micronesian island called Yap in 500 CE used large, doughnut-shaped stones named Rai as a form of currency. The Yap islanders had memorized which stone belonged to whom, so in cases of the transfer of wealth the islanders would hold an assembly and declare the transfer, thereby committing it to collective memory. The physical location of the stone did not matter because the entire population knew its ownership. The whole concept of converting currency from a physical form into a cognitive form stored in collective memory, safe from robbers and malevolent chieftains, appears extremely impressive given the fact that no type of current thought leadership or education went into constructing such a system.

In 2008 blockchain technology was put out into the world through cryptocurrency mogul Bitcoin by an anonymous person behind the name of Satoshi Nakamoto. During this year bitcoin.org was established on the internet and a paper titled 'Bitcoin: A peer-to-peer electronic cash system' was shared amongst an online group of people interested in the online cryptocurrency technology. The article was authored by Satoshi Nakamoto, and he signed his emails and messages online as such, but little is known about the person/group that invented Bitcoin and the underlying secured technology called 'blockchain'. In this paper Nakamoto states, 'What is needed is an electronic payment system based on cryptographic proof instead of trust, allowing any two willing parties to transact directly with each other without the need for a trusted third party' (Nakamoto, 2008). The elimination of a third party is the basis for blockchain technology, a shared and trusted crypto ledger that can be accessed by the parties involved in the exchange of money and goods to show complete transparency and terms (Meola, 2017). Since the creation of Bitcoin 10 years ago, blockchain has become a buzzword on how the technology can be applied to other industries. Hospitals are now doing proof of concept programmes to protect medical records and have them accessed by doctors and specialists on the shared platform backed by blockchain technology, as one example. But how can this technology be used to completely transform the supply chain world that deals with floods of paperwork, dozens of companies, and carry out a global trial for just one small product that is moving from point A to point B?

The blockchain is an open, distributed ledger that is highly efficient, secure and scalable. It is an application across all the supply chain functions from procurement, to warehousing, delivery and, of course, payments – it promises to improve efficiencies and security of supply chains more than ever before.

About this book

The intent of this book is to create a clear understanding of blockchain's applications in the supply chain so that business leaders can see the advantages that it has to offer. In the course of doing so, we have taken care to decouple blockchain from its use in cryptocurrencies, mostly because the association masks the real advantages that the technology brings to the supply chain.

The chapters that follow will explore and highlight the advantages of blockchain's use across different segments of the supply chain, including design, procurement, manufacturing, contracts, finance, consolidation, warehousing, and logistical operations including last mile delivery and reverse logistics. It will also integrate the role of IoT, machine learning, and AI as a holistic integrated technology platform for supply chain.

Some of the main questions around blockchain that the book addresses are:

- How do we apply blockchain to truly enhance the future of the supply chain?
- Can we eliminate some of the disputes and conflicts that exist today?

- How can we create better transparency through decentralized ledgers that become common ways of transacting? What would that look like?
- Should the blockchain be private or public?
- In what scenarios does blockchain become an efficient tool and in what scenarios does it become not the most efficient way of doing things?
- What are the ethical implications of this evolutionary technology on the supply chain?

All these questions and understanding of all the possibilities will be illustrated in the following chapters. We also include relevant use cases to understand how we can integrate emerging technologies like IoT to provide a truly futuristic supply chain platform. It is our wish to demystify the myth and mystify the marvels of blockchain in the supply chain.

References

Bernard, Z (2017) Everything you need to know about Bitcoin, its mysterious origins, and the many alleged identities of its creator, 2 December. [Online] www.businessinsider.fr

Gandhi, S (2016) The Silk Road, *ThingLink*. [Online] www.thinglink.com/scene/857776320405307393

Meola, A (2017) Understanding blockchain technology, bitcoins, and the rise of cryptocurrency, 25 August. [Online] www.businessinsider.fr

Nakamoto, S (2008) Bitcoin: A peer-to-peer electronic cash system. [Online] https://bitcoin.org/en/bitcoin-paper

Supply chains in 2018   02

Costly, fragile and increasingly complex

Around mid-February 2018, Kentucky Fried Chicken in the United Kingdom ran out of chicken. For over ten days in a row, the $23 billion Yum-brands-owned fast food chain had no chicken to serve its customers at about 640 of its 900-plus UK outlets. The shuttered outlets prompted KFC regulars to go on a Twitter rampage. Some even went to the police to report the perceived crime against gastronomy, until the police urged the public not to waste their time with such matters.

Meanwhile, the British media had a field day with puns; newspapers published front-page headlines screaming 'fowl' and 'a giant cock-up' followed by accounts of consumers 'clucking about' or feeling 'peckish', often mixed with some variant of the 'Why did the chicken cross the road' joke. It took about a fortnight for all the stores to restore supplies of chicken and gravy and for the crisis to go away. The restaurant chain suffered losses averaging $1.27 million per day, not to mention the incalculable damage it caused to brand KFC.

What had gone wrong with KFC's supply chain? By all reported accounts, the root of the problem was KFC's decision to change its delivery suppliers from Bidvest Logistics, a food logistics service provider, to DHL and QSL (Quick Service Logistics). DHL was to manage the warehousing and physical distribution and QSL the stock management and demand planning with a dedicated information technology (IT) system. While Bidvest used to operate out of six warehouses for KFC's supplies, DHL was to operate from a single warehouse at Rugby.

Early reports of the shortage pointed to a series of accidents that happened on 14 February involving seven vehicles at three junctions close to DHL's Rugby warehouse. Because of the mishaps, DHL's lorries got stuck in the traffic as soon as they left the depot, which led to the shortage that triggered the crisis. However, the particular event on its own couldn't explain the widespread disruption caused to KFC's supply chain that lasted for days, even after the M6 motorway was cleared.

As publications such as the *Telegraph* and the *Guardian* investigated further into the crisis – with little help from KFC and DHL, both of whom understandably laid low – it emerged that it was not the design of the new warehouse network or the accidents that caused the shortage. After all, scores of food and retail companies, such as Marks and Spencer, operate from centrally located warehouses. And there were reports of vans dumping KFC-branded crates of chicken at the roadsides after the loads had been rejected by the restaurant bosses. Clearly, there was something bigger than the new warehousing network design at play.

It turned out that the 'teething pains', as KFC later put it, were caused by the transition to the new system. Tech analyst Chris Green said in a *Guardian* article, 'DHL and its software partner, Quick Service Logistics, appeared to have failed to properly match up data from KFC's ordering process to its new system.'

In essence, the new system couldn't provide accurate traceability of orders and deliveries, and once a blip in the supply chain occurred, as it did on 14 February, the order processing system went into a tailspin, precipitating a large-scale crisis. The UK edition of *Wired* had an expert explain the cause thus: 'What makes up those supply chains is lots of different companies, lots of different relationships, all trying to manage processes, infrastructure, equipment, information systems and its staff, to make all of that perform in a synchronised way, so that the customer gets the chicken they want.'

The KFC fiasco is a recent testimony to a deeper problem that besets supply chain organizations of today, even after decades of technological advancement and globalization. The problem is of asynchrony between the two primary flows of supply chain – the physical flow and the information flow. The Council of Supply Chain Management Professionals' definition (given below) of supply chain puts the 'link' between the two flows as critical to the functioning of supply chain.

What is supply chain management?

There are two core principles behind supply chain management (SCM):

- Practically every product in the world that reaches the consumer requires the cumulative efforts of multiple organizations. Collectively, these organizations make up the supply chain.

- SCM is the active management of supply chain activities to maximize customer value and achieve a sustainable competitive advantage. Supply chain activities cover everything from product development, to sourcing and production, to logistics, as well as the information systems needed to coordinate these activities.

The organizations that make up the supply chain are 'linked' together through physical flows and information flows, forming partnerships that add value to the customer experience. Physical flows involve the transformation, movement and storage of goods and materials. Information flows allow the various supply chain partners to coordinate their long-term plans and to control the day-to-day flow of goods and material up and down the supply chain.

The Council of Supply Chain Management Professionals' definition of supply chain adequately encapsulates the new reality of supply chain management in how the past 40 years of rapid globalization has expanded its functional and geographic universe and introduced the discipline of global supply chain management.

Today's global supply chain operations encompass (but do not seamlessly integrate) a dizzying array of administrative exchanges and financial transactions performed over several geographies involving numerous trading partners, where most of the work is overwhelmingly paper-based and some of it done via electronic data interchange, a 55-year-old technology. The presence of these myriad islands of information and the swarms of middlemen causes frictions that slow down the supply chain.

The stakes are high

Industries such as textile, automotive, aviation, electronics, healthcare and pharmaceuticals that use materials from multiple sourcing locations spread out over large distances are especially prone to such frictions.

In 2016 America's largest retailers, Walmart and Target, had to offer its customers millions of dollars in refunds after discovering that the Egyptian cotton sheets sourced from an Indian textile manufacturer, Welspun India, were not Egyptian. The problem was later traced to a combination of supply chain issues that still ail the global textile industry – the involvement of multiple vendors and intermediaries across geographies and administrative overlaps. Welspun undertook a slew of measures over the ensuing months to fix the tracking and traceability issues responsible for the crisis, but not before losing close to $60 million of business and its largest customer, Target, in the process.

Losses caused due to frictions and mismatches between data points in supply chain are not only limited to those of revenue or business reputation, but they also cause widespread environmental damage, as has been seen in the palm oil supply chain, and at least in one case the deaths of newborns. In August 2017 more than 60 infants died in a hospital in a small town in Uttar Pradesh, India after the facility's oxygen supply ran out. The hospital's oxygen supplier had stopped the supply of oxygen after he was not paid for several months and his repeated mails for replenishment were lost in the tangle of bureaucratic exchanges.

The $62 billion palm oil industry has been plagued by concerns about destruction of rainforests and human rights abuses in Indonesia and Malaysia, which provide over 85 per cent of all palm oil. Plantations built on deforested land are used to supply palm oil to scores of household brands that also include McDonald's, Mars, Kellogg's and Procter & Gamble. In July 2017 a *Guardian* article reported that Pepsico, Unilever and Nestlé have been accused of complicity in the destruction of Sumatra's last tract of rainforest shared by elephants, orang-utans, rhinos, and tigers together in one ecosystem.

The palm oil supply chain is highly complex since the product is often mixed – it often reaches a supplier as a blended product from many different sources. Various initiatives have been launched to streamline the production of palm oil and nullify its impact on the environment, but most of them have not made much difference. The primary reason is that palm oil is very difficult to trace back to a specific plantation. A supply chain resilience report released by Business Continuity Institute in November 2017 looked at supply chain disruptions across 65 countries and reported that unplanned information and communications technology outage was the top cause for supply chain disruptions. A more revealing finding was that 69 per cent of respondents did not have full visibility of their supply chains. Nick Wildgoose, the Global Supply Chain Product Leader of Zurich Insurance, who has been involved with the report since its first edition in 2009, said, 'That doesn't surprise me. In fact, I'm more surprised that so many organizations claim to have full visibility of their supply chains, as it's almost impossible to know about every single supplier.'

Steve Cottrell, a pharmaceutical industry expert and the head of the life sciences consulting firm Maetrics, cited the study in a Pharmaexec.com article to say:

Given that the pharmaceutical supply chain is one of the most complex of its type in the world – managing the operational challenges of working and interacting with huge numbers of suppliers contributing ingredients and components to drug production on a global scale – it is clear that the stakes are high if poor visibility is not addressed.

Supply chain frictions caused due to asynchrony are also responsible for the inordinately long product lead times ranging from weeks to months that are common in these industries. Whereas the physical distance between the point of sourcing or production to the point of production or consumption may be not more than a few thousand miles that could be covered in days by air and a couple of weeks by sea. The majority of delays, wastages and disruptions, amounting in some cases to 45 to 50 per cent of total supply chain costs, are caused due to frictions in administrative processes, independent financial transactions and problems arising from manual interventions, including the presence of intermediaries, manmade errors, iterations and, many times, plain inactivity.

Australian lean consultant and author Tim Mclean, in a recent article, put down sources of unnecessary lead time to preventable factors such as delays in order processing by the purchasing staff (particularly when they lock themselves in to long ordering cycles or try to accumulate large orders to get a lower price), delays in order processing by suppliers, process-related delays along the multiple shipping routes and ports due several clearances, cross-docking and freight forwarding. Add to that the multiple loops of financial transaction that take place between the purchaser, the supplier, the government agencies and all the layers of intermediaries.

A World Bank report, *Enabling Trade: Valuing growth opportunities* presented in 2013 several case studies to illustrate how process-related bottlenecks in global supply chains offset significant labour cost advantages for many countries and inflate overall supply chain costs. Examples included the following:

- In Brazil, managing customs paperwork for exports of agricultural commodities can take 12 times longer than in the European Union (a full day versus a couple of hours).

- Poor-quality services can increase the input material costs of consumer goods by up to 200 per cent in certain African countries.

- Obtaining licences and lack of coordination among regulatory agencies in the United States lead to delays in up to 30 per cent of chemical shipments for one company – each late shipment costs US$ 60,000 per day.

- In Russia, product testing and licensing in the computer sector can lead to high administrative costs and delay time-to-market anywhere from 10 days to eight weeks.
- Adopting electronic documentation for the air cargo industry could yield US$ 12 billion in annual savings and prevent 70–80 per cent of paperwork-related delays.

In the UK alone, the average business reported losing £88,725 ($113,765) per year through clunky payment practices causing friction in their supply chain, according to a 2017 report by Tungsten Network. This equates to almost 6,500 man hours chasing purchase order numbers, processing paper invoices and responding to supplier enquiries. The surveyed businesses estimated that they spend on average per week around 55 hours doing manual, paper-based processes and checks; 39 hours chasing invoice exceptions, discrepancies and errors and 23 hours responding to supplier enquiries. They also spent five hours on compliance-related challenges such as handling international taxes and three hours tackling invoice fraud.

Rick Hurwitz, Tungsten Network CEO, commented:

Numerous processes in the financial world remain cumbersome and time consuming when they needn't be. Technology means we can do away with the tiresome and menial tasks that clog business work streams and instead boost productivity and efficiency. It is surprising that in this tech enabled day and age businesses are still spending so many hours per week managing a process that could be automated.

The top five friction-causing factors were named as:

- a high proportion of paper invoices received;
- too many non-purchase order based invoices;
- a high volume of supplier enquiries regarding invoice or payment status;
- a lack of automated exceptions;
- a lack of automated approval.

Globally, manifestations of the rising trade frustrations among powerful economies through crises such as the US–China trade row and Brexit continue to put already distended global supply chains under added strain. That explains the sense of the immediacy with which scholars, supply chain specialists and academicians are exploring ways to rethink, retool and remodel supply chains.

An argument for blockchain

Blockchain was born at the peak of the 2008 financial crisis when an anonymous person or a group of individuals using the name Satoshi Nakamoto drafted a paper creating a protocol for a digital cryptocurrency called Bitcoin and subsequently mined the first block of bitcoins, known as the 'genesis block'. This was born out of a need for people to establish trust and do transactions without a third party. Another popular blockchain, Ethereum, was developed by a Canadian named Vitalik Buterin in July 2015, when he created its genesis block. Ethereum introduced various new capabilities, one of which was the ability to build smart contracts – computer protocols that verify or enforce contracts. A smart contract is a self-executing agreement that handles all the stages of a contract, including the management, enforcement, performance and payment.

To describe the technology in simple terms, the blockchain is a digitized, decentralized, tamper-proof ledger platform that records and verifies transactions and cuts out the middlemen.

The financial services sector was the first to realize its game-changing potential, particularly in the way it could reduce costs, make processes more efficient and support a lot of their operations. Banks often term blockchain 'distributed ledger technology' (DLT) to distinguish it from Bitcoin's blockchain.

They were drawn to DTL because of the following attractive features, as laid out in *The Fintech 2.0 Paper*, a 2015 report from Santander InnoVentures produced in collaboration with Oliver Wyman and Anthemis Group, also widely regarded as the first comprehensive declaration of the blockchain promise for enterprises:

- Transactions can be made to be irrevocable, and clearing and settlement can be programmed to be near-instantaneous, allowing distributed ledger operators to increase the accuracy of trade data and reduce settlement risk.

- Systems operate on a peer-to-peer basis and transactions are near-certain to be correctly executed, allowing distributed ledger operators to eliminate supervision and IT infrastructure, and their associated costs.

- Each transaction in the ledger is openly verified by a community of networked users rather than by a central authority, making the distributed ledger tamper-resistant; and each transaction is automatically administered in such a way as to render the transaction history difficult to reverse.

- Almost any intangible document or asset can be expressed in code, which can be programmed into or referenced by a distributed ledger.
- A publicly accessible historical record of all transactions is created, enabling effective monitoring and auditing by participants, supervisors and regulators.

The last three years in particular have witnessed an intensified race among companies across industries and geographies to deploy blockchain to transform their supply chains.

Globally, organizations have been taking advantage of blockchain technology to improve traceability in their supply chains.

In December 2017 Unilever launched a one-year pilot project that leveraged blockchain technology to track supply chains for tea sold by the consumer goods giant and the British supermarket Sainsbury's. The company partnered with big banks and technology start-ups to track tea farmers in Malawi, who supply tea for Unilever brands. The project used technology to maintain transparency on the supply chain, so both the company and the consumer knew the origins of their tea. 'Malawian tea is the start, not the end,' said Andrew Voysey, Director of Sustainable Finance at the University of Cambridge Institute for Sustainability Leadership at the project launch. Up to 10,000 farmers in Malawi were eligible to join the pilot, which aimed to reward those who produced a fairer, more sustainable brew, with financial incentives such as preferential loans and access to credit.

Consumer goods and retail companies are facing increasing pressure to find better ways to certify that their supply chains are environmentally sustainable and free from worker-rights abuse and corruption.

Coca-Cola Co and the US State Department, along with two other companies, announced in March 2017 that they were launching a project using blockchain's digital ledger technology to create a secure registry for workers that would help fight the use of forced labour worldwide. The Bitfury Group, a US tech company, built the blockchain platform for this project, while Emercoin provided blockchain services.

In late 2017 a group of 10 large food and retail companies, including Nestlé, Unilever, and Tyson Foods joined an IBM project to study how blockchain systems can help track food supply chains and improve safety.

Here's how Walmart, on its own, intends to use blockchain to improve food safety across its complex global food supply chain. Frank Yiannas, Walmart Vice President of Food Safety and Health, revealed to an audience at an MIT Technology Review Business of Blockchain conference in Cambridge, Massachusetts that blockchain was able to shorten the time it took to track produce from six days to two seconds. Walmart was recently awarded a patent for a system that would store medical records on a blockchain from a medical device. Walmart has also filed a patent for a blockchain-based customer marketplace for reselling its goods.

The shipping industry has joined the race with a flourish. In August 2018 IBM and Maersk launched a blockchain-based shipping platform, TradeLens, with 94 early adopters that include more than 20 port and terminal operators. TradeLens' permission-driven blockchain ledger will allow all the participants to view real-time details of cargo shipments, such as shipment arrival times, customs releases, commercial invoices and bills of lading. TradeLens can track critical data about every shipment in a supply chain and create immutable records for all the participants.

TradeLens is not the only player in the fray. Tradeshift, a supply chain payments and marketplaces startup valued at over $1 billion, recently reported a 350 per cent increase in gross merchandise volume on Tradeshift's platform compared with the previous year and a 315 per cent year-over-year rise in new bookings. Tradeshift also earned the distinction of being the first platform to incorporate supply chain payments, finance and blockchain-based early payments all into one unified solution. Currently, the Tradeshift platform can integrate with both Ripple blockchain payments and R3's Corda.

Worldwide spending on blockchain solutions is on a rise. IDC estimated that blockchain spending would reach $2.1 billion in 2018, more than double the $945 million spent in 2017. The study said that the United States would see the largest blockchain investments and deliver more than 40 per cent of worldwide spending. Western Europe will be the next largest region for blockchain spending, followed by China.

In August 2018 the USC Marshall Centre for Global Supply Chain Management brought together industry leaders, tech investors and innovators at its Sixth Annual Global Supply Chain Summit to launch IBISK, an initiative with an aim to partner and collaborate with governments and multinational companies to drive the future best practices and standards for the adoption of blockchain.

Limitations of blockchain

Like any new technology, blockchain has limitations that must be considered.

The issue of scalability and the need for incentives

Blockchain, in the form that it exists, is not scalable because it is constrained by the available computational power of the network, which means that it cannot be used in its current form for high-volume transactions.

The network constraint also makes the creation of the individual blocks of the blockchain an inherently slow process. The time required for a single block to become a part of the public blockchain could vary from a few seconds to several days. Let's see how. A block (known as a record) in the blockchain is a series of sequential transactions. The complete process of creation of a block comprises two steps. First, every individual transaction has to be validated by mining computers on the network (called 'miners') by solving a complex mathematical puzzle. A Bitcoin blockchain software processes about seven transactions per second, and Ethereum blockchain does 15. Compare it to the speed of VisaNet (Visa's processing system) that could handle 47,000 transactions per second.

A single blockchain block can contain 2,000 transactions. The entire process of validation of a block is called the 'block time'. The block time for Bitcoin, which limits the size of each block to 1 megabyte due to network computer concerns, is 10 minutes. The average block time in Ethereum is faster, about 20 seconds, because its block sizes are much smaller at around 20–30 kilobytes, but it has other complex variables that we will cover in the later chapters.

The second step of adding the block on the public ledger is the one that takes an uncertain amount of time, ranging from seconds to days. This is due to two variables: network activity and the blockchain fee. The blockchain fee, also called as the 'transaction fee' or the 'miners' fee' is the money users pay to the miners when performing transactions. Usually it is $1 but it increases with the surge in the network activity as it did during the cryptocurrency bull run of December 2017 when users had to pay over $60 just to have the transactions confirmed. The speed and the scalability issues of the blockchain raise concerns that the technology is not suited for high-speed or high-throughput transaction networks. There are a number of new solutions, such as SegWit, Lightning Network and #Metahash, that promise to solve these challenges, but it's too early to see any impact.

An energy guzzler

All the nodes of a blockchain network have to perform computationally intensive procedures to create block, a process that requires large amounts of computing power.

In a report released in June 2018, the Swiss-based Bank for International Settlements (BIS), a financial body owned by 60 central banks, called the blockchain an 'environmental disaster'. To quote from the document, 'At the time of writing, the total electricity use of Bitcoin mining equalled that of mid-sized economies such as Switzerland, and other cryptocurrencies also use ample electricity. Put in the simplest terms, the quest for decentralised trust has quickly become an environmental disaster.'

In 2017 alone, according to a research conducted by the UK-based energy comparison tariff service PowerCompare, the average electricity used to mine Bitcoin surpassed the annual energy usage of some 159 countries. The website Digiconomist estimates verifying transaction on the Bitcoin block-chain consumes about 200kWh, enough to power an average home for over four weeks.

The 51 per cent attack

The blockchain is designed to follow a model of democratic governance, and it faces the same problem that real-world democracies face. In what is called a '51 per cent attack', a group of miners can defraud the system by gaining control of more than 50 per cent of the network's mining hashrate, or the computational power. Cryptocurrency networks like Bitcoin Gold, Verge and Monocoin were all hit with the 51 per cent attack during a single week in May 2018, and coins of estimated worth in the millions were stolen.

There are several other drawbacks and limitations of blockchain, such as 'forks', which are disruption caused due to software incompatibility of min-ing nodes, its tainted legacy where it enables transactions for criminal activ-ity and is perceived as an anti-establishment construct, the 'pseudonominity' of users and miners and others. But all of these issues can be resolved within the framework of permission-based blockchain networks such as the ones that are being used and will be used for the supply chain.

Blockchain in the supply chain – increased efficiency and effectiveness

As blockchain technology research has up to now predominantly focused on technological questions of design and features, while neglecting applica-tions, value creation and governance (Risius and Spohrer, 2017), there is for practitioners little to go by in terms of practical guidance for blockchain technology adaptation in the supply chain. Questions such as 'Which supply chain processes should we focus on?' or 'What performance metrics will be influenced?' are, however, relevant and need to be answered in a structured and meaningful way.

Therefore, we propose in this chapter a framework that takes both increased efficiency and effectiveness into consideration. A limitation of this framework is that it doesn't take into consideration the potential effect blockchain technology can have on business models. This will be discussed in more detail in Chapter 9. In that same chapter we will also synthesize both the efficiency and effectiveness model based on the Supply-Chain Operations Reference (SCOR) model with that of the business innovation model.

In the remaining part of this chapter we discuss supply chain management objectives and the SCOR process reference model at a conceptual level.

Supply chain management objectives

The efficiency and effectiveness of a supply chain can be measured using a range of performance objectives. Based on case study analysis, Kshetri (2017a) identified a number of supply chain objectives that can be positively affected by blockchain technology. These include cost, speed, product quality, dependability, risk reduction, sustainability and flexibility. The SCOR[1] reference model provides another, but to some extent similar, set of objectives, termed performance attributes, that are linked to performance metrics. We will use the SCOR reference model as our base as it not only provides specific metrics for each of the perform attributes but also detailed process descriptions dependent on the type of production strategy applied. It also has the advantage that it has seen widespread adoption from practitioners and researchers.

The first SCM objective is system-wide costs minimization (Simchi-Levi *et al*, 2000). While both Kshetri (2017b) and the SCOR reference model use the terms cost and costs, respectively, we think it is important to emphasize the system-wide aspect; simply reducing inventories or minimizing transportation costs is not enough. These decisions should be made taking into account the whole system, as there are trade-offs between different costs, such as storage and order processing costs. As administrative transactions add an estimated $250 to the physical transport costs of a container

(Marine Transport International, 2018), automating these transactions using blockchain technology has the potential to reduce the marginal costs of an additional transaction to almost zero (Kshetri, 2017b).

Responsiveness (SCOR) or the speed (Kshetri, 2017b) with which transactions can be executed is another important objective. Current paper-based transactions that lie at the heart of today's supply chain are extremely time consuming. For example, a container takes approximately 36 hours to physically get from the port of Singapore to Jakarta, Indonesia. However, information and financial settlement can take up to seven days. Smart contracts enabled machine-to-machine transactions reduce human interaction and communication. Not only do these machines not need holidays, and work uninterrupted 24/7, they are also never sick and, unlike humans, once properly programmed they do not make mistakes. All this results in a dramatic increase in transaction speed, while also reducing transaction costs.

Dependability or reliability (SCOR) of a supply chain is its ability to satisfy a customer's delivery date, for instance the percentage of all orders sent on or before the promised delivery date (Kshetri, 2017b). As the ability to predict accurate delivery dates is critical to many companies in today's markets, access to reliable and up-to-date data is a necessary condition. Furthermore, early indications of exceptions that occur in the execution of the plan allow (for example) re-scheduling of production orders or changes in mode of transport, so that agreed upon service levels can still be reached. Blockchain technology's ability to provide validated data and identities can improve the outcomes of scheduling algorithms as their outcomes are sensitive to the quality of the data being processed. Furthermore, real-time validated data from IoT devices and sensors on equipment will allow for better management of exceptions, such as delays.

A special measure of reliability is perfect order fulfilment. The SCOR model defines the various components that combined make up perfect order fulfilment. Product quality is one of those components that can be much affected during transportation. For example, the quality of food and medicine can be affected by changes in temperature and humidity. By having access to immutable tracking, humidity and temperature data, producer and consumers can be more confident that the product they buy has been transported under the correct conditions.

The supply chain is a dynamic system that evolves over time (Simchi-Levi *et al*, 2014). The introduction of products with short lifecycles, heightened customer expectations, political uncertainty and globalization put ever-greater pressure on supply chain relationships. This is reflected in the level of agility (SCOR) of the supply chain; ie its ability to deal with external influences to gain or maintain its competitive advantage. However, today's complex business-to-business supply chain integration technology lacks the required flexibility to cope with these changes (Korpela *et al*, 2017). Furthermore, with the rise of machine-to-machine based IoT transactions, the level of data exchange within the supply chain is expected to increase dramatically and become much more decentralized and distributed. This will further increase the need for more flexible forms of secure data exchange. Blockchain technology is very much suited to fulfil these requirements.

The final SCOR performance attribute is asset management efficiency. Assets can be both physical, such as trucks, warehouse space, inventory and production facilities, as well as working capital, such as cash and outstanding invoices. As discussed in the previous chapter, blockchain technology not only allows for improved integration of the physical, information and financials flows within the supply chain which positively affects working capital efficiency, it could also provide for better planning, through more accurate data and better exception handling, using decentralized markets to trade under-used physical assets, such as berthing space or empty loading space on board trucks, trains or boats.

Consumers, non-governmental organizations, governments and corporates show an increase in demand for information regarding their products and materials. This is not only because of food-safety related concerns, such as the bovine spongiform encephalopathy disease and avian influenza (Setboonsarng *et al*, 2009), but also because parties in supply chains face stakeholder demands for product information, and require the means to verify sustainability claims such as fair trade, animal welfare and carbon footprint reductions (BSR, 2014). Closely related to this problem is the misuse of trademarks and fake products, which is hurting consumers and companies (Martinez de Andino, 2014).

Blockchain technology provides validated data and identities as well as an immutable audit trail that would allow for more quantifiable and meaningful sustainability indicators (Kshetri, 2017b), while at the same time reducing the monitoring costs of doing so. While not a separate performance attribute in the SCOR reference model, a special application of the SCOR model has been developed, called SustainableSCOR, and this is based on the GRI Sustainability Reporting Standards that are within the scope of the SCOR model (APICS, 2017).

Global supply chains are complex networks of facilities and organizations with often different, conflicting objectives (Simchi-Levi *et al*, 2014).

As a result, the supply chain members have to deal with multiple uncertainties. These uncertainties lead to risks that require active management. Among the various risks that organizations face is the 'self-interest seeking behaviour' of individuals, which necessitates continuous monitoring of supply chain members and the negotiation and enforcement of contractual terms. Smart contracts would allow upfront compliance by means of stipulating the conditions necessary for transfer of title and subsequent payment. While risk management is pervasive within the SCOR reference model, it is not a separate performance attribute. Instead it is tied to the Agility performance attribute, the Enable process and the Best Practices.

The SCOR process model

SCOR is a process reference model. The purpose of such a process reference model, or business process framework, is to define process architecture in a way that aligns with key business functions and goals (APICS, 2017). The model consists of four major sections:

- Performance: standard metrics to describe process performance and define strategic goals.
- Processes: standard descriptions of management processes and process relationships.
- Practices: management practices that produce significantly better process performance.
- People: standard definitions for skills required to perform supply chain processes.

Our framework for analysis explicitly references to the performance and processes sections, while practices are implicitly included through the role blockchain technology can play in a particular process and the blockchain mechanisms used. For example, if we look at the sS1.2 process 'Receive Product', we can see the various metrics (RL.3.18 % Orders/Lines Processed Completely, etc) associated with this process. For this process, various best practices are defined, one of them being BP.012 'Lot Tracking'. As various use-cases described in Chapters 7 and 8 of this book involve the use of blockchain technology for inventory (lot) tracking in combination with Internet of Things (IoT) devices, this would constitute the mechanism through which inventory (lot) tracking data is provided.

We have not included at this point the People aspect in our framework, as the primary question of this chapter is 'why blockchain technology?' The People question is, in our opinion, so expensive that it falls outside of the scope of this book. However, as blockchain technology, AI and IoT are expected to dramatically change business models, we believe that this in turn will impact the People component, with new supply chain jobs emerging as these new technologies take hold.

While SCOR does not attempt to describe every process or activity, it does include (APICS, 2017):

- all customers interactions, from order entry to paid invoice;
- all physical transactions, including supplier's supplier to customer's customer, including equipment, raw materials and intermediate products, spare parts, services, software, etc;
- and all market interactions, from the understanding of aggregate demand to the fulfilment of each order.

As shown in Table 2.1, the model is designed to support supply chain analysis at multiple levels. SCOR focuses on the top three process levels, which

Table 2.1 SCOR hierarchical process model

Level	Description	Comments
1	The major processes level contains the major SCOR processes, ie Plan, Make, Source, Deliver, Return and Enable.	This level sets, amongst other things, the scope and supply chain management objectives.
2	The process categories level contains the major operations strategies as defined by SCOR, being make-to-stock, make-to-order, engineer-to-order and retail.	Each operations strategy has its own unique configuration of the major SCOR processes.
3	The process elements level defines the company's individual configuration for each of the processes.	The ability to execute these processes defines the competitive ability of its supply chain.
4	This level defines the improvement tools and activities, such as lean and six sigma, and best practices such as electronic data interchange and material resource planning	While SCOR does define various best practices per process category and/or process element, it does not describe how these best practices should be implemented.

are industry neutral. The model does not attempt to prescribe how an organization should conduct its business or tailor its systems/information flow. Every organization that implements supply chain improvements using SCOR will need to extend the model, at least to Level 4, using industry, organization, and/or location-specific processes, systems and practices.

Our framework for analysis has focused on the process elements as the unit of analysis for as far as the Plan, Source, Make, Deliver, and Return processes are concerned. For the Enable process, our unit of analysis was the process category, primarily because for most of the Enable process elements[2] no metrics were defined on the process elements level. As a result, the framework for analysis is less precise. A future extension of the model could be to define the metrics for the Enable process at the process elements level by means of the various practices defined at the Enable process elements level.

It is important to note that because of the focus on the process elements, our framework doesn't address the (potential) role and mechanisms of blockchain technology in terms of the operations strategy. In order to assess blockchain technology's role in adopting novel approaches to commercializing its underlying assets, we refer to Chapter 9 of this book.

As a detailed description of the SCOR process model is beyond the scope of this book, we encourage those readers unfamiliar with the model to download the latest version of the SCOR reference model, at the time of writing version 12.0, from the APICS website (www.apics.org), as throughout this book we will adhere to the definitions and descriptions of the SCOR reference model.

The SCOR processes and blockchain

Having introduced both SCM objectives and the SCOR model at a conceptual level in the previous paragraphs, we will now discuss some of the practical applications of blockchain technology within these processes. For a detailed analysis of blockchain roles and mechanisms in supply chain processes we refer to Chapter 6 of this book. As the SCOR model also provides performance metrics for each of the process elements, we also get a better understanding of where the potential business case can be for applying blockchain technology. This should help in battling organizational scepticism based on the notion that blockchain technology is 'technology in search of a problem'.

Plan processes

SCOR defines the Plan process as the processes associated with determining requirements and corrective actions to achieve supply chain objectives (APICS, 2017).

Complete and real-time visibility of supply chain processes and assets can exponentially increase the effectiveness of the Plan process. Blockchain can help companies share information about warehousing, delivery and maintenance of products with suppliers and vendors. Companies are already doing that. BHP Billiton, the world's largest mining firm, has announced it will use blockchain to record movements of wellbore rock and fluid samples, and improve the security of the real-time data that is generated during delivery. According to BHP geophysicist R Tyler Smith, the new system increases internal efficiency and allows the company to collaborate more effectively with partners.

Source processes

SCOR defines the Source process as the processes associated with ordering, delivery, receipt and transfer of raw material items, sub-assemblies, product and/or services (APICS, 2017).

Blockchain-based innovations can transform procurement and supplier management by improving the traceability and security of products, particularly in industries and regions that have multiple layers of suppliers. The technology has game-changing implications for procurement through the applications of smart contracts, real-time payment settlements and enhanced purchase order managements. *Forbes* magazine recently reported that Walmart is using blockchain to keep track of the pork it sources from China, and the blockchain records where each piece of meat came from, was processed and stored, and its sell-by date. Unilever, Nestlé, Tyson and Dole are also using the technology for similar purposes.

Make processes

SCOR defines the Make process as the processes associated with adding value to a deliverable through manufacturing or creation of a product or deliverable; or, in services industries, the creation of service deliverables (APICS, 2017).

It is worth noting that actual applications of blockchain technology, in the strictest sense of the Make process, are very limited. This is primarily a result of the fact that this process is within the 'four walls' of the focal company. Hence, there's no need for increased trust or to deploy a decentralized application. What is often referred to as potential applications of blockchain technology in the manufacturing industry, such as the Production Parts Approval process, are better captured in, for example, the Sourcing (provide incontestable proof of the origins of a product or subassembly and its transport conditions) or Return (using blockchain super audit trail in case of warranty disputes) processes.

Deliver processes

SCOR defines the Deliver process as the processes associated with performing customer-facing order management and order fulfilment activities (APICS, 2017).

Blockchain can create end-to-end visibility in freight transportation of all documents and transactions – bills of lading, invoices, proof of delivery and suchlike – for all the participants – shippers, third party logistics, transporters and consignees. The shipping industry leader Maersk and IBM have announced the creation of TradeLens, a blockchain-enabled shipping solution designed to promote more efficient and secure global trade.

Organizations like the US-based Blockchain in Trucking Alliance (BiTA) have been formed to create universal standards for blockchain's adoption in the transportation and logistics industry. BiTA members account for about 85 per cent of all truck-related transactions in the US.

Major shippers like Shaw Industries and JD.com have joined BiTA to collaborate with parcel carriers like FedEx and UPS, truckload carriers like JB Hunt, Schneider, 3PLs like Coyote, Echo, software companies like TMW, McLeod, and Descartes, finance organizations such as Triumph Capital, insurance companies, law firms, tech startups and telematics providers.

'Blockchain has multiple applications in the logistics industry, especially related to supply chains, insurance, payments, audits and customs brokerage,' said Linda Weakland, UPS Director of Enterprise Architecture and Innovation at the time of joining BiTA. 'The technology has the potential to increase transparency and efficiency among shippers, carriers, brokers, consumers, vendors and other supply chain stakeholders.'

Other sector leaders concur. 'We're quite confident that blockchain has big, big implications in supply chain, transportation and logistics,' FedEx CEO Frederick Smith said at the news site CoinDesk's 2018 blockchain technology summit, Consensus 2018.

Return processes

SCOR defines the Return process as the processes associated with moving material from a customer back through the supply chain to address defects in product, ordering or manufacturing, or to perform upkeep activities (APICS, 2017).

The reverse process of supply chain is highly challenging for companies because its main components are scattered geographically, often controlled by multiple parties that don't communicate with one another, and therefore coordination is a tedious, time-consuming and costly activity.

Blockchain's ability to immutably record the product history and its associated financial transactions across the supply chain can transform the reverse process of supply chain. The automotive sector can particularly improve their reverse logistics chains that involve include repairs and maintenance activities with the help of blockchain. Blockchain can also help improve the recycling processes, from collection to manufacturing, proving compliance with sustainability guidelines and recycling certification schemes.

The UK-based recycling software seller FRED is incorporating blockchain into its offering to help connect parties involved in the recycling supply chain, from supplier and shipper right through to port operator. The integration has been done as part of a proof of concept trial being conducted by Marine Transport International, the developer of blockchain-enabled technology for the container logistics industry. In the trial, FRED software used by supplier Parry & Evans Recycling captures data from shipments including weight, container number, commodity, seal number, piece count, load and container imagery, Annex VII documents, port of call and truck driver particulars. Through Marine Transport International's blockchain connection, this information is then shared with haulier, shipper, port operator and ocean carrier instantly. Without the connection to the blockchain network, all the data would need to be uploaded into the individual parties' systems, entailing dozens of emails and ways of formatting the information. Phil Short, managing director of Increase Computers, the developers of FRED, said in a press release,

By incorporating blockchain into a live process, we're tapping into a major opportunity to help the recycling industry hugely simplify the way it transports material. There has been a huge amount of hype about blockchain – with this proof of concept we're involved in a real, practical application with significant global potential.

Enable processes

SCOR defines the Enable process as the processes associated with establishing, maintaining and monitoring information, relationships, resources, assets, business rules, compliance and contracts required to operate the supply chain as well as monitoring and managing the overall performance of the supply chain (APICS, 2017).

Based on the examples of the use of blockchain technology in the previous paragraphs we can see that implementation of the technology in the Plan, Make, Source, Deliver and Return processes also affects the Enable sub-processes, such as business rules, manage data and information and manage supply chain risks. This is explained in more detail in Chapter 6.

Notes

1 SCOR is a process reference model developed and endorsed by the Supply Chain Council as the cross-industry standard diagnostic tool for supply chain management.

2 The metrics were only defined at the process element level for the sE5 'manage supply chain assets' and sE9 'manage supply chain risk'.

References

APICS (2017) SCOR quick reference guide. [Online] https://www.apics.org/docs/default-source/scc-non-research/apicsscc_scor_quick_reference_guide.pdf

BSR (2014) BSR UNGC Guide to traceability. [Online] https://www.bsr.org: https://www.bsr.org/reports/BSR_UNGC_Guide_to_Traceability.pdf

Korpela, K, Hallikas, J and Dahlberg, T (2017) Digital supply chain transformation toward blockchain integration, Hawaii International Conference on System Sciences, volume 50.

Kshetri, N (2017a) Blockchain's roles in strengthening cybersecurity and protecting privacy, *Telecommunications Policy*, **41** (10), pp 1027–38

Kshetri, N (2017b) Blockchain's roles in meeting key supply chain management objectives, *International Journal of Information Management*, 39, pp 80–89

Marine Transport International (2018) [Online] https://unctad.org/en/PublicationsLibrary/rmt2018_en.pdf

Martinez de Andino, JM (2014) Counterfeits in the supply chain: A big problem and it's getting worse. [Online] http://www.industryweek.com/inventory-management/counterfeits-supply-chain-big-problem-and-its-getting-worse

Risius, M and Spohrer, K (2017) A blockchain research framework: What we (don't) know, where we go from here, and how we will get there, *Business and Information Systems Engineering*, 59 (6), pp 385–409

Setboonsarng, S, Sakai, J and Vancura, L (2009) *Food Safety and ICT Traceability Systems: Lessons from Japan for developing countries,* technical report, ADBI Working Paper Series

Simchi-Levi, D, Kaminsky, P and Simchi-Levi, E (2000) *Designing and Managing the Supply Chain*, McGraw-Hill, London

Simchi-Levi, D, Schmidt, W and Wei, Y (2014) From superstorms to factory fires: Managing unpredictable supply chain disruptions. [Online] https://hbr.org/2014/01/from-superstorms-to-factory-fires-managing-unpredictable-supply-chain-disruptions

Basics of blockchain

03

Digital transactions – the problem of double spend

One of the most promising applications of the World Wide Web has been e-commerce – allowing buyers and sellers to transact business easily over long distances. The use of credit cards and third-party payment processing services have been essential to allow the transfer of money from buyer to seller in return for the goods and services received, but there has always been some friction and significant overhead associated with the transaction as these require that both end points have in common a trusted, centralized third party. Another challenge faced by today's systems is that the maintaining of personal financial data about customers, including credit card numbers at merchant servers, introduces security vulnerabilities, with many reports of data breaches over the years resulting in credit card theft.

Technologists have thus sought for some time to develop a form of electronic cash that can be truly distributed, not requiring a centralized third party to validate and complete the transaction. Some early efforts in this direction include Digicash from David Chaum and HashCash from Adam Back (Narayanan and Clark, 2017). The main hurdle to implementing such a form of truly distributed digital currency has been the problem of double-spend. Unlike traditional paper cash or metal coins, which represent value in the form of uniquely designed, counterfeit-resistant material objects, if naively implemented digitally as any unique sequence of bits, electronic cash or digital coins can always be copied. The problem of double spend that remained open and unsolved for a long time is how to ensure that a buyer doesn't make two or more copies of the same digital coin to pay multiple vendors, rendering it an ineffective currency.

As mentioned in Chapter 1, on 31 October 2008 a person or possibly a group of people under the pseudonym Satoshi Nakomoto published on the internet a paper titled 'Bitcoin: A peer-to-peer electronic cash system'

(Nakamoto, 2008), which proposed, for the first time, an algorithm to implement a truly distributed digital currency. Shortly thereafter, in January 2009, the Bitcoin network was started and made available along with an open-source software implementation.

As we shall see below, the Bitcoin algorithm not only provided a solution to double-spend, to enable decentralized electronic cash, it also introduced and spurred the development of powerful related ideas that have other applications, including the creation of a distributed, ordered, add-only ledger/database that is nearly impossible to change (immutable), the notion of 'smart contracts' which allow agreements between users to be implemented in code in a distributed way, as well as the creation and scalable maintenance of business networks.

The Bitcoin protocol

At the core of the Bitcoin protocol is a simple but elegant idea: if all monetary transaction records (ie who sent how much to whom) are replicated widely, then there is no concern about double-spend. Whenever someone gets money (bitcoins) from a sender, they can look through the commonly available record for themselves to decide whether this is a valid or invalid (double-spend) transaction, in particular by simply verifying if someone is trying to send more bitcoins than they have (Figure 3.1).

Bitcoin is composed of a set of building blocks put together in a careful manner to achieve decentralized trust. In the following we briefly explain some of the building blocks.

Hashing

A basic cryptographic ingredient in Bitcoin is the use of hash functions to hash data. A hash function takes some data as input and typically outputs a smaller amount of random-looking data of fixed length (n bits, see Figure 3.2). It is a one-way function in that it is not possible to recover the input data from the fixed-length output (called hash). Even though the number of possible strings is much larger than the number of possible hashed values, it is possible that a given hashed value corresponds to multiple input values; with a well-designed hash function it is extremely hard to generate an input that would give the same hash as another input, so for all intents and purposes the hash is a unique 'fingerprint' of the input data. Further, a

Figure 3.1 How the Bitcoin protocol works

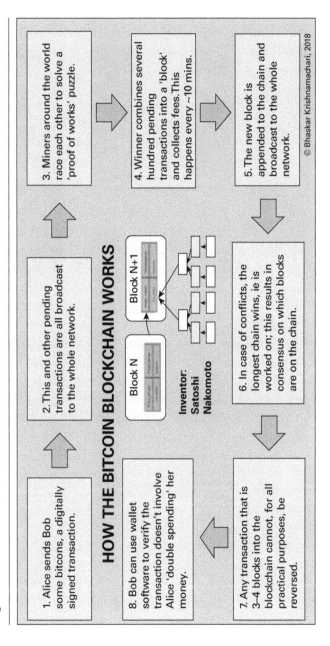

HOW THE BITCOIN BLOCKCHAIN WORKS

1. Alice sends Bob some bitcons, a digitally signed transaction.

2. This and other pending transactions are all broadcast to the whole network.

3. Miners around the world race each other to solve a 'proof of works' puzzle.

4. Winner combines several hundred pending transactions into a 'block' and collects fees. This happens every ~10 mins.

5. The new block is appended to the chain and broadcast to the whole network.

6. In case of conflicts, the longest chain wins, ie is worked on; this results in consensus on which blocks are on the chain.

7. Any transaction that is 3–4 blocks into the blockchain cannot, for all practical purposes, be reversed.

8. Bob can use wallet software to verify the transaction doesn't involve Alice 'double spending' her money.

Block N   Block N+1

Inventor: Satoshi Nakomoto

© Bhaskar Krishnamachari, 2018

Figure 3.2   Illustration of hash functions

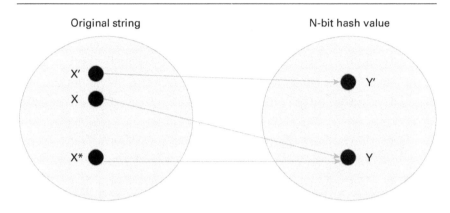

minor modification to the input (eg from X to X" in the figure) typically results in a significant modification of the hash value (from Y to Y'). The utility of hashing lies in being able to verify that some data has not been tampered with or modified. If one has the hash of the original data, it is possible to compare the hash of a given input to see if it matches the original hash. If it does, then the original data has not been modified, with very high probability. If the hashes don't match, then for sure the original data has been modified in the given input. Further, trying to identify a modification of a given input through a nonce value in order to generate a hashed value with a specific property such as a given number of zeros at the start is a computationally challenging 'puzzle' that can be used as a form of proof of work. Bitcoin makes use of the SHA256 hashing function (Dang, 2012) for its proof of work.

Asymmetric key cryptography

Another essential cryptographic scheme used in Bitcoin is the idea of asymmetric key cryptography (Figure 3.3). As the name suggests, it consists of a pair of different keys, referred to as public and private keys, that are mathematically linked to each other. A piece of data encrypted by a public key can only be decrypted by the corresponding private key. Likewise, a piece of data encrypted by the private key can only be decrypted by the corresponding public key. The private key is held as a secret by one individual, while that individual makes its corresponding public key as widely known as possible. Anyone wishing to send that individual an encrypted message uses the

Figure 3.3   How asymmetric key cryptography works

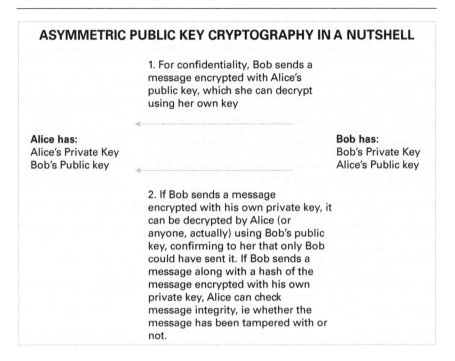

ASYMMETRIC PUBLIC KEY CRYPTOGRAPHY IN A NUTSHELL

1. For confidentiality, Bob sends a message encrypted with Alice's public key, which she can decrypt using her own key

Alice has:
Alice's Private Key
Bob's Public key

Bob has:
Bob's Private Key
Alice's Public key

2. If Bob sends a message encrypted with his own private key, it can be decrypted by Alice (or anyone, actually) using Bob's public key, confirming to her that only Bob could have sent it. If Bob sends a message along with a hash of the message encrypted with his own private key, Alice can check message integrity, ie whether the message has been tampered with or not.

public key to encrypt that message, which no one else can decode (since they do not have the private key that can decrypt it, only the public key, which cannot decrypt that message). The most famous and widely used asymmetry key cryptography algorithm is RSA (Rivest *et al*, 1978).

Digital signature

If the person encrypts a message with their private key, it can be decoded by anyone at all with the public key (thus it is not an effective scheme for confidentiality), but it has the property that everyone can verify exactly who sent the message since it must have been encrypted with the private key that only the given individual should possess (Figure 3.4); thus it acts as digital signature (Rivest *et al*, 1978). This idea combined with hashing can be used to create a more efficient digital signature – the sender first hashes the original message and then encrypts that hash with its private key and sends it to a recipient along with the original message in plain text. The recipient runs

Figure 3.4   How digital signatures work

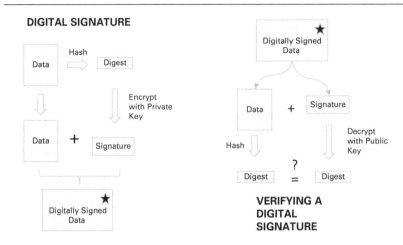

the received plain text message through the same hash and compares it against the decrypted hash to:

1 Verify that the correct sender sent the message.

2 Verify it has not been tampered with. Signing a hashed version or digest of the message also has the benefit that encrypting the hashed version is typically quite a bit faster, computationally (because the hash is a lot smaller in size than the original message).

The blockchain

An essential idea at the heart of the Bitcoin protocol is the blockchain. This is a one-way data structure that can be seen in Figure 3.5. The idea is to take a block of data (say numbered n), then include a hash of that block into the next block n+1. The process is repeated starting from block 1 onwards. The benefit of this scheme is that now, if someone were to modify some block in the middle, say block k, they would also have to modify every block afterwards. Why? We can reason as follows. Since they have modified block k, its hash would now be different from the hash stored in block k+1, so unless they change k+1 to replace the old hash with the new hash of the modified block k, their modification would be noticed. But now, for the same reason, unless they modify block k+2 the change made in k+1 will be noticed, and so on. Now, if there is some way to make the modification or creation of a block really challenging, then an adversary would find it difficult to modify blocks that are

Figure 3.5 The blockchain is a one-way data structure, with each new block containing a hash of the previous one

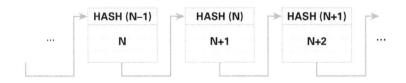

sufficiently 'deep' into the chain because of all the work they would have to do to modify all the blocks from the starting point until the last block.

Proof of work

So how could one make the creation or modification of a block challenging? The Bitcoin protocol uses an idea called HashCash, which was originally developed for stopping email spam (Back, 2002). The idea is to create a computational puzzle by adding a field called a 'nonce' into the data that is being hashed and then imposing a requirement on the output of the hash (requiring, for example, that it start with a certain number of 0s). The puzzle consists of figuring out what bits should go in the nonce field to ensure that the hash meets that requirement. This turns out to be a hard problem that can only be solved by trial and error. Adding a nonce field to each block and imposing the requirement on the hash that is stored in the next block then makes the creation or modification of a block computationally difficult. Finding (through trial and error) the nonce that makes a block with a hash meeting this property is referred to as 'mining' a block.

Transactions and blocks

But what exactly is a block? In the Bitcoin protocol it is a collection of transactions, which are essentially each a combination of from and to addresses along with the number of bitcoins being exchanged. In Figure 3.6, consider transaction 3; the total number of bitcoins (BTC) being sent into that transaction is 2.3 BTC, coming from the combined partial outputs (as shown) of transactions 1 and 2. The number of bitcoins sent out from that transaction to various addresses (including potentially a transaction fee) total 2.3 BTC as well. The total number of transactions in each block depends on the size

Figure 3.6 Bitcoin transactions

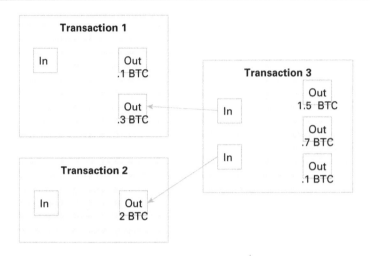

of each transaction that is added, as there is a limit on the total block size (1 MB in the original protocol). Each transaction is broadcast to the whole network.

Distributed mining and mining difficulty

In the Bitcoin protocol, all nodes get to mine simultaneously. Each node gets to choose which transactions to include in a block and then attempts to mine that block and add it to the chain. A block is mined roughly once every ten minutes, with a decentralized algorithm that changes the difficulty level of the puzzle (which translates to how many zeros are required at the beginning of the hash) as needed to ensure that the time to mine is about ten minutes. Thus, if there are a lot of miners or a lot of computation available for mining, then the difficulty level is likely to go up, and if the number of miners decreases then the difficulty level can even be adjusted downwards. Figure 3.7 shows the adjustment of mining difficulty over time on Bitcoin.

Once a block is mined it is added to the blockchain and the updated blockchain is broadcast to all other nodes in the network. Because mining is distributed, it is possible that a 'fork' occurs. This happens when more than one miner mines a block at the same round and for some time there may be two (or more) different versions of the blockchain. To resolve this conflict, a policy of 'pick the longest blockchain' is used by miners, ie they always prefer to add a block to the chain with the greatest number of blocks. Any chains that are not long will tend to have fewer miners working on them

Figure 3.7 Bitcoin mining difficulty level over time

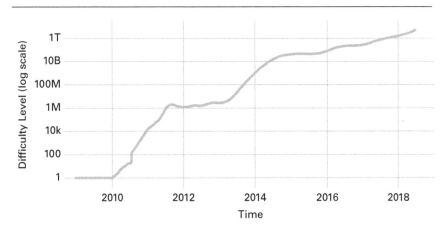

(the ones that have not seen the longest chain for some reason) and these chains will take longer to add new blocks to, making them even shorter than the longest chain over time. Over time this policy ensures consensus on one version of the blockchain. Typically, once a block is about five to six blocks deep into the chain, it is likely to be on the longest blockchain, and thanks to the difficulty of the proof of work puzzle it becomes very difficult for an adversary to modify a block that deep into the blockchain and still keep up with the longest chain, which acts as a security measure.

Incentives

Miners are offered two kinds of incentives to participate in the Bitcoin network. First, there is a block mining reward, which started at 50 in 2009 and is halved every four years (210,000 blocks to be precise). This reward allows new bitcoins to come in to existence. This geometric progression of block rewards means that the total number of bitcoins that will ever exist has a finite bound. Second, there is a reward from transaction fees. Each transaction that is broadcast has a transaction fee associated with it that is chosen autonomously by the sender of the transaction. A miner has an incentive to select the highest fee transactions in choosing which ones to include in the block.

Thus, at times when there are a lot of pending transactions, the average transaction fee associated with a transaction that makes it into the block tends to go higher, and vice versa. In turn, senders of transactions may self-select and choose not to send transactions during times that the transaction queue (called mempool) is high. This provides a feedback loop, keeping the number of pending transactions in check.

Another feedback loop present in the Bitcoin protocol has to do with the price of electricity. Mining is power-hungry. When the cost of electricity gets high, a miner may decide to drop out of the network because it is no longer profitable to be mining. Then, as the number of miners goes down, the difficulty level is likely to be adjusted down, reducing the computation cost, making mining profitable again.

The Sybil attack

By imposing a computational cost, proof of work mitigates a security vulnerability that can exist in anonymous distributed systems, called the Sybil attack (Douceur, 2002). A Sybil attack is mounted by an adversary who creates many spurious identities to gain advantage over a system. In the case of Bitcoin, anyone that is part of the protocol as a miner must do computational work. Thus even if someone generates a large number of identities, they cannot gain any advantage in terms of being able to increase their ability to mine a block, because computational work has to be done for each identified miner, which means there is no gain from assuming those additional identities.

The 51 per cent attack

One known vulnerability of the Bitcoin protocol is that if an adversary somehow gains more than 51 per cent of the network's computational capability, they can potentially start modifying blocks and introducing double-spend transactions, subverting the network. While there is no defence against such an eventuality, to some it is an unlikely event, and it is hoped that someone with this level of control over the network would have an incentive to keep the network stable and not maliciously disrupt it.

Sending bitcoins

With the above building blocks in place, we can see how one sender can send bitcoins to a recipient using the protocol. The sender creates a signed transaction with its address, the address of the recipient. The receiver checks to see if the sender address has a positive balance to make this a valid transaction, and typically waits for the block to be about five to six to verify that the transaction is correct. Transactions are stored in each block using a data structure called the Merkle tree (Nakamoto, 2008) that makes it easy to verify that a transaction is present.

Smart contracts

The term 'smart contracts' was first coined by Nick Szabo (Szabo, 1997). Essentially, they refer to algorithmic contracts that determine what should be done in a transaction as a function of whether certain conditions are met, without requiring the intervention of a human third party or reliance on legal recourse. Because transactions in blockchain-based cryptocurrencies are verified computationally, it is easy to expand their capabilities to allow for programmable smart contracts. The Bitcoin protocol also provides a script language that allows such smart contracts to be implemented. A simple example of a smart contract is a multi-signature account, which require multiple users to sign before a transaction is sent, with the number of required signatures being a parameter. This can allow the creation of escrow services and facilitate the operation of group funds.

Smart contracts on Ethereum

Ethereum introduced a more sophisticated implementation of programmable smart contracts that allows for more general computations through the addition of the Ethereum virtual machine (Wood, 2014). Smart contracts are coded in a language such as Solidity, and compiled into a bytecode, that every node on the Ethereum network can run (Dannen, 2017). Smart contracts maintain state variables and provide methods that allow changes to be made to those variables through messages sent by users or other smart contracts. In order to ensure that the cost associated with executing and communicating information needed for smart contracts is covered, there is a 'gas' payment associated with key smart contract operations. This programming capability added to blockchains allows the development of a wide array of novel decentralized applications ranging from voting systems to domain registration systems to securitizing digital assets to creating new token economies. There are even standards for types of smart contracts such as the ERC-20 standard for tokens. Ethereum also provides for standard APIs that allow the development of web and mobile or desktop client software that can interact easily with smart contracts on the Ethereum blockchain.

Figure 3.8   An example of an Ethereum Solidity smart contract

```
contract SimpleCoin {
      address leader;
      mapping (address => uint) remaining;

      function SimpleCoin () {
            leader = msg.sender;
      }

      function createCoin (address owner, uint amount) {
            if (msg.sender != leader) return;
            remaining[owner] += amount;
      }

      function sendCoin (address receiver, uint amount) {
            if (remaining[msg.sender] < amount) return;
            remaining[msg.sender] -= amount;
            remaining[receiver] += amount;
}}
```

Figure 3.8 shows an example smart contract on Ethereum written using Solidity – a contract is similar to a class in an object-oriented language like C++ or Java (Solidity, nd). It defines two sets of variables – one an address for a leader (which ends up being the node that deploys and initiates this contract), the other a mapping of addresses to balance amounts. It defines a *createCoin* transaction that can be performed by the leader, to generate coins for a given owner, and it defines a *send* transaction that can be used by owners of coins to send coins to others. Ethereum provides APIs such as web3.js for decentralized applications that can send transactions and receive notifications from smart-contracts deployed on to the Ethereum blockchain.

The decentralized applications that can be created in this way have two main benefits. First, since the underlying information is not stored on a central server it is robust to denial of service compared to traditional server-based applications. Second, since at least the bytecode for the smart contract is publicly available on the blockchain and can be read by all, along with the values of the underlying state variables, it allows for greater transparency and trust that a given program is truly doing what it claims to.

Beyond Bitcoin – blockchains

While the Bitcoin protocol itself is an astonishing breakthrough invention allowing for the first time a truly decentralized currency, what has been the source of even greater excitement is the following key capabilities and properties of blockchain protocols like Bitcoin and Ethereum, which can give rise to entirely new applications:

- Value transfer: The transactions allow movement of monetary value directly between parties.

- Data storage: The transactions and smart contracts can include data fields to store other information in the blocks, potentially useful for quite different applications.

- Programmable contracts and transactions: Blockchains allow the implementation of smart contracts and decentralized transaction-based applications with increased transparency as the code is consistently applied without possibility of manipulation.

- Decentralized: By having everyone in the network maintain a consistent copy of the blockchain, one no longer needs a centralized entity to maintain the ledger containing all transactions. At a minimum, this provides robustness to failure of nodes.

- Trustless: Allows two individuals anywhere to engage in a transfer of value without having to trust a third party; this is in itself a consequence of the decentralization. Similarly, the maintenance of the ledger doesn't require a trusted third party.

- Temporally ordered: The ordering of hashed blocks in the chain conveys that the data in block n must have been in existence when block n+1 was created (since the latter must include a hash of block n). This gives a temporal ordering to the information stored in the blockchain.

- Immutable: Transactions placed sufficiently deep into the blockchain are effectively immutable, and thus the blockchain is an add-only data store (no data-modifying updates or deletes possible). This in turn means that one can use information stored in a blockchain without concerns that it has been tampered with or modified surreptitiously.

- Archival: The entire history of transactions and data is always available. It is possible to trace back any set of activities stored on the ledger to the very beginning.

- Transparent: Unless explicitly encrypted, information about transactions is available for anyone to read and verify, increasing the trust in the stored content.

- Anonymous: In principle, the addresses used to send and receive bitcoins are anonymous sets of numbers, so anyone can participate without revealing their identity. While the transaction graph (which address transacted with which one) could be analysed to infer identities to some extent, newer schemes like Monero and Zcash have offered further ways to hide the addresses involved in transactions. Now, this is not always completely desirable, particularly in the context of business applications where the entities interacting with each other do not wish to be anonymous. For such applications, secure and verified digital identities can be used.

- Confidential: Currently, while in the original Bitcoin protocol, the amount being transferred has to be public, any other data stored on the chain can be encrypted. So long as the parties that need to see that data have the corresponding cryptographic keys they can communicate confidentially. Newer protocols have enabled setting up private 'channels' that allow multiple parties to be easily able to exchange confidential information with each other and no other parties.

Permissioned blockchains

Keeping in mind the above key properties as the essential benefits of block-chain technology, researchers and developers identified an alternative architecture for blockchain technology that generally eliminates anonymity, not allowing anyone that is not known to others to submit transactions. In this *permissioned* architecture, suitable for business networks in which the participating entities are known and identified from the start, the core components of having a distributed blockchain-based ledger, with programmability, are retained; however, the process by which the distributed ledger is maintained is changed. One reason for this is that the Sybil attack is no longer a concern if there is a permissioning process to join the network so that all parties are known and cannot assume false identities. Therefore, it is not essential to run the proof of work algorithm to provide a defense against the Sybil attack and to achieve consensus through the longest chain strategy. Instead, the identified participants can run a deterministic distributed consensus algorithm to agree on the last block to be added to the chain.

This has several advantages. First, thanks in part to extensive research in the academic community on distributed consensus protocols, the consensus process is quite fast and allows for much higher transaction volumes. Today, permissioned blockchain systems are capable of thousands of transactions per second compared to tens of transactions per second for open, permissionless chains. Second, the algorithms can potentially provide provable guarantees with respect to fault tolerance. There are a number of known algorithms that are guaranteed to be tolerant to arbitrary 'Byzantine' failures (which include the possibility of malicious adversaries) so long as at least two-thirds of the participants behave correctly without faults.

Such private, permissioned blockchains are gaining in popularity for many business and enterprise applications and operations spanning multiple organizations such as reconciling records between banks and establish distributed ledgers for supply chain. Examples of such permissioned blockchain systems include Hyperledger Fabric, Ripple and Enterprise Ethereum.

Hyperledger

The Hyperledger project is an open source effort of the Linux Foundation that includes many frameworks and tools. One particularly popular and well-maintained framework within the project is Hyperledger Fabric, an open source permissioned blockchain developed and contributed initially by IBM (Cachin, 2016; Androulaki *et al*, 2018). It has a modular architecture allowing different consensus algorithms and different permissioning and ordering schemes to be swapped in a plug and play manner. Hyperledger Fabric 1.0, released on July 2017, includes channels for allowing parties to exchange confidential information, an ordering service that ensures validating peers get consistently ordered transactions, endorsement policies for transactions, CouchDB to support a range of queries, and a bring-your-own membership service provider model. It also allows the definition and deployment of programmable smart contracts (called chaincode in Hyperledger Fabric terminology).

Measurements indicate that with about a dozen nodes serving as endorsers, responsible for maintaining and verifying the full copy of the distributed ledger, Hyperledger Fabric is today capable of transaction throughputs on the order of several thousand transactions per second.

For rapid modelling and development of business applications, the project includes Hyperledger Composer, which starts with a template to model and develop applications involving business networks to be run in a decentralized fashion using Hyperledger Fabric, or in principle even other blockchains/distributed ledger technologies (Dhillon *et al*, 2017). In Hyperledger Composer, the core data of a business network including the business model, transaction logic and access controls are packaged in the form of a business network archive that can be deployed easily to a runtime. We discuss below how Hyperledger Composer can be used, with an example.

Figure 3.9   Overview of Hyperledger Fabric, a permissioned blockchain system

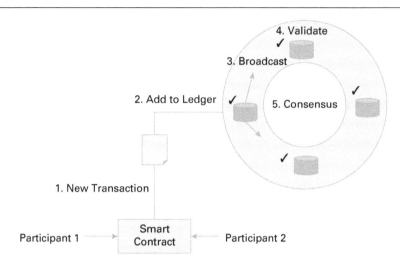

In Hyperledger composer one can define a business network and an application to put on the distributed ledger by identifying the set of participants in the network (with permissions allocated based on their roles), a set of a assets that they will transact, and the transactions that can be applied to the assets, which are represented in the form of code. Other key components include access control and queries, as shown in Figure 3.9. Consider the following illustrative example in which blockchain could be used to help customers go to a car service merchant to replace or repair the engine on their car if within the manufacturer's warranty (Verhoelen, 2018).

In this business network, the assets include engines and cars. The participants include manufacturers (who make cars and engines), merchants (who sell cars and repair/install engines), and customers (who own cars). The assets are described by relevant attributes such as their own ID, corresponding car/engine ID, current owner, and the participants are each permissioned with their own corresponding identity numbers. The possible transactions include the following: createEngine, createCar, installEngine, repairEngine, transferCar, sellCar, transferEngine.

Let us track what may happen to a particular car. When it is first created, a createCar transaction records the creation date, assigns it an ID and records this creation on the ledger. When an engine is created a similar record

Figure 3.10 Hyperledger Composer: key elements of a business network definition

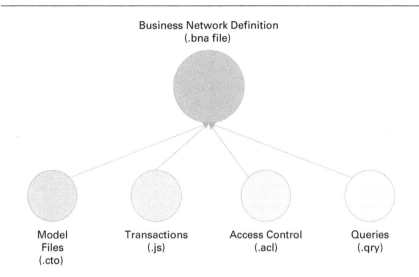

Business Network Definition
(.bna file)

Model Files (.cto)   Transactions (.js)   Access Control (.acl)   Queries (.qry)

is created for it using the createEngine transaction. When an engine is first installed in the car, the installEngine transaction is used to pair the engineID with the carID. All records are time-stamped. When the car is sent from the manufacturer to the merchant, a transferCar transaction may be used to record that. And when a customer is sold the car, a sellCar transaction is called which updates the ownership of the car and its installed engine along with the sale date.

Now, say the engine is covered by a three-year warranty. At any time within the warranty period if the customer comes to the merchant with a complaint about the engine, the merchant can quickly verify whether the warranty holds. If so, the merchant may repair the engine if possible locally, and record the repair on the ledger using the repairEngine transaction. Or perhaps the engine may need to be replaced. In this case, the merchant may get a new engine (recorded on the ledger using a transferEngine transaction to note its ownership changing from the manufacturer to the merchant) and install it on the customer's car. An installEngine transaction would transfer ownership of the new engine to the customer, and pair that new engine's ID with the car ID, replacing the older ID. Thus, the records on the blockchain can keep a faithful record of events in the real world.

References

Androulaki, E, Barger, A, Bortnikov, V, Cachin, C, Christidis, K, De Caro, A, ... and Muralidharan, S (2018) Hyperledger Fabric: A distributed operating system for permissioned blockchains, arXiv preprint arXiv:1801.10228

Back, A (2002) Hashcash: A denial of service counter-measure. [Online] http://www.hashcash.org/papers/hashcash.pdf

Cachin, C (2016) Architecture of the Hyperledger blockchain fabric, *Workshop on Distributed Cryptocurrencies and Consensus Ledgers*, July

Dang, QH (2012) Secure hash standard (shs) (No. Federal Inf. Process. Stds.(NIST FIPS)-180-4)

Dannen, C (2017) *Introducing Ethereum and Solidity*, Apress, Berkeley, CA

Dhillon, V, Metcalf, D and Hooper, M (2017) The Hyperledger project, in *Blockchain Enabled Applications*, Apress, Berkeley, CA, pp 139–49

Douceur, JR (2002) The Sybil attack, in *International Workshop on Peer-to-Peer Systems*, Springer, Berlin, Heidelberg, March, pp 251–60

Hyperledger Fabric: A blockchain platform for the enterprise at the Linux Foundation. [Online] https://hyperledger-fabric.readthedocs.io

Nakamoto, S (2008) Bitcoin: A peer-to-peer electronic cash system. [Online] http://bitcoin.org/bitcoin.pdf

Narayanan, A and Clark, J (2017) Bitcoin's academic pedigree, *Communications of the ACM*, **60** (12), pp 36–45

Rivest, RL, Shamir, A and Adleman, L (1978) A method for obtaining digital signatures and public-key cryptosystems, *Communications of the ACM*, **21** (2), pp 120–26

Solidity (no date) [Online] https://solidity.readthedocs.io/

Szabo, N (1997) The idea of smart contracts, *Nick Szabo's Papers and Concise Tutorials*, 6

Verhoelen, J (2018) Implementierung einer Blockchain-Anwendung mit Hyperledger Fabric und Composer. [Online] https://www.informatik-aktuell.de/betrieb/virtualisierung/eine-blockchain-anwendung-mit-hyperledger-fabric-und-composer.html

Wood, G (2014) Ethereum: A secure decentralised generalised transaction ledger, *Ethereum Project Yellow Paper*, **151**, pp 1–32

Internet of Things, data analytics and other information technologies

04

In this chapter we explore a number of emerging computational technologies that are relevant to a wide range of supply chain applications. These technologies complement blockchain technologies to provide ways to improve tracking and efficiency of supply chain operation.

The Internet of Things

The Internet of Things (IoT) is the name given to a diverse set of technologies that work together to provide networked sensing and actuation capabilities for applications that span the cyber and physical worlds (Unemyr, 2017). The term is intended to be a contrast with the fact that the original internet, which is still largely what we have today, was primarily intended for people to communicate with each other. Most end-to-end traditional internet applications, whether it be email or websites or social media, have humans both generating data and consuming it. Thus the internet is primarily for connecting humans to each other today. By contrast, with the wide availability of embedded microcontrollers that can read live measurements from digital electronic sensors, it is now possible to deploy such embedded sensors for various uses and have them generate data that could be of meaningful use to some application. For example, an embedded sensor that measures the temperature of a box used to transport fresh food products, connected to the internet, could provide a live stream of readings that are useful to monitor and assess the condition of the goods during shipment. Likewise, it is also now possible to connect embedded actuators to the internet, so that it is possible to take some action on the physical world remotely – for example, to move a robot arm or turn on a cooling fan.

Thus, smart 'things', whether they be sensors or actuators, or other electronic devices can be connected to the internet and operated remotely. As the numbers of embedded controllers grow dramatically, such uses of the internet involving communications between things and people as well as between things and other things, referred to also as machine to machine (M2M) communications, are going to outnumber the original person-to-person communication uses of the internet, accounting for the phrase 'the Internet of Things'.

Architecturally, the Internet of Things can be viewed as seen in Figure 4.1. On one end are the 'things' layer at the 'edge' consisting of sensors, actuators, cameras and other things; but they may also possibly include some human input sources such as mobile applications or dash buttons. These may be locally connected through a single-hop or mesh wireless network. The local edge network also typically has a local hub or gateway node that provides access to the wider internet, and possibly includes also some local edge computation capabilities that are more substantial in principle than what may be possible to fit on resource-constrained things.

Figure 4.1 Internet of Things architecture

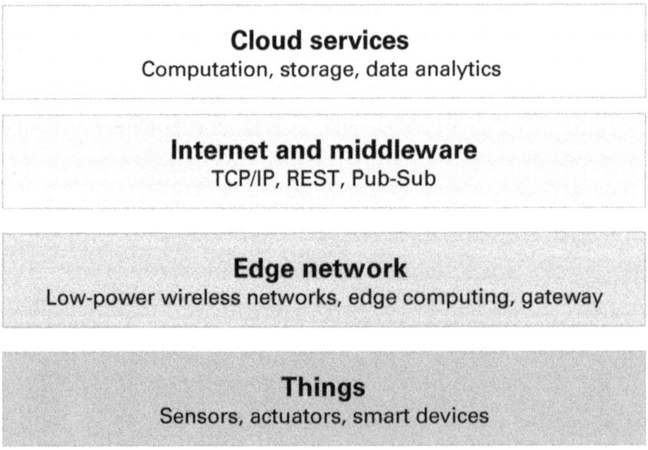

Cloud services
Computation, storage, data analytics

Internet and middleware
TCP/IP, REST, Pub-Sub

Edge network
Low-power wireless networks, edge computing, gateway

Things
Sensors, actuators, smart devices

There are often technical challenges affecting the capability of sensors that measure relevant physical readings in order to communicate them to applications over the internet. The things at the edge are often resource constrained due to limitations on form factor and energy availability. Low-power operation of sensor devices sometimes requires that they be periodically put to sleep, resulting in low-frequency sensing, so that their batteries can last longer. Energy-driven constraints on processor, memory, storage and radio capabilities can further limit performance, so that each individual sensor may only collect and communicate at the rate of a few bytes per second.

Consider the following few examples of IoT sensors that may be useful in the context of supply chain applications:

- Location tracking of assets using global positioning systems (GPS): GPS devices can infer the position of an object by collecting and processing signals from geo-positioning satellites (Misra and Enge, 2006). Because the satellites are located quite far from the earth and due to limitations on their transmission power, the received signal is quite weak and therefore GPS systems typically only work well in outdoor, line of sight environments (even foliage cover of trees can affect reception of GPS signals). They typically provide meter-scale accuracy of location, and can be used for asset tracking applications such as keeping tabs on the location of a fleet of shipping/delivery trucks. Note that GPS sensor readings must still be communicated from the device to the monitoring application (typically over the internet) so that there is also the need for a wireless communication mechanism. When used to track vehicles, power is typically provided directly from the vehicle, although lighter-weight battery-operated GPS devices could also be deployed for tracking in a more flexible manner.

- Location tracking using passive radio frequency identification (RFID) devices: Passive RFID tags (Lai and Cheng, 2014; Gao *et al*, 2004) reflect electromagnetic radio-frequency signals from a reader in such a way that they can be uniquely identified. Typically they can only be detected and read over a short range due to power limitations on RFID readers. Ultra high frequency RFID tags used on pallets or cases for supply chain applications are typically readable over a short range of about 10 metres or less.

- Location tracking using active radio frequency (RF) beacon devices: Slightly more sophisticated and with higher range are battery-operated radio beacon devices that can be measured as high as 100m away. They also require potentially less expensive, potentially mobile readers, and can be used, in conjunction with RF-based location algorithms, for localization of assets in larger indoor spaces such as warehouses (Hightower and Borriello, 2001).

- Temperature sensors: For applications such as cold-chains, which are temperature-controlled supply chains needed for perishable goods such as food, and certain pharmaceuticals and chemicals, it is important to monitor the temperature of the goods in movement (Dada and Thiesse, 2008; Pang *et al*, 2015). This can be done with temperature sensors connected to embedded wireless devices placed in the containers. The frequency and accuracy of sensing can vary on factors such as power consumption and supply, cost of the system, sophistication of calibration mechanisms, etc.

- Accelerometers: Another sensor that can be useful in the context of supply chain applications is an accelerometer. Typically these provide the acceleration in three dimensions, but may also be part of a 9-axis inertial motion unit (IMU) that combine 3-axis accelerometer, with 3-axis gyroscope and 3-axis magnetometer readings. The gyroscope provides information about rotations, while the magnetometer provides magnetic field readings that can be used to compensate for and correct drift due to errors in the sensing as well as provide compass heading. A 9-axis IMU can provide accurate position and angle information about tracked objects, and even a basic accelerometer can help detect undesirable events such as jostling of a delicate or fragile package as it moves through the supply chain (Pang *et al*, 2015).

The data from sensors is typically collected and stored locally at an embedded microcontroller device. While in principle these devices could be read from at any time by connecting them to a reading device (such as phone or laptop in wireless range or connected by a wire), for useful applications where the data is needed at a remote point in real time, it is essential that there be a way for the sensor device to send data over the internet. The sensor itself may have a low-power radio on board. Examples of wireless technologies commonly encountered for the link to/from a sensor device are the following:

- RFID: For passive RFID tags, the data is actually measured and collected at the reader (which essentially emits and reads RF electromagnetic signals scattered from the device) and not the tag itself. The reader itself may be connected to the internet through a wired LAN connection or wirelessly through WiFi or cellular connectivity.

- WiFi: The sensor devices may have a WiFi chip on board, allowing them to talk directly to a nearby access point that is internet connected. While traditionally WiFi is not designed to be energy-efficient, there are now low-power WiFi chips available that allow for battery operated sensors to use WiFi for communication (albeit often at lower data rates).

- Cellular data: The device may have a traditional cellular data connection supported by a SIM card. Typically, using a traditional cellular data connection has a higher energy cost and thus is best suited for sensors that have adequate access to power supply.

- Bluetooth and Bluetooth low energy: Bluetooth is a wireless standard that is well suited for direct short range communication, typically with a small set of devices. The newer Bluetooth low energy (BLE) standards (Gomez *et al*, 2012) allow for very low-power consumption and are used for example in beacons and to communicate data from other low-power active sensors. In many cases, BLE and Bluetooth are used because they provide an easy access to be paired with smartphones that are nearly always Bluetooth enabled, but they could also be connected more directly with Bluetooth readers or hubs that can communicate with multiple devices at once.

- IEEE 802.15.4/Zigbee: Another standard for low-power wireless communications that dates back to the 2000s is IEEE 802.15.4, associated with the Zigbee alliance (Baronti *et al*, 2007). This standard provides for short-range wireless communications on the order of 10 metres or even less with very low power consumption on the order of tens of milliwatts. It is well suited for battery-operated wireless embedded devices. It can be used to develop a multi-hop mesh low-power wireless network that routes the data from one node through multiple intermediate nodes before reaching a gateway. Newer variants of this protocol such as IEEE 802.15.4e along with IETF standards such as 6TiSCH that allow for time-slotted channel hopping allow for more predictable, reliable communications so long as the wireless network is deployed at sufficient density.

- Long-range radio (LoRA) and SigFox: LoRA is a relatively newer proprietary standard launched by Semtech and supported by the LoRA Alliance (Sornin *et al*, 2015; Augustin *et al*, 2016). It allows for low-power communication with wireless IoT sensors over very long distances (as much as 10km in rural areas with line of sight communications). Another proprietary standard for low-power long-range wireless communication with IoT devices that is also emerging recently is Sigfox, which shares some similarities with cellular wireless networks (Centenaro *et al*, 2016).

- Narrowband IoT (NB-IoT) and LTE-M: The NB-IoT system (Chen *et al*, 2017) is a low-power wide area network standard developed recently by the 3GPP cellular standards body, being deployed by cellular providers. LTE-M is another standard for low-power WAN that works with the LTE standard. These standards provide a way for IoT devices to be connected directly to the widely deployed cellular networks.

The sensor data from low-power wireless embedded devices is typically sent over a wireless single- or multi-hop network to a gateway node close to where the IoT sensor devices are located. From this point, the data is typically further communicated over the internet for cloud-server or end user devices to consume.

Traditionally, as seen in Figure 4.2, communication networks are typically organized into five main layers on the internet: physical, data link, network, transport, and application (Keshav, 1997). We have already described how various wireless physical, link and network layer communication standards are likely to be used to move data from low-power embedded sensors to a local gateway. Further, at the network layer, traditional intra-domain and inter-domain Internet Protocol (IP) routing protocols are used to move the data to the desired destination using IP address-based routing mechanisms. Increasingly for IoT devices, the newer version of IP called IPv6 is used because it provides a sufficiently large address space for as many as 2^{128} devices (a number so vast that there is no danger of ever running out of addresses for end-devices, as had started to happen with the previously deployed version that it was designed to replace, called IPv4).

Figure 4.2   Five layers on the internet

Layer Number	Layer Name	Protocols	Data Unit	Addressing
5	Application	HTTP, MQTT,...	Messages	–
4	Transport	TCP, UDP	Segments, datagrams	Port number
3	Network	IP	Packets	IP address
2	Data link	802.11 (WiFi), 802.15.4 (Zigbee), ...	Frames	MAC address
1	Physical	802.11, 802.15.4, ...	Bits	–

At the transport layer, there are essentially two main choices on the internet – User Datagram Protocol (UDP) and Transmission Control Protocol (TCP). UDP is intended for best effort delivery of data that is loss-tolerant and has lower overhead as it doesn't established any persistent connection between end points across the internet. TCP, on the other hand, is designed to provide more robust, reliable, in-order delivery but incurs a higher overhead.

At the application layer, there are several protocols and mechanisms that can be used to communicate IoT data across the internet. These include REST and Pub-Sub application-layer systems, described below.

- REST-based IoT applications: REST stands for REpresentational State Transfer and is an architecture for end-to-end web services applications on the internet that use a client-server model (Fielding and Taylor, 2002). It is easiest to understand as a generalization of HTTP, the protocol used for browsing the web. The client in case of HTTP is the browser, and the server is a software associated with the website. The client communicates with the server through simple, uniform, stateless, operations/commands/requests including GET, POST, PUT, UPDATE, DELETE among others (see Figure 4.3). The client requests and modifies resources located at the server using these commands. The resources are referred to using a uniform resource link (URL) that the server can use to identify relevant information to serve up to the browser client. The 'statelessness' consists in the fact that the server doesn't need to maintain any memory of past requests, all necessary information to satisfy a given

Figure 4.3 REST-based web services

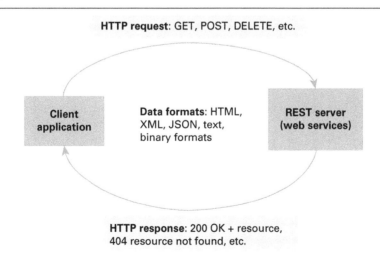

HTTP request: GET, POST, DELETE, etc.

| Client application | Data formats: HTML, XML, JSON, text, binary formats | REST server (web services) |

HTTP response: 200 OK + resource, 404 resource not found, etc.

request is contained within that request itself. In the context of IoT sensing systems, REST-based applications can be developed in two directions. The first requires the gateway to effectively act as the server that receives requests from remote nodes such as cloud compute points or user mobile devices and serves them accordingly. The second requires the gateway to connect to a cloud-based server to send its data onwards to the cloud-based server. While HTTP and REST primarily work over reliable TCP connections, there are also newer lower-overhead implementation of REST-like communications such as CoAP that use simple UDP.

- Publish–Subscribe Middleware for IoT applications: Because of their unique characteristics, such as data coming from many sensor devices that are potentially intended for a large number of end consumption points, IoT applications are often built using Publish–Subscribe Middleware such as message queue telemetry transport (MQTT), an ISO standard (Banks and Gupta, 2014). In Publish–Subscribe protocols such as MQTT (see Figure 4.4), end devices that produce or consume information act as clients that connect to a server that acts as a message broker. Devices that produce information such as sensors 'publish' (send) messages to the broker with a given topic or channel ID. Any devices that are interested in one or more topics can connect to the broker and 'subscribe' to those topics. Any messages received by the broker on any given topic are forwarded to all subscribers to that topic. Each topic thus has one or more publishers that can send a real-time stream of messages with that topic, and one or more subscribers that can receive those streams. Besides MQTT (implemented in the open-source mosquitto broker as well as RabbitMQ) there are other Pub–Sub Middleware protocols and systems such as AQMP, XMPP, DDS and Apache Kafka

Figure 4.4   MQTT Publish–Subscribe protocol

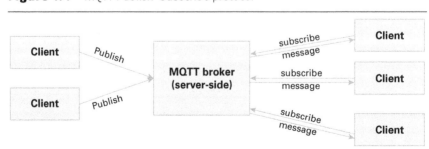

with different levels of scalability and performance. There are also proprietary cloud real-time Publish–Subscribe based messaging service solutions such as PubNub and Satori. Pub–Sub systems typically implement the message broker functionality on a server and provide software application programming interfaces (APIs) and software development kits (SDKs) to allow the design of publish and subscribe clients that can run on every kind of device from low-power embedded devices to mobile devices to servers. Because of their flexibility, scalability, ability to support a wide range of dynamic real time flows, such Pub–Sub Middleware systems are starting to be deployed quite widely in the context of IoT systems.

The data coming from sensor systems can be streamed and aggregated to a cloud computing system where it can be stored, queried, visualized, and used to drive analytics for online decision systems including diagnostics, anomaly detection, classification, inference and predictive analytics. We next describe the role that cloud computing systems play in IoT and data management for supply chain applications.

Cloud computing

The usage of the words 'cloud computing' were popularized in the 2000s with the introduction of Amazon web services (AWS), followed soon by similar general-purpose cloud offerings by other major providers such Microsoft Azure, Google Cloud Platform, IBM Cloud, Oracle Cloud, DigitalOcean and others. At its core, cloud computing (Armbrust *et al*, 2010) is about allowing server-side code to run on compute servers made available at large-scale data centers that can remotely do processing and data management for client-side applications. One reason for the popularity of cloud services has been the growth in mobile applications where it is often essential to have data storage, management and other services to be provided from one or more powerful computer servers in an easily scalable manner.

An important predecessor to cloud computing was the development of the service-oriented architecture (Erl, 2005) in software engineering, which emphasizes the modular design of software in such a way as to capture within each service a logical (business) activity that is self-contained and works as a black box for its consumers. Each service may itself be composed of other services. Cloud computing enables applications to scale rapidly by placing such black box services online on data centres, where various functions such as reliability (dealing with node failures), security management, account management, scaling of computation to meet demand, latency management by replicating services, software upgrading, account management and authorization, etc can be handled in a scalable and flexible manner by leveraging the capabilities and experience of cloud providers. While there was some resistance in the early days to moving business-sensitive data and computations to third-party cloud provider servers, the benefits of scale and trust that have developed over the years have changed the equation, and many companies have started to entrust nearly all their data and computation to such providers.

There are several layers of cloud-computing services (Figure 4.5), as described below:

- Infrastructure as a service (IaaS): The simplest, lowest capability one can leverage from a cloud provider is to essentially rent from them raw computation, memory, storage and load-balancing capabilities. When using a cloud provider in this manner, the application developer or company that is obtaining that service is fully responsible for deciding on, licensing or designing (as needed), installing and operating all the software and data systems on their own and have the freedom to run arbitrary software. The provider typically allows the customer application developer to custom-select machines with desired capabilities and operating systems, in a way that could be scaled as needed over time, for example, to meet a growing demand for their product. Typically, customers can even select the geographic location of one or more compute points needed to best serve their customers. Traditionally, cloud computing infrastructure

Figure 4.5   Levels of cloud service

	No cloud	IaaS	PaaS	SaaS
	Application and data	Application and data	Application and data	Application and data
Self-managed	Runtime and operating system	Runtime and operating system	Operating system and runtime	Runtime and operating system
Vendor-managed	Virtualization	Virtualization	Virtualization	Virtualization
	Servers and networking	Servers and networking	Servers and networking	Servers and networking

was provided only through virtual machines where an entire operating system is provided within each instance. Typically, such large resource consuming virtual machine instances are managed and coordinated over the underlying bare-metal servers (host machines) in the provider's data centres using software called hypervisor, which have their own significant overhead. However, in recent years, lower overhead alternatives known as containers have gained in popularity. Containers provide isolation for applications without requiring each to have its own separate operating system (OS), instead running directly on the host OS with lower overhead. Besides allowing smaller pieces of code to be deployed with low overhead, the use of containers can also bring down set-up time of software from hours to minutes. A widely used tool to package applications into containers that can be run on any Linux server is Docker. Orchestration software such as Docker Swarm and Kubernetes provide the capability of launching and managing the running of Docker containers on a collection of end hosts or virtual machines with built-in capabilities such as fail-over management. Examples of cloud-based container services include Amazon's Elastic Container Service, Azure Container Service, and the Google Kubernetes Engine. Another infrastructure that is provided by cloud providers is storage, such as provided by Amazon S3, Azure storage, Oracle cloud storage, etc.

- Platform as a service (PaaS): One step up from infrastructure, this provides the customer application developers with collections of pre-built software tools that simplify the process of designing and deploying their applications. These could include program execution environments, databases, Pub–Sub or messaging middleware, web-server. While the customer application developer retains the ability to configure and customize their application using the platform and associated SDKs and APIs, this approach provides a higher-level abstraction to the customer, in that they need not rent/allocate resources manually for supporting their application, instead benefiting from automatic scaling solutions provided for them. One additional benefit of procuring PaaS over IaaS is that software upgrades and security mechanisms needed to protect the product become the responsibility of the platform provider. One example of a platform as a service offering is PubNub, which hosts a real-time Pub–Sub messaging cloud platform for applications as varied as ride-sharing, fleet management and product tracking for supply chains. Another example is presented by structured query language (SQL) database services offered by different cloud providers. Yet another family of PaaS solution are represented by mobile backend as a service (MBaaS) solutions, which provide unified APIs to access common functionalities needed for mobile applications such as push notifications, database store and query, and social network integration. An example of an MBaaS is Firebase. More recently, in the context of blockchain applications, there has been a trend to provide blockchain as a service (currently there are already such offerings, for instance, by IBM Cloud, Azure, AWS, and Oracle), in which instances of full-nodes of the desired blockchain (such as Hyperledger Fabric or Ethereum) are run by cloud providers based on parameters specified by the customer(s).

- Software as a service (SaaS): A final step in abstraction with respect to cloud computing services is to host the entire software for an full end-to-end application on the cloud accessible only through thin clients such as browsers. All the functionality and basic configuration of the full software stack is handled in this case by the cloud service provider. Some simple examples of this are office software such as Google docs or email software services such as MS Outlook and Gmail. Another example is the customer relationship management (CRM) software provided by Salesforce, which provides a range of functionalities from sales and partner relationship management to assistance with marketing, customer service, and more. SaaS applications can be sold directly to end-customers, scalably, on a subscription basis. From a business perspective, the growth of SaaS solutions has helped them reallocated IT resources as there is less need to maintain hardware and software installations, maintenance and upgrade in-house.

Big data: computation and storage

With the rapid growth in data-driven applications, software systems for supply chain management have to deal with data complexity in many ways. The field of big data management has been developing to meet these challenges (Provost and Fawcett, 2013). There are three essential dimensions to consider in the context of big data:

1 Volume: Big data applications are characterized by large volumes of data coming particularly from the growing numbers of IoT devices. Software systems must be designed to store and process an increasing volume of data over time.

2 Velocity: The data being sent from sensor devices in a supply chain is often in the form of dynamic data streams, and for many applications that are latency and time sensitive, it is important to be able to process and act on these high throughput streams in real time. Thus the software systems handling data must have significant bandwidth and compute capability.

3 Variety: Unlike traditional data management systems, the other major challenge in modern big data systems is the need to handle vastly different types of data, ranging from numbers and text representing sensed data and context to sound, images and videos. Meaningful inferences may need to be drawn by processing, combining and fusing very different types and modalities of data.

The above-mentioned three Vs provide a way to think about the challenges of big data systems; various data analytics solutions are needed to clean, process and derive meaningful inferences, predictions and decisions from raw data.

From a computational perspective, the rise of big data applications has resulted in innovative parallel and distributed computing paradigms that can take advantage of the scalable compute resources available on cloud platforms. MapReduce (Dean and Ghemawat, 2008), implemented by Apache Hadoop, is one paradigm for computation over massive data sets that leverages the availability of parallel computing by dividing the computations into two stages – a mapping stage that groups input values by pertinent keys, and a reduce function that can process the values for each key in a way that lends itself naturally to parallelization. More recently, a generalization of map reduce, the representation of computations in the form of directed acyclic graphs (DAGs) has been found to be more broadly useful for complex pipelined computations. This is the basis, for example, of the Google Cloud Data Flow distributed computing system as well as Apache Spark. Apache Spark (Zaharia *et al*, 2016) is a fully functional big data analytics engine that provides a number of other capabilities including stream processing, stream querying, a machine learning library, GraphX, an API for graphs and graph parallel-computation.

Traditional relational SQL databases (eg Oracle SQL, MySQL, PostgreSQL) are highly structured with well-defined schemas (Figure 4.6). Due to the changes in the nature of data being stored and processed with a need for greater flexibility, support for diverse types of data, and scalability have given rise to a new class of NoSQL databases (Han *et al*, 2011), as shown in

Figure 4.6   SQL vs NoSQL databases

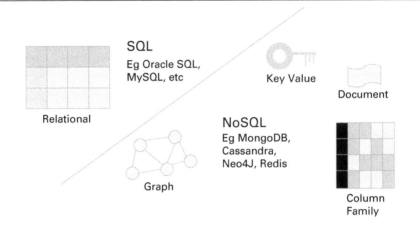

Figure 4.6. Examples of NoSQL databases that are being used for various big data are Apache Cassandra, MongoDB, and CouchDB, each with unique features and capabilities. Apache Ignite is a fast distributed database designed to be highly available and fault-tolerant, uses RAM memory for storage and in-memory computation and supports both traditional SQL and NoSQL capabilities.

Two different philosophies or models in database design are ACID and BASE. The ACID properties are atomicity (either all elements of a transaction go through or none), consistency (only valid data is entered), isolation (different transactions in parallel don't affect each other) and durability (transactions are not lost). BASE systems exhibit basic availability in the presence of failures, soft state and eventual consistency. Compared to ACID-compliant systems, BASE-compliant databases trade off consistency for availability. While traditional SQL systems are typically ACID-compliant, NoSQL systems tend to be BASE-compliant in most cases, as a way of dealing with the larger volume and velocity of data. In systems designed with BASE-compliant databases it may be necessary to build applications with additional events to signal when certain important consistent states are achieved.

Data analytics and machine learning

There are many types of algorithms for data analytics, learning and prediction that have emerged in the context of big data systems. We briefly overview some of the different types of machine learning solutions and their capabilities that have been maturing rapidly in recent years in the following, but a thorough treatment of this vast subject is certainly beyond the scope of this small section of a chapter. For such a treatment, the interested reader may wish to consult books such as Kelleher *et al*, 2015 and Müller and Guido, 2016.

Data representation

As readers familiar with computer file formats may know, different types of digital data are often represented in different ways. For building complex software systems for supply chain it is important to standardize and normalize these representations so that computational systems at different points in the supply chain can all interoperate with each other. For sensor data that can be represented as text (ie primarily numbers and strings), one widely used language-independent format is Javascript Object Notation (JSON), which essentially represents data in the form of name-value (or key-value) pairs in a very lightweight and human-readable format. IoT data may also sometimes be represented more compactly in non-human-readable binary representations such as Concise Binary Object Representation (CBOR). There are, of course, other standard binary standards for particular kinds of data such as images (JPEG, PNG), audio and video (WAV, MPEG), rendered web pages and documents (HTML, PDF), etc. Standards like SensorML further standardize how particular sensor types, values and units should be represented. There is also a trend towards using models and formats such as resource description framework (RDF, a W3C standard) and JSON with linked-data (JSON-LD) for representing relationships between different types of data and objects that they may represent; these allow for richer, semantically meaningful queries over complex interlinked data.

Data compression

When are there significant resource limitations in a system with respect to storage and bandwidth, data may need to be compressed. Data may be compressed in a lossless manner or in a lossy manner. In the former case, all information is retained. An example of a universal lossless compression system is the well-known 'zip' system, which can be applied to all kinds of digital data. An example of a lossy compression mechanism is the JPEG algorithm, which is used to represent images in an irreversibly compressed manner in a way that allows for a tunable tradeoff between compression efficiency and the quality of the image.

Data cleaning

In many applications the raw data that is made available for processing and analytics must first be 'cleaned' before it can be used. There may be many problems with the input data – for example, it may have missing and incomplete elements or there may be noise mixed in with the data, or it may be available in inconsistent formats. There are many existing techniques for dealing with some of these problems, such as interpolation approaches for missing data, or the use of digital filters for denoising audio data. Some machine learning tools may be applied to deal with certain kinds of erroneous data (for example, spelling errors or similar but inconsistent ways of referring to the same names might be easily fixable using a language processing tool). In other applications, ad-hoc cleaning approaches may need to be devised by engineers and experts based on their domain knowledge.

Data clustering and unsupervised machine learning

Given a set of data inputs, each described in terms of multiple attributes (dimensions), there are algorithms that can automatically cluster the data points and detect if they naturally fall into different categories (Figure 4.7). Algorithms for this kind of clustering in high dimensions that require no prior domain knowledge or human annotations are categorized as unsupervised

Figure 4.7   Data clustering and unsupervised machine learning

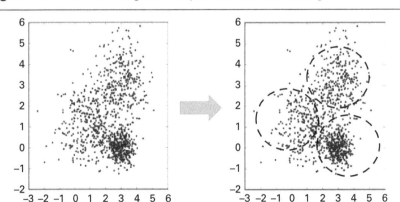

machine learning techniques. Examples of such techniques include K-means clustering, hierarchical clustering, clustering using mixture models.

Model-based Bayesian statistical inference and estimation

In some applications involving random variables that are linked to each other in ways that can be modelled using conditional probabilities and prior probabilities, certain inferences and estimations based on data-driven observations can be made using Bayesian techniques. As a concrete example, in tracking assets using RF beacons, observations of signal strength at particular known points can be used to estimate the location of the beacon using such an approach if the model for the conditional probability of getting some particular set of signal strength observations if the beacon is located at a particular point is known, or such a model can itself be learned and improved over time based on measurements.

Supervised machine learning for classification and prediction

One of the most successful applications of machine learning in recent years has been to problems related to detection and classification of complex, high dimensional inputs using what are called deep neural networks. Without dwelling on these systems in detail, it is important to note that neural networks require annotated data. For instance, a neural network to detect the presence of a particular type of item such as a shipping container in an image requires a number of images that have been previously annotated (typically by a human) to indicate whether or not they contain that shipping container. As more training data becomes available, the performance of such a classification system improves.

Typically, there are two main stages or phases in developing such a supervised machine learning system for classification – the model training phase and the model-based classification phase (Figure 4.8). Typically, the model training phase is computationally intensive for complex problems as a wide range of parameters may have to be explored and a non-linear optimization problem must be solved in order to get good performance. Once a model is trained, it can be deployed to provide classification of inputs in the second phase. The latter phase is typically less intensive. In some applications, after some time, based on the collection of new data or due to some changes in

Figure 4.8   Supervised machine learning

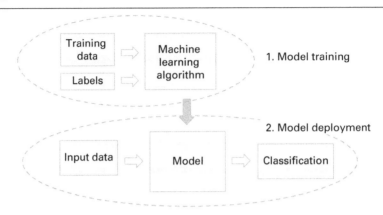

1. Model training

2. Model deployment

the underlying environment, the model may need to be re-trained. One domain that has seen particular success with supervised machine learning is computer vision, ie processing of images, using convolutional neural networks to detect objects in the images, applied, for instance, to autonomous driving and other applications. Other domains that have also benefited from neural networks are audio and speech processing, anomaly detection for software security and many others, including time-series prediction (where different architectures such as recurrent neural networks are often employed). There are several popular software frameworks for neural networks such as Google's TensorFlow, and there are also software tools with simple high-level APIs that provide an easy interface to be used to train them, such as Keras. For certain applications ready-made, pre-trained neural network based systems can be deployed rapidly, such as the real-time object detection system called YOLO, which can detect specified objects and identify their bounding boxes in a given image and high speeds. Beyond image recognition, it is important to know that neural networks can be applied any domain where there is some amount of annotated high dimensional data (such as those obtained from multiple IoT devices in a supply chain application) available, for problems as varied as detection, classification, prediction, estimation, and function approximation (regression).

Natural language and speech processing

As has been mentioned, besides image recognition, another domain that has been revolutionized by supervised machine learning is natural language and speech processing. Speech to text recognition, human language and grammar comprehension, translation capabilities, text to speech conversion, voice imitation, have all advanced rapidly in recent years, and are even available as ready-made PaaS/SaaS offerings from cloud providers such as Google, Oracle, Amazon and IBM Watson. Chatbot systems for having meaningful automated conversations with humans are now available from many companies to be customized and programmed for particular domains.

Reinforcement learning

Today's AI systems can not only learn to do classification and inference from data, they can also learn entire policies to act on the data that they encounter, in a closed loop. Applied to the problem of learning to play video games through an informed trial and error process, recent deep reinforcement learning algorithms (which use neural networks at their core, to approximate an optimized high dimensional mapping between states to actions) have had tremendous success, outperforming even expert human players. These systems have broad applicability. By working with 'digital twins' of real-world control systems and learning by trial and error through simulations, such systems can even learn to operate everything from industrial machinery and robotics to making online decisions with respect to pricing and trading, and much more. Reinforcement learning, in many ways, represents the best hope for the AI vision of autonomous systems that learn to operate themselves optimally and adapt to changes in the environment.

Data visualization

A final aspect of data analytics that bears discussion is data visualization. From real-time measurements to summarized statistics, it is often helpful to visualize the rich streams of data that are collected and analysed. Tools like Grafana provide ways to build dashboards for real-time data that allow for humans in the loop to monitor and identify relevant trends by visualizing multiple relevant metrics over time. By improving user interfaces/user experience (UI/UX) for data consumers and decision makers, such tools help tell more compelling stories with data. Another emerging trend is the use of augmented reality techniques to overlay IoT system data and inferences from that data over physical systems such as industrial plants or warehouses.

Security, privacy and trust

As we move towards an increasingly digital future for supply chains, it is important to keep in mind that computer-based information systems can be potentially vulnerable from a cyber-security perspective. Traditionally, computer security has developed ways to deal with issues related to the triad (see Figure 4.9): confidentiality and integrity of data (using encryption algorithms, transport layer security schemes and hashing mechanisms), as well as availability (through mechanisms to deal with centralized and distributed denial of service). Data-centric systems need to be careful also of privacy concerns, particularly in light of regulations such as the General Data Protection Regulation (GDPR), which can impose stiff penalties on businesses that don't treat privacy-sensitive data with a lot of care. This is a frontier where new developments are still very much in progress. Algorithmic techniques such as differential privacy (which carefully adds noise to data to provide certain privacy guarantees), partial and fully homomorphic encryption and trusted execution environments (such as Intel SGX, which provide ways to preserve the confidentiality of computations), and systems that limit data storage and provide ways to allow users to retract and delete data about them are currently being developed.

Blockchain protocols and blockchain-based systems, built as they are over cryptographic primitives, are being designed to incorporate many of these capabilities, and often provide some measure of security protection against a fraction of nodes not only failing but acting adversarially. However, they still remain vulnerable to traditional problems such as zero-day bugs in the protocol and smart contract software (that have not been previously discovered or fixed). Fundamentally, blockchain-based systems aim to

Figure 4.9   Data security and related concepts

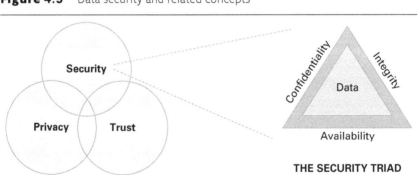

THE SECURITY TRIAD

provide a level of distributed trust, so that interactions between self-interested parties that cross traditional trust boundaries can be enabled with less friction, an important capability for supply chain systems. While block-chain technologies provide the guarantee that data, once entered on a distributed ledger is immutable, however, they cannot guarantee that the data was valid/correct in the first place. Particularly if data is being sent to a blockchain from sensors, additional tamper-proofing, verification, validation and correction measures may be needed to ensure that it is correct and valid. This can be a hard problem to solve in some settings.

Integration of IoT and other technologies for supply chain with blockchain

As blockchain technologies mature for supply chain applications, they are likely to be integrated seamlessly with the IoT, cloud computing, data analytics and security technologies described in this chapter. As two examples of such integrations consider a) the combination of IoT-based Publish–Subscribe systems and blockchain technologies, and b) decentralized marketplaces for IoT data.

Publish–Subscribe and blockchain

Traditionally, as described above, Publish–Subscribe is implemented using a client-server approach whereby publish and subscribe clients communicate with a broker that is hosted on a server (Figure 4.10). In the context of supply

Figure 4.10   Distributed Publish–Subscribe brokers with blockchain

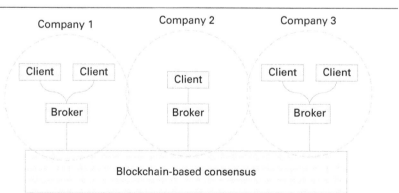

chain, where there may be IoT and other data-streaming devices deployed in many organizations and there is a need to share the streams in a trusted manner, such a centralized approach may not always be a good fit. One approach that has been proposed is to replace the single central broker with a collection of distributed brokers that maintain consistent state through a consensus process. A well-known Pub–Sub system that is capable of providing such a capability is Apache Kafka, which includes a component called Apache Zookeeper which provides for consensus, more specifically a capability called atomic broadcast, among multiple nodes so that each is guaranteed to provide data in the same order. Apache Zookeeper provides for atomic broadcast in a way that is resilient to less than N/2 crash failures (nodes leaving the network). A stronger form of trusted Publish–Subscribe could be provided by connecting a distributed collection of traditional Pub–Sub brokers hosted by different consortium members using a Byzantine fault-tolerant consensus protocol. Trinity (Ramachandran *et al*, 2018a) (Figure 4.10) is one such system recently proposed and demonstrated, which connects different MQTT Publish–Subscribe brokers to the permissioned Tendermint Byzantine fault-tolerant consensus-based blockchain in order to guarantee that each broker's subscribers see the same verified stream of information from publishers to any/all the broker, consistently, and in the same order. Trinity can be enhanced with smart contract logic that allows individual nodes to make autonomous decisions based on IoT device measurements.

Figure 4.11   Streaming data payment protocol

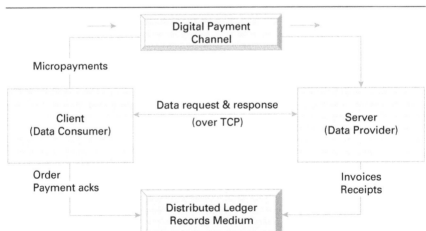

Decentralized marketplaces for IoT data

By enabling micro-payments for digital data and streams, blockchain technologies are starting to allow different organizations to exchange data between providers and consumers who may be different parties in a supply chain consortium, where the data may cross trust boundaries, in a seamless manner. The Streaming Data Payment protocol (SDPP) (Figure 4.11) is an example of a payment channel-agnostic and distributed ledger technology-agnostic application layer protocol that allows the buyer and seller of a data stream to transact comprehensively over that data, with periodic micro-payments using cryptocurrencies or traditional electronic payment rails, and blockchain-based storage of records including orders, invoices and receipts (Radhakrishnan and Krishnamachari, 2018). Efforts such as Ocean protocol and the decentralized data marketplace project at the University of Southern California (Ramachandran *et al*, 2018b) have proposed ways to allow sellers to post registries using smart contracts that buyers can browse to determine and acquire data streams they would be interested in. Other elements of such decentralized IoT marketplace such as dynamic pricing, search and decentralized recommendation systems using token-curated registries, etc are still in the early stages of research and development.

References

Armbrust, M, Fox, A, Griffith, R, Joseph, AD, Katz, R, Konwinski, A and Zaharia, M (2010) A view of cloud computing, *Communications of the ACM*, **53** (4), pp 50–58

Augustin, A, Yi, J, Clausen, T, and Townsley, WM (2016) A study of LoRa: Long range and low power networks for the Internet of Things, *Sensors*, **16** (9), p 1466

Banks, A and Gupta, R (2014) MQTT Version 3.1. 1, *OASIS Standard*, 29

Baronti, P, Pillai, P, Chook, VW, Chessa, S, Gotta, A, and Hu, YF (2007) Wireless sensor networks: A survey on the state of the art and the 802.15. 4 and ZigBee standards, *Computer communications*, **30** (7), pp 1655–95

Centenaro, M, Vangelista, L, Zanella, A and Zorzi, M (2016) Long-range communications in unlicensed bands: The rising stars in the IoT and smart city scenarios, *IEEE Wireless Communications*, **23** (5), pp 60–67

Chen, J, Hu, K, Wang, Q, Sun, Y, Shi, Z and He, S (2017) Narrowband Internet of Things: Implementations and applications, *IEEE Internet of Things Journal*, **4** (6), pp 2309–14

Dada, A, and Thiesse, F (2008) Sensor applications in the supply chain: The example of quality-based issuing of perishables, in *The Internet of Things*, Springer, Berlin, Heidelberg, pp 140–54

Dean, J and Ghemawat, S (2008) MapReduce: Simplified data processing on large clusters, *Communications of the ACM*, **51** (1), pp 107–13

Erl, T (2005) *Service-Oriented Architecture*, vol 8, Pearson, India

Fielding, RT, and Taylor, RN (2002) Principled design of the modern Web architecture, *ACM Transactions on Internet Technology (TOIT)*, **2** (2), pp 115–50

Gao, X, Xiang, Z, Wang, H, Shen, J, Huang, J and Song, S (2004) An approach to security and privacy of RFID system for supply chain, in *E-Commerce Technology for Dynamic E-Business*, 2004, IEEE International Conference, September, pp 164–68

Gomez, C, Oller, J and Paradells, J (2012) Overview and evaluation of Bluetooth low energy: An emerging low-power wireless technology, *Sensors*, **12** (9), 11734–53

Han, J, Haihong, E, Le, G and Du, J (2011) Survey on NoSQL database, In *Pervasive computing and applications (ICPCA)*, 2011 6th IEEE international conference, October, pp, 363–66

Hightower, J and Borriello, G (2001) Location systems for ubiquitous computing, *Computer*, **34** (8), pp 57–66

Kelleher, JD, Mac Namee, B and D'Arcy, A (2015) *Fundamentals of Machine Learning for Predictive Data Analytics: Algorithms, worked examples, and case studies*, MIT Press, Cambridge, MA

Keshav, S (1997) *An Engineering Approach to Computer Networking: ATM networks, the internet, and the telephone network*, vol 1, Addison-Wesley, Reading

Lai, YL, and Cheng, J (2014) A cloud-storage RFID location tracking system, *IEEE Transactions on Magnetics*, **50** (7), pp 1–4

Misra, P and Enge, P (2006) *Global Positioning System: Signals, measurements and performance second edition*, Ganga-Jamuna Press

Müller, AC, and Guido, S (2016) *Introduction to Machine Learning with Python: A guide for data scientists*, O'Reilly Media, Inc, Sebastopol, CA

Pang, Z, Chen, Q, Han, W and Zheng, L (2015) Value-centric design of the Internet-of-Things solution for food supply chain: Value creation, sensor portfolio and information fusion, *Information Systems Frontiers*, **17** (2), pp 289–319

Provost, F and Fawcett, T (2013) Data science and its relationship to big data and data-driven decision making, *Big Data*, **1** (1), pp 51–59

Radhakrishnan, R and Krishnamachari, B (2018) Streaming data payment protocol (SDPP) for the Internet of Things, *Proceedings of the 1st International Workshop on Blockchain for the Internet of Things* (BIoT), held in conjunction with IEEE Blockchain, Halifax, Canada

Ramachandran, G, Wright, K-L, Zheng, L, Naveed, M, Krishnamachari, B, Dhaliwal, J, Trinity: A Byzantine Fault-Tolerant Distributed Publish-Subscribe System with Immutable Blockchain-based Persistence, IEEE International Conference on Blockchain and Cryptocurrency (ICBC), Seoul, May 2019.

Ramachandran, GS, Radhakrishnan, R and Krishnamachari, B (2018b) Towards a decentralized data marketplace for smart cities. Invited paper at 1st International Workshop on Blockchain Enabled Sustainable Smart Cities (BLESS 2018), Kansas City, MO, USA, held in conjunction with the 4th IEEE Annual International Smart Cities Conference (ISC2)

Sornin, N, Luis, M, Eirich, T, Kramp, T and Hersent, O (2015) *Lorawan Specification*, LoRa Alliance, Fremont, CA

Unemyr, M (2017), *The Internet of Things – The Next Industrial Revolution Has Begun: How IoT, big data, predictive analytics, machine learning and AI will change our lives forever*, Amazon Digital Services, November

Zaharia, M, Xin, RS, Wendell, P, Das, T, Armbrust, M, Dave, A and Ghodsi, A (2016) Apache spark: A unified engine for big data processing, *Communications of the ACM*, **59** (11), pp 56–65

Blockchain strategy 05

The why, what and how in supply chain management

Introduction

Prior to 2018, blockchain in SCM was the realm of some early adaptor companies (IBM, 2017; Campbell, 2016; Nation, 2017). And while in those early days the business case evolved around understanding the technology (TKI-Dinalog, 2016), we have seen a strong uptake in the interest for blockchain technology[1] across the supply chain industry since the beginning of 2018.

As a result, not only do more companies want to experiment with the technology, also the ambition levels of these early adaptors have increased. Considered across industries by many board members to be still very much of a hype in 2017, it is now part of the C-level agenda in what many see as one of the most conservative industries in the world, shipping (Tirschwell, 2018). Proof-of-concepts (PoC) developed within internal innovation labs or together with start-ups or IT service providers to showcase the possibilities and the limitations of the technology are rapidly succeeded by more advanced applications of the technology, including the integration of blockchain technology with other advanced digital technologies as IoT and AI. We refer to Chapter 4 for an introduction into these other technologies.

However, it is our experience that SCM practitioners still struggle with answering three fundamental business questions when it comes to blockchain technology. These are:

1 Why blockchain?
2 What SCM processes and metrics will be affected by blockchain?
3 How should we approach a blockchain project?

With this has come the need to get a better understanding of the actual SCM applications for which blockchain technology makes sense and, once identified, a way to select the right project(s). And while the implementation of blockchain projects resembles in many ways the implementation of more traditional ICT, these projects do have certain specific challenges of their own. This automatically raises the question about how best to implement such a project. Unfortunately, while blockchain technology has received a lot of popular and academic attention in the last two years, this has predominantly focused on technological questions of design and features, while neglecting applications, value creation and governance (Risius and Spohrer, 2017).

It is therefore not surprising that SCM practitioners currently have very little to go by when it comes to the identification and analysis of the business case for blockchain in SCM or the actual implementation. In the following three chapters we will take a first step towards remedying this, by introducing a blockchain strategy for supply chains; one that is linked to supply chain management objectives and supply chain management processes. Furthermore, we will pay special attention to factors that expedite or inhibit the implementation of blockchain within supply chains, such as the integration with legacy systems, interoperability of blockchain protocols and governance.

Chapter 5 starts with answering the question 'why blockchain?' We answer this question based on an analysis of the unique capabilities of the technology in relation to specific supply chain management challenges that companies face, and that have until now not been adequately addressed.

In Chapter 6 we look at what SCM processes and metrics will be affected by blockchain. Using the SCOR model (Apics, 2017), we will explore the various roles blockchain can play in SCM processes and through which mechanisms these roles are implemented. In Chapter 7 we will take an in-depth look at an SCM case that involves the Port of Rotterdam, Samsung SDS and ABN-AMRO; this case will provide practical insight into some of the challenges companies will face when implementing blockchain.

Why blockchain and not another technology?

'In half a day we came up with 50 some use-cases for blockchain!' or a blockchain based Uber-like application for tombstones (Sedgwick, 2017);

although blockchain technology can hardly be considered a familiar tool at this point, Abraham Kaplan's *law of the instrument* (Kaplan, 1964) already seems to apply. 'Give a small boy a hammer, and he will find that everything he encounters needs pounding.' For companies to avoid this mistake and consequently select the wrong use-cases while sifting through the countless ideas, we need to look carefully at the unique capabilities of blockchain technology and how they relate to the supply chain management pains.

Supply chain resilience

Although digitization of supply chains has been an important issue for the last two decades in industries such as retail, automobile, electronic, aviation and chemical, it has not received similar attention in other industries (Korpela *et al*, 2017). These forerunner industries are normally dominated by a small number of large corporations as a result of economies of scale. To achieve coordination, the dominant member in the supply chain can enforce standards and platforms on their sourcing and distribution partners with whom they have a contractual relationship. This results in a highly centralized system where the other supply chain members have little or no control over their data, offers them little or no benefits and is susceptible to collusion and the unauthorized alteration of data. The vulnerability of these centralized systems should not be underestimated, as the effect of the cyberattack on the results of the AP Møller-Maersk Group to the tune of $300 million (Novet, 2017) clearly shows. Crippling operations at a number of their container terminals in main ports such as Rotterdam for several days, it also had profound effects on the supply chain operations of their clients. While little is known about the direct and indirect damage to the supply chains affected by the attack, a report filed by the American pharmaceutical company Merck with the Security and Exchange Committee indicates that the attack severely impacted Merck's global production, research and sales operations (Security and Exchange Commission, 2017).

Blockchain, a distributed database for transaction processing:

- removes the presence of a central authority and consequently the single point of failure;
- provides a tamper-proof transaction ledger;
- provides trusted transactions based on algorithmically enforced rules without human interaction. As such, blockchain provides a secure end-to-end delivery of data.

This is likely to result in a lower susceptibility to manipulation and forgery by malicious participants. Not only does this apply to more traditional enterprise resource planning (ERP) and SCM applications, blockchain-based identity and access management systems can address some of the key challenges associated with IoT security as well (Kshetri, 2017b).

While blockchain technology is by no means a cybersecurity 'silver bullet', and many of today's cyberattacks could have been prevented with adequate ICT security policies, more rigorous patching procedures and replacement of end-of-life (operating) systems, it could provide a way to contain the effects of a security breach in a targeted way, in particular when IoT devices are involved (Kshetri, 2017b).

Business-to-business integration

Even in cases where there's a dominant member in the supply chain, their control remains limited to their first tier suppliers or distribution partners, primarily as a result of contractual agreements. However, disruptions at n^{th} tier suppliers can severely disrupt supply chains. This can be seen in light of a disruption in 2012 at a polymer plant, for Ford a second tier supplier, in Europe, which caused a shortage of a polymer used by most manufacturer-suppliers to make fuel tanks, brake components and seat fabrics. It took six months to restart production, a delay that had a large financial impact on the auto industry. As Simchi-Levi *et al* (2014) showed, when it comes to supply chain risk management the 'devil lies in the detail', with disruptions at suppliers of less expensive components having a much bigger impact on the results of the focal company than, say, expensive parts that fall into the high financial impact segment.

Currently, the data to manage the risks associated with these suppliers is simply not there in a centralized system, primarily because of costs reasons and their lack of flexibility, making it difficult to enforce sharing of data, even when there is a contractual agreement in place. Open-source blockchain technology offers data security and cost-effective transmission of transactions in peer-to-peer networks with no central system. In this way, blockchain technology simplifies business-to-business (B2B) integration (Korpela *et al*, 2017) while removing the aforementioned trust concerns.

Furthermore, B2B integration so far has primarily between two companies, either directly or via an information broker platform such as Seeberger or Descartes. However, often multiple specialized intermediate companies, such as banks and insurance companies, are needed to conduct supply chain transactions (Chauffor and Farole, 2009) with related exchange of documents and money. The involvement of multiple parties in a transaction, increases the complexity of those transactions, making them cost-ineffective and slow using existing B2B integration methods (Korpela *et al*, 2017). Blockchain, on the other hand, makes it possible to automate these transactions using smart contracts. This is addressed in more detail on page 97.

Traceability in the extended supply-chain

Closely related to the challenges of risk-management in a multi-tier supply-chain is tracking and tracing in an extended supply chain. Global Standard One (GS1), an international organization that develops and maintains data standards across various industries, defines track and trace as 'the ability to track forward the movement through specified stage(s) of the extended supply chain and trace backward the history, application or location of that which is under consideration' (Ryu, 2012). The value of better traceability is best illustrated with the example of the 2015 E coli outbreak at Chipotle Mexican Grill outlets that left 55 customers seriously ill. As supply chains become more complex, their transparency and accountability are reduced, compromising prevention or containment of such contamination (Kshetri, 2017a).

At the same time, companies face customer demands for product information and having the means to verify sustainability claims (BSR, 2014). The first is partly achieved through the use of labels and certifications, while the latter is opaque to consumers, NGOs, governments, advocacy organizations alike (El Maouchi, 2018). A major stumbling block that prevents the whole-chain traceability in the case of centralized systems is the fact that the central authority has to administer identities and data, giving it full visibility over all the relationships and data being exchanged. And even if the central authority manages to impose this on all his first tier suppliers, it will not include second tier to n^{th} tier suppliers. Not only do they not have a contractual obligation towards the central authority to provide data or show that they act sustainably, the first tier suppliers will be most hesitant to expose their relationships with their suppliers, for example out of fear that the focal company will bypass them and source directly. Blockchain allows for the preservation of privacy of the actors and make transactions unlinkable to the sender or recipient of the transaction while allowing full traceability through a single product-specific tracking key and validation of the authenticity of transactions (El Maouchi, 2018).

Know your transaction

Although 'know your transaction' (KYT) can be considered a specific case of traceability in the extended supply chain, we are of the opinion that this is such a vital, but up to now overlooked, functionality of blockchain technology that it deserves a separate paragraph.

It is not surprising that the financial industry, which was the first industry to adopt cryptocurrency and blockchain, is the one industry where KYT has received attention. The rise of cryptocurrency posed new challenges for banks and financial institutions around the world to comply with policies for the prevention of money laundering and the financing of terrorism (Camino *et al*, 2017). As existing 'know your customer' rules proved difficult to implement on digital currencies, primarily as a result of their varying ranges of anonymity, banks needed to start looking for alternative ways to ensure compliance. This has led to the development of big data driven analytics of ledger transactions, to identify unwanted behaviour such as *whaling* (hoarding of coins) and anomalous delays.

Similarly, combining data about transactions from the shared ledger allows for unwanted behaviour, such as delays or inaccurate data, to be identified in the supply chain. In turn, if this unwanted behaviour is reflected in their reputation within the network, members would be able to spot 'bad apples' and not use them in future transactions. As the reputation score is built from the ground up, based on the level of adherence to mutually agreed upon transactions, and continuously assessed, this measure provides a much better indication of actual reputation than passing a one-off know your customer process. In other words, KYT on blockchain would allow for bottom-up and upfront compliance.

Machine-to-machine integration

Up to now, digitization of supply chains has been primarily the realm of B2B transactions. Data is transferred from one data silo to the other. What happens between the physical points these silos represent remains largely unknown. 'Where's my container?' 'Under what conditions were my products transported?' 'Where's my railway carriage?' – these questions can normally not be answered until the data is available in one of the data silos. And although blockchain technology can impact B2B integration, we believe that IoT machine-to-machine integration is a much more powerful application of the technology and set to transform many industries. This is corroborated by early research (Christidis and Devetsikiotis, 2016; Kshetri, 2017b).

With each IoT device having its own identity and containing data about the physical item it represents, a virtual ecosystem is created. The 'virtual ecosystem' (Kok, 2014) is a system that supports cross-chain collaboration in the transportation of containers, or any packaging unit for that matter, such as cartons, cases, trollies and products (Figure 5.1).

Each container creates a digital shadow of itself that virtually categorizes relevant information. This virtual container uses an electronic dossier, stored on a blockchain, which contains the characteristics of the load, the location, shipping conditions, such as humidity and temperature, and the specific shipping instructions of the cargo. Encrypted data is being pushed to authorized supply chain partners, depending on their access rights in the dossier or certain parts of the dossier, based on smart contracts, upon changes in the electronic dossier. Companies now have the ability to share crucial information through the ecosystem, which can be used to make better decisions in optimizing the supply chain, for example, when it comes to truck utilization and CO_2 reduction across organizational boundaries. Note that each point, or address in blockchain parlance, in this 'virtual ecosystem' can have multiple connections with other points. Creating this n–n network using existing hierarchical systems would require all data to be available in a single hierarchical database

Figure 5.1   The virtual ecosystem

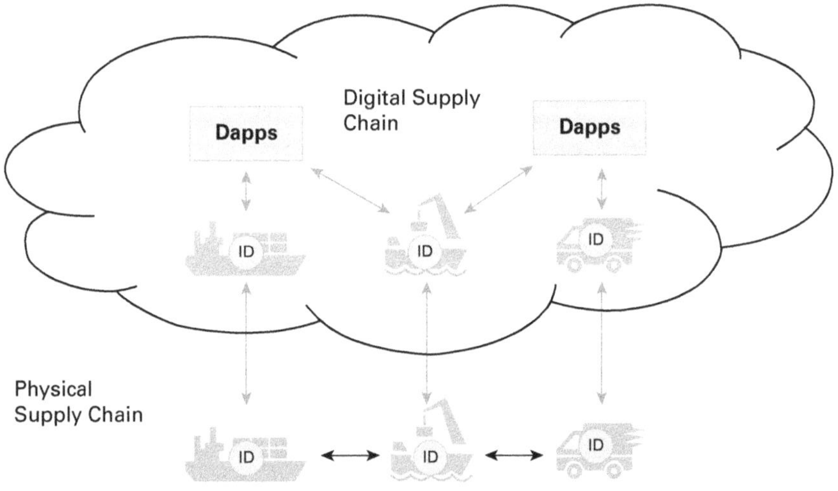

that connects to all individual items in the 'virtual ecosystem'. This would introduce an enormous single point-of-failure while at the same time giving control over the system to a single authority.

Real-time settlement of information and financial flows

A container takes approximately 36 hours to physically get from Singapore to Jakarta, Indonesia. However, information and financial settlement can take up to seven days. This is primarily due to the fact that instead of having direct access to data and being able to verify automatically whether the actual transaction (eg payment, bill-of-lading release, customs clearance, etc) happened, buyer and seller have to rely on an intricate network of trusted third parties (TTP) such as surveyors, banks, insurance companies and customs clearance agents for verification. Each transaction is only considered trustworthy once the individual ledgers of the TTP are updated and matched. As well as exchange of data, normally in the form of a document, payment(s) or some other form of value or ownership transfer are part of the transaction. While payments, and to a lesser extent invoices, might be transferred and settled automatically between organizations, the exchange of documents, such as certificates-of-origin, bill-of-ladings, waybills, is still very much a computer-paper-computer manual operation model (Korpela *et al*, 2017).

Also, as a consequence of the TTP involvement in these transactions, these are no longer simple transactions between two parties but now require the involvement of four parties, such as the buyer, the buyer's bank, the seller and the seller's bank; or the buyer, the buyer's surveyor, the seller and the seller's surveyor. This further reduces the execution speed of transactions and results in increased transaction costs. To enable real-time settlement of information and financial flows, parties must agree how this is to be done; this is where smart contract (Szabo, 1996) comes into play.[2] Szabo defines a smart contract as:

> a computerized transaction protocol that executes the terms of the contract. The general objectives of smart contract design are to satisfy common contractual conditions (such as payment terms, liens confidentiality and even enforcement), minimize exceptions, both malicious and accidental, and minimize the need for trusted intermediaries.

Through smart contracts, we cannot only digitize the document flow in the supply chain but also include 'behaviour' into these documents, allowing for automatic settlement of financial flows between two of more parties, once certain conditions are met.

A consensus-based source of truth

An efficient and effective flow of data within the supply chain is vital to achieve responsiveness to customer demand and overall customer satisfaction (Singh, 1996). Other research has shown that a supply chain that implements coordination is characterized by effective communication and data exchange. And despite technological advances, such as XML[3] and APIs[4] and the coming of age of logistics information brokers such as Descartes Seeburger and port community systems such as Portbase, sharing of information between supply chain members is still very much a cumbersome process with many organizations managing the same order, but the data is redundant and inaccurate (Kok, 2014).

A recent study from the Boston Consultancy Group (Ramachandran, 2017) clearly highlights the tremendous redundancy of data in trade finance. While the total number of data field interactions easily exceeds ~5.000, 'create/value-adding data' accounts for only ~1–2 per cent while 'ignore/ transmit to next party', accounts for ~85–90 per cent. And while we agree with Korpela *et al* (2017) that blockchain in itself cannot meet the need for standardization of electronic supply chain documents, we are of the opinion that it can be the foundation for a common 'create/value-adding' data layer, provided supply chain members are willing to look beyond their own data-silo. A perfect example of this is the bill of lading (BoL). Although, largely considered to be a maritime industry document, the data on the BoL that is actually created by the shipping line itself is quite limited. Data about the estimated time of arrival, vessel name, port of loading, port of discharge, etc, is normally captured in the booking they receive from their client while the data that is the basis for the Marks and Numbers is created by the buyer or seller.

Furthermore, most of the validation of data is done once data is transferred from one data-silo to the other. These validations don't go very deep; normally it involves some form of referencing with existing master-data such as addresses, product codes, quantities and checking whether the data transfer meets the data exchange message definition in terms of mandatory fields filled, field length and whether the data in the fields is of the right type (numeric, alfa-numeric, date, etc). However, more advanced forms of validation, such as the checking of time-stamps of the transactions, or validation of multi-party transaction data within the extended supply-chain, are still missing in today's B2B integration within the supply chain. As it turns out, these two problems are closely related and can be solved using blockchain technology, as we will describe in the following paragraph.

Blockchain and data validation

Blockchain strings together validated transactions in a way that they cannot be tempered with, and as such can be considered to provide a consensus-based source of the truth, where validation precedes the actual inclusion in the temper-proof block. As data is validated by multiple parties, based on predetermined rules, data quality within the supply chain is set to improve. The impact of better data quality on supply chain transactions should not be underestimated. According to GS1 US the use of inaccurate transactional data can cost up to 25 per cent more in labour, for instance. As with many other things, the devil lies in the detail when it comes to transactional data quality; a mere one-quarter inch error in case height measurements in freight and warehouse measurement processes could lead to 1,000 fewer product cases consigned per truckload. The result of loading 20 fewer cases per pallet equals having to use six more trucks than would otherwise be necessary. Along the same lines, participants in GS1 US's National Data Quality Program have found that making seemingly small corrections to data for a product attribute – catching a package measurement that was just 1.5 pounds off, for example – could save a company $100,000 in cost avoidance in annual transportation costs (GS1 US, 2017).

This is not only the case for transactional data, but also provenance data – metadata that records the history of the creation and operations performed in a transaction. Data provenance is crucial for data accountability, forensics and privacy (Liang *et al*, 2017). As part of the transactional data, all provenance data is collected, validated and stored in a single immutable ledger, providing a single consensus version of the truth for both transactional and provenance data.

Incentivization

Cryptocurrencies such as Bitcoin and Ethereum rely on clever technologies and incentive engineering to achieve decentralization. These incentives, in the form of cryptocurrency, are needed to ensure that nodes in the network behave honestly and only add valid blocks to the chain. Incentive-centred design is a relatively new field of research that draws heavily on economic, psychological, sociological and game theory and combines these with the design and engineering sciences of artificial intelligence, software engineering, operations research and networking. While the design of engineering incentives can get complex quickly, the basic premise is actually quite simple: 'How do we get individuals to act in line with the goals of the system?'

For many years supply chain practitioners have been told that data-sharing dramatically improves the efficiency of the supply chain (Hazen and Byrd, 2012; Croom, 2005). Yet, when it comes to actual implementation our reaction is similar to a 6-year-old whose mother says that he needs to eat his broccoli as it is good for him; the boy would rather have French fries. While this could be considered irrational and even childish behaviour, it is in fact the opposite. Why should I give up something that clearly has a value for other supply chain members and get nothing in return? In cases where there is a dominant member in the supply chain or data sharing is required for reasons of regulatory compliance, data sharing can be enforced relatively easy. But in situations such as those discussed on page 94 contractual or regulatory enforcement is near impossible. In those cases incentivization could be used to stimulate data sharing by simply rewarding people for sharing (reliable) data.

While data is an asset that is particularly suitable for incentivization, it doesn't have to stop there. Supply chains are beset with situations where parties often have conflicting goals, and where centralized solutions are difficult to implement because supply chain members are reluctant to give up autonomy or simply do not trust each other. In those cases, clever incentivization, in combination with other, more established supply chain planning and optimization solutions could help in resolving those conflicting goals.

A hybrid world

As the potential applications of blockchain technology mentioned above do not encompass all possible ICT solutions found in the supply chain it should come as no surprise that we believe that existing IT solutions such as cloud-platforms and in-house ERP[5] systems will co-exist for many years to come with blockchain solutions. Furthermore, the enormous amounts of ICT investment made over the years cannot simply be written off at the stroke of a pen. In other words, a hybrid infrastructure of blockchain and non-blockchain solutions will be the norm.

In such a world, one natural question emerges: how will all these systems interoperate? The term 'interoperability' is receiving more and more attention in the blockchain community, not only because of the rise of the number of protocols, but also because of the growing number of different chains for different industries, or even different chains within the same industry. While up to 2017 this was primarily a theoretical discussion, because it requires not one, but two already existing, stable and sufficiently powerful blockchains to build off (Buterin, 2016), the topic is quickly becoming more relevant with the first real-life blockchain applications emerging, such as IBM's Tradelens[6] and WeTrade.[7] We will discuss blockchain interoperability in more detail in Chapter 7.

However, in a hybrid world, where blockchain and non-blockchain applications exist side by side, this is not the only level of interoperability we face, if we want to take full advantage of blockchain's inherent capabilities. While one of the advantages of using platforms where cryptographic authentication is naturally baked into every single operation is that we can provide much tighter and more secure coupling between platforms than is possible with previously existing systems (Buterin, 2016), we somehow have to come to grips with the fact that a substantial part of the interaction between systems in a future supply chain will not be from one blockchain to the other, but from an ERP system or cloud platform to a blockchain or vice versa. As SCM practitioners know all too well, the chain is as strong as its weakest link, so doesn't this make blockchain a form of local optimization with little or no effect on the supply chain as a whole?

We believe that this is not the case. Not every transaction needs to be cryptographically secure. Critical transactions, such as the ones that involve transfer of value or ownership, would be most likely candidates to be moved to the blockchain, outside of the realm of ERP systems and cloud platforms. Although the transactional data would come from one or more sources that do not have cryptographic authentication naturally build into every transaction, it can be used as a starting point to create a shared view on this transaction. An example is WeTrade, which relies on data from centralized applications from buyer and seller and their respective banks to start an open account trade finance transaction but uses cryptographic authentication and smart contracts on the blockchain to ensure a shared consensus-based view on the transaction and parallel processing. Other examples of blockchain applications that run in a hybrid environment are Komgo and Vakt, two energy trade platforms underpinned by blockchain technology. Build on the Ethereum blockchain, these platforms digitize the large number of contracts, letters of credits, invoices and other paperwork currently sent around the world by email, fax or post (*Financial Times*, 2018).

Closely related to this is the use of blockchain technology as a notary at vital touchpoints between systems or organizations. For example, the bill of lading (BoL) is simultaneously an output of the export process and an input for the import process. The notary would then validate the authenticity of the BoL, for example by consulting a number of Oracles about specific data, or the signatures, in case the BoL was signed digitally. The notary then achieves consensus amongst the various Oracles on whether or not the data represents the actual transaction and then issues a signature. Furthermore, the signing of the transaction by the notary can also result in the hash of that transaction being locked, until certain conditions are met. This could be used to ensure that the original BoL remains original, and that no copies can be created. This would solve the problem related to the 'double-spending' of the BoL; ie using a single BL as a collateral for multiple loans. This problem is still very much real today, as port frauds in the Chinese metal trade show (Reuters, 2014). This is exactly one of the roles being performed by the blockchain application described in the use-case 'Deliver' in Chapter 7.

For dominant supply chain members looking to extend their control beyond tier 1 suppliers, for example, to support their risk management practices, blockchain applications can be used specifically designed for that purpose and offered as distributed application (Dapp) in a Dapp store, running on top of blockchain platforms, such as Deliver, WeTrade or Komgo. These applications could run separate from their ERP backbone used to manage their tier 1 processes, preventing expensive integration and operate on aggregated data provided by blockchain platforms such as described in Chapter 7 in the use-case 'Deliver'. Their main role would be to act as an early warning system for disruptions within their tier n supply chain, such as congestion or changes in trade flows, and provide traceability in the extended supply chain.

As already mentioned the performance of centralized systems such as ERP or advanced planning systems (APS)[8] can be greatly increased by having access to up-to-date and validated data. This sort of Oracle role is exactly what blockchain technology can provide. For example, a blockchain network can validate important events, such as estimated time of arrival, or handover of the BL, that can be used as input for transport or production planning, as well as cash-flow forecasting. Companies operating such ERP and APS systems could subscribe to such an Oracle service in order to obtain trusted and validated data. This is exactly one of the roles being performed by the blockchain application described in the use-case 'Deliver' in Chapter 7.

And while supply chain optimization algorithms that are at the heart of APS applications have seen widespread adaption in retail, logistics and manufacturing, the amount of time needed for processing these models can be a limiting factor. Especially in those cases when there are a lot of exceptions, such as congestion, unexpected outage of assets and the planning can be easily disrupted, for example, because of the late arrival of a mother vessel in case of barge planning and changes in the delivery date at final destination, the outcomes of these models can quickly become outdated. This is particularly true when there's a large interval (±24 hours) between the original outcome and the re-run of the planning. In those cases, a decentralized market could help in coordinating the transactions of the various actors in the interval.

While the above examples are certainly not exhaustive, they provide clear indication of how blockchain and non-blockchain solutions can peacefully co-exist. As such, it serves as a gentle reminder that the suitability of a certain technology is very much dependent on the situation and that there's indeed a third option between the 'you can do this on a centralized database as well' and 'put everything on the blockchain and all your troubles will be over' points of view.

A conceptual look at SCM and blockchain technology

In the previous paragraphs we have described the unique capabilities of blockchain technology in relation to specific supply chain management challenges that companies face, and that have, until now, not been adequately addressed. While this problem-related approach helps in making blockchain technology less conceptual, we believe that before we move to answering the 'what?' and 'how?' questions in the next two chapters, we need to circle back and look at SCM and blockchain technology conceptually.

So, conceptually, what does SCM stand for? Ganeshan *et al* (1999) conclude that supply chains are managed as a single entity either through a dominant member or through a system of partnerships requiring well-developed cooperation and coordination. The scope of responsibility for

Figure 5.2 Why blockchain?

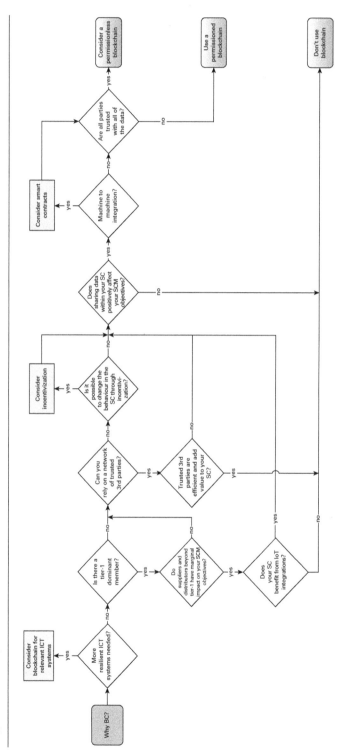

managing a supply chain is specific to the firm and its myriad of relationships with its suppliers, vendors and customers. Key words here are 'dominant member' and 'system of partnerships'. In the previous paragraphs we have seen that this is very much a question of 'centralized' versus 'decentralized'. And while we are all familiar with successful SCM cases from dominant members in the supply chain, such as Walmart, Dell and Amazon, the cases based on systems of partnerships are few and far between. This is because management of partnerships raises complex questions about autonomy, trust and 'gain-and-pain' sharing, commonly not encountered in a centralized supply chain. Up to now we haven't been able to answer these questions in a satisfactory way as the default answer of 'a trusted third party' leads to loss of autonomy and reduces flexibility. Furthermore, while the extra transaction costs as a result of a TTP can be assessed quite easily, the advantages of collaboration are much harder to gauge (Ralston *et al*, 2017). We address the business case for collaboration in some detail in Chapter 6 of this book.

We consider blockchain to be the enabling technology for peer-to-peer collaboration, a technology that allows suppliers, vendors and customers to efficiently manage the supply chain as a single entity, without the need for a dominant member or trusted third party, and so maintain autonomy, trust and flexibility. In this way, it will allow supply chains to not only reach new levels of effectiveness and efficiency, but will also create new business model opportunities for new entrants, but also existing supply chain members. To facilitate decision making we have developed a flow-chart based on the previous paragraphs (Figure 5.2).

Notes

1 Although we do not consider distributed ledger technology (DLT) and blockchain as synonyms, we will refer to them in this, and the following chapter, as 'blockchain technology'.
2 Szabo's article precedes Satoshi Nakamoto's Bitcoin blockchain by almost a decade. Among other things, Szabo describes the cryptographic building blocks needed to run these smart contracts. However, the Bitcoin blockchain made the idea practical.
3 XML (extensible markup language) is a markup language that defines a set of rules for encoding documents in a format that is both human-readable and machine-readable (Wikipedia).
4 Just as a graphical user interface makes it easier for people to use programs, application programming interfaces make it easier for developers to use certain

technologies in building applications. By abstracting the underlying implementation and only exposing objects or actions the developer needs, an API reduces the cognitive load on a programmer. (Wikipedia)

5 ERP systems create an enterprise-wide transaction backbone and integrate manufacturing, financial and other systems.

6 https://www.tradelens.com/

7 https://we-trade.com/

8 APS systems are decision support tools for planning and scheduling that use computer-based optimization (www.ortec.com).

References

BSR (2014) [Online] https://www.bsr.org/reports/BSR_UNGC_Guide_to_Traceability.pdf

Buterin, V (2016) [Online] https://static1.squarespace.com/static/55f73743e4b051cfcc0b02cf/t/5886800ecd0f68de303349b1/1485209617040/Chain+Interoperability.pdf

Camino, R, State, R, Montero, L and Valtchev, P (2017) Finding suspicious activities in financial transactions and distributed ledgers, *IEEE International Conference on Data Mining Workshops*, ICDMW, pp 787–96

Campbell, R (2016) Modum.io's temperature tracking blockchain solution wins accolades at kickstarter accelerator 2016, 14 November. [Online] https://bitcoinmagazine.com: https://bitcoinmagazine.com/articles/modum-io-s-tempurature-tracking-blockchain-solution-wins-accolades-at-kickstarter-accelerator-1479162773/

Chauffor, J-P and Farole, T (2009). Trade finance in crisis market adjustment or market failure? July. [Online] http://documents.worldbank.org/: http://documents.worldbank.org/curated/en/673931468336294560/Trade-finance-in-crisis-market-adjustment-or-market-failure

Christidis, K and Devetsikiotis, M (2016). Blockchains and smart contracts for the Internet of Things, *IEEE Access*, **4**, pp 2292–303

Croom , SR (2005) The impact of e-business on supply chain management: An empirical study of key developments, *International Journal of Operations and Production Management*, **28** (1), pp 55–73

El Maouchi, M (2018, 02) Decouples: A privacy-preserving solution for traceability in supply chains, Masters Thesis, Technical University, Delft

Financial Times (2018) [Online] www.ft.com: https://www.ft.com/content/648c3dda-bb47-11e8-8274-55b72926558f

Ganeshan, R, Jack, E, Magazine, MJ and Stephens, P (1999) *A Taxonomic Review of Supply Chain Management Research*, Springer, New York

GS1 US (2017) Invest in high-quality product data to support your growth strategy. [Online] https://www.gs1us.org/DesktopModules/Bring2mind/DMX/ Download.aspx?Command=Core_Download&EntryId=934&language=en- US&PortalId=0&TabId=134

Hazen, BT and Byrd, TA (2012) Toward creating competitive advantage with logistics information technology, *International Journal of Physical Distribution and Logistics Management*, **42** (1), pp 8–35

IBM (2017) Maersk and IBM unveil first industry-wide cross-border supply chain solution on blockchain, March. [Online] https://www-03.ibm.com/press/us/en/ pressrelease/51712.wss

Kaplan, A (1964) *The Conduct of Inquiry: Methodology for behavioral science*, Transaction Publishers

Kok, AD (2014) *Cross Chain Collaboration in the FMCG Supply Chain*, TKI- Dinalog

Korpela, K, Hallikas, J and Dahlberg, T (2017) Digital supply chain transformation toward blockchain integration, *Hawaii International Conference on System Sciences (HICSS)*, Volume 50

Kshetri, N (2017a) Blockchain's roles in meeting key supply chain management objectives, *International Journal of Information Management*, 39, pp 80–89

Kshetri, N (2017b) Blockchain's roles in strengthening cybersecurity and protecting privacy, *Telecommunications Policy*, **41** (10), pp 1027–38

Liang, X *et al* (2017) ProvChain: A blockchain-based data provenance architecture in cloud, *17th IEEE/ACM International Symposium on Cluster, Cloud and Grid Computing*, pp 468–77

Nation, J (2017) 2 June. [Online] https://www.ethnews.com: https://www.ethnews. com/walmart-tests-food-safety-with-blockchain-traceability

Novet, J (2017) 16 August. [Online] https://www.cnbc.com/: https://www.cnbc. com/2017/08/16/maersk-says-notpetya-cyberattack-could-cost-300-million.html

Ralston, PM, Richey, RG and Grawe, SJ (2017) The past and future of supply chain collaboration: A literature synthesis and call for research, *International Journal of Logistics Management*, **28** (2), pp 508–30

Ramachandran, SE (2017) *Digital Innovation in Trade Finance*, BCG, Boston

Reuters (2014) [Online] https://www.cnbc.com/2014/08/03/legal-fight-chills-china- metal-trade-after-port-fraud-probe.html

Risius, M and Spohrer, K (2017) A blockchain research framework: What we (don't) know, where we go from here, and how we will get there, *Business and Information Systems Engineering*, pp 385–409

Ryu, J (2012) November. [Online] https://www.gs1.org/docs/traceability/Global_ Traceability_Standard.pdf

Security and Exchange Commission (2017) July. [Online] https://www.sec.gov/ Archives/edgar/data/310158/000110465917047544/a17-18477_1ex99d1.htm

Sedgwick, K (2017) December. [Online] https://news.bitcoin.com/: https://news.
bitcoin.com/the-most-pointless-cryptocurrency-tokens-ever-invented/

Simchi-Levi *et al* (2014) January. [Online] https://hbr.org/2014: https://hbr.
org/2014/01/from-superstorms-to-factory-fires-managing-unpredictable-supply-
chain-disruptions

Singh, J (1996) The importance of information flow within the supply chain,
Logistics Information Management, **9** (4)

Szabo, N (1996) [Online] http://www.fon.hum.uva.nl/rob/Courses/
InformationInSpeech/CDROM/Literature/LOTwinterschool2006/szabo.best.
vwh.net/smart_contracts_2.html

Tirschwell, P (2018) Blockchain theory's path to reality in shipping is beset by
details and distrust, 16 May. [Online] https://www.joc.com/print/3428386?utm_
source=Eloqua&utm_medium=email&utm_campaign=CL_JOC%20Daily%205/
17/18%20TF%206%3A46am%20%20_PC9156_e-production_E-9774_
DB_0517_0646

TKI-Dinalog (2016) Logistics sector to make concrete progress using blockchain
technology, November [Online] https://www.dinalog.nl/en/logistics-sector-to-
make-concrete-progress-using-blockchain-technology/

What supply chain management processes and metrics will be affected by blockchain?

06

Introduction

While having examined in the previous chapter the various meaningful applications of blockchain technology in the supply chain, we are still left with a wide-ranging number of possible use cases. SCM practitioners need a way to identify where they can expect to find 'the biggest bang for their buck'. In this chapter we will provide a framework, based on the Supply Chain Operational Reference model, that can help in finding those supply chain processes where greater efficiency and effectiveness can be realized by using blockchain technology as well as provide insight on what metrics will be affected. Our approach is a practical one; by looking at today's supply chain processes and pains we look at the business case in the 'here-and-now' and not in 'what-could-be'.

And while we do believe that technologies such as blockchain will lead to new business models and even destroy existing ones, this process will be, as Iansiti and Lakhani pointed out (2017), a transitional one, as the technology further matures and we get to grips with the way the technology impacts the underlying processes and transactions in the supply chain. This should not be underestimated. The analogy between the early years of Transmission Control Protocol/Internet Protocol (TCP/IP)[1] and blockchain technology is in that respect very powerful (Iansiti and Lakhani, 2017); the first, and for quite some time only, TCP/IP based killer-app was email. Now this technology allows us to rent out our apartment to strangers from the other side of the globe.

Key to the successful implementation of technology is that we have to look at familiar problems from a different perspective, otherwise we continue to treat the symptoms and not cure the disease. And while a full coverage of innovation or change management is beyond the scope of this book, we would like to illustrate the importance of this point by citing two anecdotes.

Early 2018 I (Aljosja Beije) gave a presentation about the impact of innovation on the road haulage industry in the Netherlands. Having finished my presentation I asked whether there were any questions. A gentleman in the audience raised his hand, and after thanking me for the interesting presentation he said that his industry has different problems right now, and that in particular the current shortage of truck-drivers in the Netherlands was the one that was keeping him up at night. I then asked him whether he had ever looked at the problem the other way around; how about if we don't have a shortage of truck-drivers, but simply too many trucks? Which is not a stretch to imagine considering that average loadfactor in the Netherlands for trucks hovers at around the 60 per cent.

It is safe to say that the invention of the shipping container has transformed the physical flow in the supply chain. Today's global trade volumes would not be possible without it, nor would they be as efficient. Surprising enough, however, the flow of information and money that run parallel to the physical flow are still based on paper documents, whose origins can be traced back to medieval world. Yes, we have managed to digitize these documents, but digitization is not the same as automation; digitization leads to 'machine-to-paper-to machine' processes, as anybody who has ever observed somebody printing out a BoL and entering it manually in a system will readily endorse. Automation results in 'machine-to-machine' transactions.

The outline for this chapter is as follows. Based on the individual building blocks introduced in Chapter 2, ie SCM objectives and the SCOR process, we will provide a summary of how the blockchain capabilities mentioned in the previous chapter are linked to SCM objectives. This is done by systematically linking the blockchain capabilities to the various value creation mechanisms at work and their interaction, using the theoretical building blocks as discussed Chapter 2. This summary will in turn provide insight into the impact a blockchain project has on the SCM objectives. While not a business case in terms of dollars and cents or pounds and pence, the framework does provide a way to make the business case for blockchain technology more tangible.

Supply chain management objectives and the SCOR reference model

As blockchain technology research has up to now predominantly focused on technological questions of design and features, while neglecting applications, value creation and governance (Risius and Spohrer, 2017), there's little practical guidance for supply chain management practitioners on blockchain technology adaptation in the supply chain. To bridge that gap, we have developed a framework based on the SCOR model that links blockchain roles and mechanisms to supply chain management objectives.

Our framework for analysis has focused on the process elements as the unit of analysis for as far as the Plan, Source, Make, Deliver, and Return processes are concerned. For the Enable process, our unit of analysis was the process category, primarily because for most of the Enable process elements[2] no metrics were defined on the process elements level. As a result, the framework for analysis is less precise. A future extension of the model could be to define the metrics for the Enable process at the process elements level by means of the various practices defined at the Enable process elements level.

It is important to note that because of the focus on the process elements, our framework doesn't address the (potential) role and mechanisms of blockchain technology in terms of the operations strategy. As a detailed description of the SCOR process model is beyond the scope of this book, we encourage those readers unfamiliar with the model to download the latest version of the SCOR reference model, at the time of writing version 12.0, from the APICS website as throughout this book we will adhere to the definitions and descriptions of the SCOR reference model.

To correctly assess blockchain's role and the mechanisms involved requires use case descriptions with a high level of detail. Unfortunately, while there's a lot of information available about blockchain pilots, they generally lack the necessary level of detail. Therefore, further case study research is needed to more accurately assess the relationship between the supply chain management objectives and the blockchain roles and mechanisms. In Chapter 7 we provide a first example of such an analysis based on the results of the Deliver pilot. As the Deliver pilot progresses and more use cases become available at the required level of detail, we will continue building on this model.

Plan processes

SCOR defines the Plan process as the processes associated with determining requirements and corrective actions to achieve supply chain objectives (APICS, 2017). For this, demand and supply data are aggregated for a specific time horizon (eg a year, a month or a week), and at a specific corporate hierarchy (eg division, product line, stock keeping unit (SKU)). This requires up-to-date and accurate data from, for example, internal and external processes and transactions, capital assets, transport capacity and inventory. As such, the Plan process establishes/communicates plans for the other SCOR execution processes of Source, Make and Deliver and the Return process. For example, the Source and Make planning provides information about the quantities of raw materials and semi-finished products needed in the production process, the sources of these supplies, their stocking-points, available production capacity and routing across multiple production sites. A Deliver plan fulfils the estimated demand (forecast) and considers the available transportation and storage capacities, while the Return planning process provides information about the needed return resources, such as couriers and the location and capacity of repair sites to meet anticipated and unanticipated return requirements. Regulatory requirements and compliance, company specific business rules and supply chain performance metrics defined in the Enable process set the confines for the supply chain in which to operate. In the end, the full supply chain plan must tie in with the financial plan of the specific corporate hierarchy. Given the strong emphasis the Plan process puts on reliable and real time data it should come as little surprise that blockchain technology can have a substantial impact on the Planning process metrics.

In terms of the supply chain management objectives, companies should look at blockchain for the use in their Plan process if they want to:

- have lower system-wide costs through a reduction in inventory levels;
- become more responsive through a reduction in planning cycle time;
- become more dependable through more accurate forecasting.

We have summarized the outcome of our analysis in Table 6.1. For a full overview, including the description of the processes, we refer to Appendix of this chapter (page 140).

Table 6.1 Plan process – summary of blockchain's roles and metrics affected

Blockchain's roles	Processes	Process metrics affected
Only parties mutually accepted in the network can engage in transactions, facilitating the identification of all sources of demand and supply	sP1.1, sP1.2, sP2.1, sP2.2, sP3.1, sP4.1, sP4.2	AM.2.2 – Inventory Days of Supply RL.3.37 – Forecast Accuracy RS.3.44 – Identify, Prioritize and Aggregate Supply Chain Requirements Cycle Time RS.3.39 – Identify, Prioritize and Aggregate Supply Chain Requirements Cycle Time RS.3.41 – Identify, Prioritize and Aggregate Supply Chain Requirements Cycle Time RS.3.38 – Identify, Prioritize and Aggregate Supply Chain Requirements Cycle Time RS.3.36 – Identify, Assess and Aggregate Production Resources Cycle Time RS.3.40 – Identify, Prioritize, and Aggregate Delivery Requirements Cycle Time RS.3.37 – Identify, Assess, and Aggregate Delivery Resources Cycle Time
Integrate data from 2nd tier to n tier supply chain members	sP1.1, sP1.2, sP2.1, sP2.2, sP3.1, sP4.1, sP4.2	RL.3.37 – Forecast Accuracy RS.3.44 – Identify, Prioritize and Aggregate Supply Chain Requirements Cycle Time RS.3.39 – Identify, Prioritize and Aggregate Supply Chain Requirements Cycle Time AM.2.2 – Inventory Days of Supply RS.3.41 – Identify, Prioritize and Aggregate Supply Chain Requirements Cycle Time RS.3.38 – Identify, Prioritize and Aggregate Supply Chain Requirements Cycle Time RS.3.36 – Identify, Assess and Aggregate Production Resources Cycle Time RS.3.40 – Identify, Prioritize, and Aggregate Delivery Requirements Cycle Time RS.3.37 – Identify, Assess, and Aggregate Delivery Resources Cycle Time

(continued)

Table 6.1 (Continued)

Blockchain's roles	Processes	Process metrics affected
Blockchain's append only ledger can address challenges associated with self-reported data from supply chain members	sP1.1, sP1.2, sP2.1, sP2.2, sP3.1, sP4.1, sP4.2	RL.3.37 – Forecast Accuracy RS.3.44 – Identify, Prioritize and Aggregate Supply Chain Requirements Cycle Time RS.3.39 – Identify, Prioritize and Aggregate Supply Chain Requirements Cycle Time AM.2.2 – Inventory Days of Supply RS.3.41 – Identify, Prioritize and Aggregate Supply Chain Requirements Cycle Time RS.3.38 – Identify, Prioritize and Aggregate Supply Chain Requirements Cycle Time RS.3.36 – Identify, Assess and Aggregate Production Resources Cycle Time RS.3.40 – Identify, Prioritize, and Aggregate Delivery Requirements Cycle Time RS.3.37 – Identify, Assess, and Aggregate Delivery Resources Cycle Time
Reward supply chain members for sharing reliable data	sP1.3, sP2.3, sP2.4, sP3.3, sP4.3	RL.3.36 – Fill Rate RS.3.15 – Balance Supply Chain Resources with Supply Chain Requirements Cycle Time AM.2.2 – Inventory Days of Supply RS.3.29 – Establish Sourcing Plans Cycle Time RS.3.12 – Balance Product Resources with Product Requirements Cycle Time RS.3.13 – Balance Production Resources with Production Requirements Cycle Time RL.3.37 – Forecast Accuracy
Provide a secure, peer-to-peer collaborative planning and forecasting platform without centralized control	sP1.1, sP1.2, sP1.3, sP2.3, sP2.4, sP3.3, sP3.4, sP4.3, sP4.4	RL.3.37 – Forecast Accuracy RS.3.44 – Identify, Prioritize and Aggregate Supply Chain Requirements Cycle Time RS.3.39 – Identify, Prioritize and Aggregate Supply Chain Requirements Cycle Time AM.2.2 – Inventory Days of Supply RL.3.36 – Fill Rate RS.3.15 – Balance Supply Chain Resources with Supply Chain Requirements Cycle Time RS.3.12 – Balance Product Resources with Product Requirements Cycle Time RS.3.29 – Establish Sourcing Plans Cycle Time RS.3.36 – Identify, Assess and Aggregate Production Resources Cycle Time RS.3.13 – Balance Production Resources with Production Requirements Cycle Time RS.3.28 – Establish Production Plans Cycle Time

Description	Processes	Metrics
Simplify business-to-business integration	sP1.2, sP2.1, sP3.1	RS.3.39 – Identify, Prioritize and Aggregate Supply Chain Requirements Cycle Time AM.2.2 – Inventory Days of Supply RL.3.37 – Forecast Accuracy RS.3.41 – Identify, Prioritize and Aggregate Supply Chain Requirements Cycle Time
Can provide data that can be used to monitor inventory objects	sP1.3	RL.3.36 – Fill Rate RS.3.15 – Balance Supply Chain Resources with Supply Chain Requirements Cycle Time AM.2.2 – Inventory Days of Supply
Blockchain's append only ledger, provides a single source of truth for data on which to build the supply chain plan	sP1.4	AM.2.2 – Inventory Days of Supply RS.3.30 – Establish Supply Chain Plans Cycle Time
The outcomes of the supply chain plan are immediately available to those supply chain partners accepted on the network	sP1.4, sP2.4, sP3.4, sP4.4	AM.2.2 – Inventory Days of Supply RS.3.30 – Establish Supply Chain Plans Cycle Time RS.3.29 – Establish Sourcing Plans Cycle Time RS.3.28 – Establish Production Plans Cycle Time RL.3.36 – Fill Rate
Reputation based vendor selection on the basis of transaction data in the network	sP2.3, sP2.4	RS.3.12 – Balance Product Resources with Product Requirements Cycle Time RS.3.29 – Establish Sourcing Plans Cycle Time

Source processes

SCOR defines the Source process as the processes associated with ordering, delivery, taking receipt and transfer of raw material items, sub-assemblies, product and/or services from suppliers (APICS, 2017). Unlike the SCOR Planning process hierarchy, which includes the supply chain and the various SCOR processes (Source, Make, Deliver and Return), the Source process hierarchy is structured around the concept of the customer order decoupling point (see Figure 6.1). This decoupling point also provides the process hierarchy for the Make and Deliver processes.

In a Make-to-Stock environment the end customer orders are filled from the stocks of inventory of finished goods that are stored in the various stocking points within the supply chain. Consequently, the intention of Source-to-Stock is to maintain a certain level of inventory for these materials, sub-assemblies of products based on predicted demand. The ability to accurately predict demand is key in this environment. The granularity (SKU, product-line, etc) of this demand forecast differs based on the time-bucket (month, week, day) and region/stocking point(s) (country, warehouse, shop, etc). Typically, throughout the sourcing process the product cannot be referenced to the customer order (APICS, 2017).

Figure 6.1   Customer order decoupling point

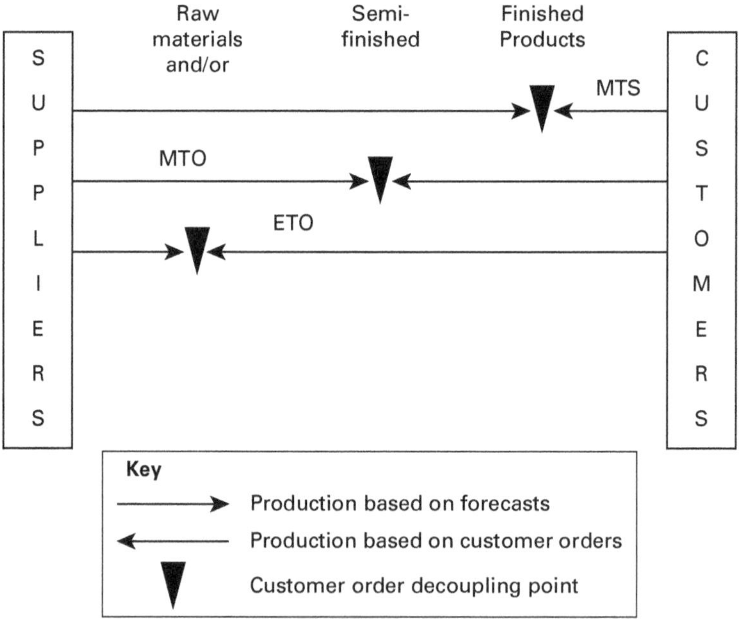

In a Make-to-Order environment, it is the confirmed customer order that triggers the flow of materials in the supply chain. Because of this, the customer has to wait longer for his product than is the case with Make-to-Stock; the upside is that the product can be made more to the taste of the customer, for example by allowing them to select certain higher quality components or other forms of personalization. Very little or no inventory is maintained of the finished goods or component materials. The intention of Source-to-Order is to maintain inventory ordered (and/or configured) specifically for customer orders only. The product is typically identifiable throughout the sourcing process by the reference to the customer order (APICS, 2017).

Engineer-to-Order is a strategy of manufacturing whereby finished goods are manufactured up to the specification of customer orders. It calls for higher lead time to design and manufacture as per exact specifications of the customer. The intention of the Source-Engineer-to-Order is to ensure that parts, assemblies or specialized products are sourced based on the requirements or specifications of a specific customer order (APICS, 2017).

In terms of the supply chain management objectives, companies should look at blockchain for the use in their Source process, if they want:

- system wide cost minimization through a reduction in inventory levels;
- to become more reliable, through a reduction of variation in the sourcing process. For example, by reducing transaction and documentation errors and changes in schedules;
- to become more responsive through a reduction in lead and cycle times.

We have summarized the outcome of our analysis in Table 6.2. For a full overview, including the description of the processes, we refer to Appendix of this chapter (page 152).

Make process

SCOR defines the Make process as the processes associated with adding value to a deliverable through manufacturing or creation of a product or deliverable; or, in services industries, the creation of service deliverables (APICS, 2017). The Make process can take on various forms; for example distilling, blending, machining and assembly. As already mentioned, the Make process hierarchy is centred around the customer order decoupling point. Make-to-Stock products can be completed prior to the receipt of a customer order, and are generally produced to a planned schedule in accordance with a sales forecast (APICS, 2017).

Table 6.2 Source process – summary of blockchain's roles and metrics affected

Blockchain's roles	Processes	Process metrics affected
Provide a secure, peer-to-peer collaborative planning and forecasting platform without centralized control	sS1.1, sS1.2, sS2.1, sS2.2, sS3.3, sS3.6	RL.3.27 – % Schedules Changed within Supplier's Lead Time RS.3.10 – Average Days per Schedule Change RS.3.122 – Schedule Product Deliveries Cycle Time RL.3.18 – % Orders/Lines Processed Complete RL.3.20 – % Orders/Lines Received On-Time to Demand Requirement RL.3.23 – % Orders/Lines Received with Correct Shipping Documents RS.3.113 – Receiving Product Cycle Time RL.3.25 – % Product Transferred On-Time to Demand Requirement RL.3.26 – % Product Transferred Without Transaction Errors RS.3.139 – Transfer Product Cycle Time AM.2.2 – Inventory Days of Supply
Provide lot tracking data	sS1.2, sS2.2	RL.3.18 – % Orders/Lines Processed Complete RL.3.20 – % Orders/Lines Received On-Time to Demand Requirement RL.3.23 – % Orders/Lines Received with Correct Shipping Documents RS.3.113 – Receiving Product Cycle Time
Supplier delivery performance analysis based vendor selection on the basis of transaction data in the network	sS1.2, sS2.2, sS3.1, sS3.2	RL.3.18 – % Orders/Lines Processed Complete RL.3.20 – % Orders/Lines Received On-Time to Demand Requirement RL.3.23 – % Orders/Lines Received with Correct Shipping Documents RS.3.113 – Receiving Product Cycle Time RS.3.35 – Identify Sources of Supply Cycle Time AM.3.2 – % Materials that have a Valid Bill of Materials AM.3.3 – % Materials that are Recyclable/Reusable RL.3.17 – % Suppliers with an EMS or ISO 14001 Certification RS.3.125 – Select Supplier and Negotiate Cycle Time

Enable fully automated processing ('straight through processing') of transfer of ownership and payment of inventory managed or owned by vendors	sS1.3, sS1.4, sS2.3, sS2.4	RL.3.19 – % Orders/Lines Received Defect Free
		RL.3.21 – % Orders/Lines Received with Correct Content
		RL.3.24 – % Orders/Lines Received Damage Free
		RS.3.140 – Verify Product Cycle Time
		RL.3.25 – % Product Transferred On-Time to Demand Requirement
		RL.3.26 – % Product Transferred without Transaction Errors
		RS.3.139 – Transfer Product Cycle Time
		AM.2.2 – Inventory Days of Supply
Elimination of paper records reduces human interaction and communication	sS1.3, sS1.4, sS2.3, sS2.4, sS3.4	RL.3.19 – % Orders/Lines Received Defect Free
		RL.3.21 – % Orders/Lines Received with Correct Content
		RL.3.24 – % Orders/Lines Received Damage Free
		RS.3.140 – Verify Product Cycle Time
		RL.3.25 – % Product Transferred On-Time to Demand Requirement
		RL.3.26 – % Product Transferred without Transaction Errors
		RS.3.139 – Transfer Product Cycle Time
		AM.2.2 – Inventory Days of Supply
		RL.3.18 – % Orders/Lines Processed Complete
		RL.3.20 – % Orders/Lines Received On-Time to Demand Requirement
		RL.3.23 – % Orders/Lines Received with Correct Shipping Documents
		RS.3.113 – Receiving Product Cycle Time

(continued)

Table 6.2 (*Continued*)

Blockchain's roles	Processes	Process metrics affected
Can provide real time, secure and validated data that can be used to monitor transport conditions of the product	sS1.3, sS1.4, sS2.3, sS2.4, sS3.4, sS3.5	RL.3.19 – % Orders/Lines Received Defect Free RL.3.21 – % Orders/Lines received with correct content RL.3.24 – % Orders/Lines received damage free RS.3.140 – Verify Product Cycle Time RL.3.25 – % Product Transferred On-Time to Demand Requirement RL.3.26 – % Product Transferred Without Transaction Errors RS.3.139 – Transfer Product Cycle Time AM.2.2 – Inventory Days of Supply RL.3.18 – % Orders/Lines Processed Complete RL.3.20 – % Orders/Lines Received On-Time to Demand Requirement RL.3.23 – % Orders/Lines received with Correct Shipping Documents RS.3.113 – Receiving Product Cycle Time
Enable fully automated processing ('straight through processing') of the authorization of payment and the payment itself	sS1.5, sS2.5, sS3.7	RS.3.8 – Authorize Supplier Payment Cycle Time
Reputation based vendor selection on the basis of transaction data in the network	sS3.1, sS3.2	RS.3.35 – Identify Sources of Supply Cycle Time AM.3.2 – % Materials that have a Valid Bill of Materials AM.3.3 – % Materials that are Recyclable/Reusable RL.3.17 – % Suppliers with an EMS or ISO 14001 Certification RS.3.125 – Select Supplier and Negotiate Cycle Time
Invitation to tender can be made immediately available to those qualified supply chain partners accepted to the network	sS3.1	RS.3.35 – Identify Sources of Supply Cycle Time AM.3.2 – % Materials that have a valid Bill of Materials AM.3.3 – % Materials that are Recyclable/Reusable

Table 6.3 Make process – summary of blockchain's roles and metrics affected

Blockchain's roles	Processes	Process metrics affected
Elimination of paper records	sM1.7, sM2.7, sM3.7	RL.3.57 – Waste Processing Errors RS.3.141 – Waste Accumulation time AM.3.15 – Hazardous waste as % of Total Waste
Provide a decentralized market place for waste/ surplus materials	sM1.7, sM2.7, sM3.7	RI.3.57 – Waste Processing Errors Rs.3.141 – Waste Accumulation Time Am.3.15 – Hazardous Waste As % Of Total Waste

Make-to-Order is the process of adding value to a deliverable either as manufacturing or creation of a product or deliverable, or in the services industries, creation of service deliverables, for a specific customer order (APICS, 2017). In the case of the Engineer-to-Order process, the delivery object is not fully defined at the start of the process and requires a considerable amount of design, engineering analysis and testing time.

Table 6.3 provides an overview of the processes and the affected metrics. It is worth noting that actual applications of blockchain technology in the strictest sense of the Make process are very limited. This is primarily a result of the fact that this process is within the 'four walls' of the focal company. Hence, there's no need for increased trust or to deploy a decentralized application. For a full overview, including the description of the processes we refer to Appendix of this chapter (page 139).

Deliver process

SCOR defines the Deliver process as the processes associated with performing customer-facing order management and order fulfilment activities. The Deliver process hierarchy includes not only the Make-to-Stock, Make-to-Order and Engineer-to-Order, but also the Retail sub-process (APICS, 2017).

The process Deliver Stocked Product is the process of delivering a product that is sourced or made based on aggregated customer orders, projected orders/demand and inventory re-ordering parameters. The intention of Deliver Stocked Product is to have the product available when a customer order arrives, to prevent the customer from looking elsewhere (APICS, 2017). The intention of the process Deliver-Make-to-Order Product is to have the product or service delivered as quickly as possible upon the receipt of the customer order.

The Deliver-Engineer-to-Order Product process will only begin after the receipt and validation of a firm customer order. The intention of this process is to have the product or service delivered as quickly as possible upon the receipt of the customer order (APICS, 2017).

Deliver Retail Products are the processes used to acquire, merchandise and sell finished goods at a retail store. A retail store is a physical location that sells products (and services) direct to the consumer, using a point of sale process (manual or automated) to collect payment. Merchandising at a store level is the stocking and restocking of products in designated storage locations to generate sales in a retail store (APICS, 2017).

In terms of the supply chain management objectives, companies should look at blockchain for the use in their Deliver process if they want:

- system-wide cost minimization through a reduction in inventory levels and order management costs;
- to become more reliable, through a reduction of variation in the deliver process. For example, by reducing transaction and documentation errors;
- to become more responsive through a reduction in lead and cycle times;

We have summarized the outcome of our analysis in Table 6.4. For a full overview, including the description of the processes we refer the reader to Appendix of this chapter (page 166).

Return process

SCOR defines the Return process as the processes associated with moving material from a customer back through the supply chain to address defects in product, ordering, or manufacturing, or to perform upkeep activities. The Return process hierarchy includes the Source and Return of Defective Products, Maintenance, Repair and Overhaul (MRO) products and Excess products (APICS, 2017).

The Return Defective Product process supports the return, receipt and determination of any type of product not conforming to specifications (including order non-conformance such as late or otherwise improper delivery); company business rules determine the definition of defective and can include warranty claims, product recalls, non-conformity of a product and/ or other similar policies including appropriate replacement (APICS, 2017).

Table 6.4 Deliver process – summary of blockchain's roles and metrics affected

Blockchain's roles	Processes	Process metrics affected
Provide order tracking data	sD1.1, sD1.4, sD1.12, sD2.1, sD2.4, sD2.12, sD3.1, sD3.12	RS.3.100 – Process Inquiry and Quote Cycle Time CO.3.14 – Order Management Costs RL.3.33 – Delivery Item Accuracy RL.3.34 – Delivery Location Accuracy RL.3.35 – Delivery Quantity Accuracy RS.3.18 – Consolidate Orders Cycle Time CO.3.15 – Order Delivery and/or Install Costs RL.2.1 – % of Orders Delivered in Full RL.2.2 – Delivery Performance to Customer Commit Date RS.3.126 – Ship Product Cycle Time CO.2.4 – Cost to Deliver
Blockchain serves as a single consensus based source of truth	sD1.1, sD2.1, sD3.1	RS.3.100 – Process Inquiry and Quote Cycle Time CO.3.14 – Order Management Costs RS.3.93 – Obtain and Respond to Request for Quote/Request for Proposal Cycle Time
Elimination of paper records	sD1.2, sD2.2, sD3.2	RL.3.33 – Delivery Item Accuracy RL.3.34 – Delivery Location Accuracy RL.3.35 – Delivery Quantity Accuracy RS.3.94 – Order Fulfilment Dwell Time RS.3.112 – Receive, Enter and Validate Order Cycle Time RS.3.92 – Negotiate and Receive Contract Cycle Time CO.3.14 – Order Management Costs

(continued)

Table 6.4 (*Continued*)

Blockchain's roles	Processes	Process metrics affected
Simplify business-to-business integration	sD1.2, sD2.2, sD3.2	RL.3.33 – Delivery Item Accuracy RL.3.34 – Delivery Location Accuracy RL.3.35 – Delivery Quantity Accuracy RS.3.94 – Order Fulfilment Dwell Time RS.3.112 – Receive, Enter and Validate Order Cycle Time RS.3.92 – Negotiate and Receive Contract Cycle Time CO.3.14 – Order Management Costs
Enable fully automated order processing ('straight through processing')	sD1.2, sD2.2, sD3.2	RL.3.33 – Delivery Item Accuracy RL.3.34 – Delivery Location Accuracy RL.3.35 – Delivery Quantity Accuracy RS.3.94 – Order Fulfilment Dwell Time RS.3.112 – Receive, Enter and Validate Order Cycle Time CO.3.14 – Order Management Costs RS.3.92 – Negotiate and Receive Contract Cycle Time
Provide inventory tracking data	sD1.3, sD2.3, sD3.3	RL.2.1 – % Orders Delivered in Full RL.2.2 – Delivery Performance to Customer Commit Date RL.3.36 – Fill Rate RS.3.94 – Order Fulfilment Dwell Time RS.3.116 – Reserve Resources and Determine Delivery Date Cycle Time RS.3.115 – Reserve Inventory and Determine Delivery Date Cycle Time CO.3.14 – Order Management Costs RL.3.33 – Delivery Item Accuracy RL.3.34 – Delivery Location Accuracy RL.3.35 – Delivery Quantity Accuracy RS.3.25 – Enter Order, Commit Resources and Launch Program Cycle Time

Provide a secure, peer-to-peer collaborative platform without centralized control for order management	sD1.4, sD1.5, sD1.6, sD2.4, sD2.5, sD2.6, sD3.5, sD3.6	RL.3.33 – Delivery Item Accuracy RL.3.34 – Delivery Location Accuracy RL.3.35 – Delivery Quantity Accuracy RS.3.18 – Consolidate Orders Cycle Time CO.3.14 – Order Management Costs CO.3.15 – Order Delivery and/or Install Costs RS.3.16 – Build Loads Cycle Time RS.3.117 – Route Shipments Cycle Time CO.2.4 – Cost to Deliver
Provide a secure, peer-to-peer collaborative platform without centralized control for order management and inventory financing	sD1.7, sD2.7, sD3.7	RL.3.16 – % Suppliers Meeting Environmental Metrics/Criteria CO.3.14 – Order Management Costs CO.3.15 – Order Delivery and/or Install Costs CO.2.4 – Cost to Deliver RS.3.124 – Select Carriers and Rate Shipments Cycle Time
Enable fully automated product receipt ('straight through processing')	sD1.8, sD2.8, sD3.8	CO.3.12 – Indirect Cost Related to Production RS.3.108 – Receive product from Make / Source Cycle Time
Enable fully automated processing ('straight through processing') of the billing process, including authorization of payments and the payment itself	sD1.15, sD2.15, sD3.15	RL.2.3 – Documentation Accuracy RL.3.11 – % Faultless Invoices RS.3.48 – Invoice Cycle Time CO.3.14 – Order Management Costs AM.2.1 – Days Sales Outstanding

(continued)

Table 6.4 (*Continued*)

Blockchain's roles	Processes	Process metrics affected
Elimination of paper records reduces the human interaction and communication	sD1.8, sD1.11, sD1.13, sD2.8, sD2.11, sD2.13, sD3.8, sD3.11, sD3.13	RS.3.108 – Receive product from Make/Source Cycle Time
		RL.2.2 – Delivery Performance to Customer Commit Date
		RL.2.3 – Documentation Accuracy
		RL.3.31 – Compliance Documentation Accuracy
		RL.3.33 – Delivery Item Accuracy
		RL.3.34 – Delivery Location Accuracy
		RL.3.35 – Delivery Quantity Accuracy
		RL.3.43 – Other Required Documentation Accuracy
		RL.3.45 – Payment Documentation Accuracy
		RL.3.50 – Shipping Documentation Accuracy
		RS.3.51 – Load Product and Generate Shipping Documentation Cycle Time
		CO.3.12 – Indirect Cost Related to Production
		RL.2.4 – Perfect Condition
		RL.3.41 – Orders Delivered Damage Free Conformance
		RL.3.32 – Customer Commit Date Achievement Time Customer Receiving
		RS.3.102 – Receive and Verify Product by Customer Cycle Time
		RL.3.42 – Orders Delivered Defect Free Conformance
		RS.3.103 – Receive and Verify Product Cycle Time

Can provide real-time, secure and validated data that can be used to monitor transport conditions of the product	sD1.8, sD1.13, sD2.8, sD2.13, sD3.8, sD3.11, sD3.13	RS.3.110 – Receive Product from Source or Make Cycle Time
		RL.2.2 – Delivery Performance to Customer Commit Date
		RL.2.4 – Perfect Condition
		RL.3.32 – Customer Commit Date Achievement Time Customer Receiving
		RL.3.33 – Delivery Item Accuracy
		RL.3.34 – Delivery Location Accuracy
		RS.3.108 – Receive product from Make/Source Cycle Time
		RL.3.35 – Delivery Quantity Accuracy
		RL.3.43 – Other Required Documentation Accuracy
		RL.3.45 – Payment Documentation Accuracy
		RL.3.50 – Shipping Documentation Accuracy
		RS.3.51 – Load Product and Generate Shipping Documentation Cycle Time
		CO.3.12 – Indirect Cost Related to Production
		RL.3.41 – Orders Delivered Damage Free Conformance
		RL.3.42 – Orders Delivered Defect Free Conformance
		RS.3.102 – Receive and Verify Product by Customer Cycle Time
		RS.3.103 – Receive and Verify Product Cycle Time

The Return MRO Product process supports the deliver, receipt and determination of MRO products or company assets for the purpose of servicing, repairing or upgrading it, as defined by Maintenance Plans or the occurrence or anticipation of risk of failure. Generally, company assets managed through a MRO process are expected to be refurbished to a useable condition and returned to service. The Return Defective Product and Return MRO Product processes do not represent the actual maintenance, repair or overhaul activities; these are generally represented by the Make process (APICS, 2017).

The Return Excess Product process supports the delivery, receipt and determination of excess or ageing inventory or obsolete products as defined by the terms and conditions of a customer/supplier contract. The intention of excess product returns is to reallocate inventory to a location or organization that can sell the product that is considered in excess in the current location. The blockchain roles and mechanisms associated with the Make process closely match the capabilities of Excess Material Exchange,[3] a Dutch blockchain start-up.

In terms of the supply chain management objectives, companies should look at blockchain for the use in their Return process, if they want:

- system-wide cost minimization through a reduction in inventory levels of defective, MRO and excess products;
- to become more responsive through a reduction in lead and cycle times;

We have summarized the outcome of our analysis in Table 6.5. For a full overview, including the description of the processes we refer to Appendix of this chapter.

Enable process

SCOR defines the Enable process as the processes associated with establishing, maintaining and monitoring information, relationships, resources, assets, business rules, compliance and contracts required to operate the supply chain as well as monitoring and managing the overall performance of the supply chain. Enable processes interact and manage alignment with processes in other domains; for example, financial processes, human resource processes, ICT, and product and process design processes (APICS, 2017).

Table 6.5 Return process – summary of blockchain's roles and metrics affected

Blockchain's roles	Processes	Process metrics affected
Blockchain's 'super audit trail' can address challenges associated with self-reported data that are provided with supply chain partners	sSR2.1, sSR1.1	AM.3.42 – % Unserviceable MRO Inventory in Identification AM.3.29 – % Defective Inventory in Disposition
Business rules implemented on the blockchain using smart contracts	sSR2.1, sSR2.3, sDR1.1, sDR2.1, sDR3.1, sSR1.1, sSR1.3	AM.3.42 – % Unserviceable MRO Inventory in Identification AM.3.41 – % Unserviceable MRO Inventory in Return Authorization RS.3.5 – Authorized Defective Return Cycle Time RS.3.7 – Authorize MRO Product Return Cycle Time RS.3.6 – Authorize Excess Product Return Cycle Time AM.3.29 – % Defective Inventory in Disposition AM.3.30 – % Defective Inventory in Return Authorization
Elimination of paper records	sSR2.3, sSR1.3	AM.3.41 – % Unserviceable MRO Inventory in Return Authorization AM.3.30 – % Defective Inventory in Return Authorization
Elimination of paper records while preparing the scheduling documentation and automation of the scheduling administration	sSR2.4, sSR1.4	RL.3.28 – % Shipping Schedules that Support Customer Required Return by Date AM.3.43 – % Unserviceable MRO Inventory in Scheduling AM.3.32 – % Defective Product Inventory in Scheduling
Provide order tracking data	sSR2.5, sDR1.4, sDR2.4, sDR3.4, sSR1.2, sSR1.5	RL.3.5 – % Error-Free Returns Shipped RL.3.47 – Return Shipments Shipped on Time AM.3.40 – % Unserviceable MRO Inventory in Transportation RS.3.104 – Receive Defective Product Cycle Time RS.3.138 – Transfer MRO Product Cycle Time RS.3.137 – Transfer Excess Product Cycle Time AM.3.29 – % Defective Inventory in Disposition

(continued)

Table 6.5 (Continued)

Blockchain's roles	Processes	Process metrics affected
Provide a secure, peer-to-peer collaborative platform without centralized control for scheduling of the return	sDR1.2, sDR2.2, sDR3.2	CO.2.5 – Cost to Return RS.3.121 – Schedule MRO Return Receipt Cycle Time RS.3.119 – Schedule Excess Return Receipt Cycle Time
Elimination of paper records reduces the human interaction and communication	sDR1.3, sDR2.3, sDR3.3	RS.3.118 – Schedule Defective Return Receipt Cycle Time RS.3.104 – Receive Defective Product Cycle Time RS.3.106 – Receive MRO Product Cycle Time RS.3.105 – Receive Excess Product Cycle Time
Can provide real-time, secure and validated data that can be used to monitor transport conditions of the product	sDR1.3, sDR2.3, sDR3.3	RS.3.104 – Receive Defective Product Cycle Time RS.3.106 – Receive MRO Product Cycle Time RS.3.105 – Receive Excess Product Cycle Time
Enable fully automated product receipt ('straight through processing')	sDR1.3, sDR2.3, sDR3.3	RS.3.104 – Receive Defective Product Cycle Time RS.3.106 – Receive MRO Product Cycle Time RS.3.105 – Receive Excess Product Cycle Time
Provide a decentralized market place for waste / surplus materials	sDR1.4, sDR2.4, sDR3.4	RS.3.104 – Receive Defective Product Cycle Time RS.3.138 – Transfer MRO Product Cycle Time RS.3.137 – Transfer Excess Product Cycle Time

The Enable process hierarchy consists of the following sub-processes:

1 Business Rules.

2 Manage Supply Chain Performance.

3 Manage Data and Information.

4 Manage Supply Chain Human Resources.

5 Manage Supply Chain Assets.

6 Manage Supply Chain Contracts/Agreements.

7 Manage Supply Chain Network.

8 Manage Regulatory and Voluntary Compliance.

9 Manage Supply Chain Risk.

10 Manage Supply Chain Procurement.

11 Manage Supply Chain Technology.

For a full overview, including the description of the processes, we refer to Appendix of this chapter (page 131).

Business rules

SCOR defines the Enable Business Rules process as the process of establishing, documenting, communicating and publishing supply chain business rules. A business rule is a statement or parameter that defines or constraints some aspect of the business and is generally used in decision making (APICS, 2017). Business rules are intended to influence the outcome of operating the supply chain and can apply, for example, to people, processes and, owing to 'smart contracts', now also to transactions. An example of a business rule can be 'invoices are not accepted if there is no signed proof of delivery'. The development of the policies on which the business rules are based generally falls out of the scope of this process; it translates policies into business rules applied to supply chain processes (APICS, 2017).

In terms of the supply chain management objectives, we can see from Table 6.6 that blockchain is expected to impact:

- responsiveness, through a reduction in the overall cycle time needed to manage these business rules;
- agility, through the immediate availability or de-activation of business rules;
- reliability, through automating the business rules using 'smart contracts'.

Table 6.6   Enable process – summary of blockchain's roles and metrics affected

Blockchain's roles	Processes	Process metrics affected
Document business rules at the transactional level to enable 'straight through processing'	sE1, sE2	RS.3.54 – Manage Business Rules for Plan Processes Cycle Time RS.3.55 – Manage Business Rules for Return Processes Cycle Time RS.3.57 – Manage Deliver Business Rules Cycle Time RS.3.79 – Manage Production Rules Cycle Time RS.3.86 – Manage Sourcing Business Rules Cycle Time
Business rules are immediately available to those supply chain partners accepted on the network	sE1	RS.3.54 – Manage Business Rules for Plan Processes Cycle Time RS.3.55 – Manage Business Rules for Return Processes Cycle Time RS.3.57 – Manage Deliver Business Rules Cycle Time RS.3.79 – Manage Production Rules Cycle Time RS.3.86 – Manage Sourcing Business Rules Cycle Time
Business rules on the network can be immediately de-activated	sE1	RS.3.54 – Manage Business Rules for Plan Processes Cycle Time RS.3.55 – Manage Business Rules for Return Processes Cycle Time RS.3.57 – Manage Deliver Business Rules Cycle Time RS.3.79 – Manage Production Rules Cycle Time RS.3.86 – Manage Sourcing Business Rules Cycle Time
Provide data that can be used to access useful, meaningful and representative indicators for performance	sE2	RS.3.2 – Assess Delivery Performance Cycle Time RS.3.3 – Assess Supplier Performance Cycle Time RS.3.65 – Manage Integrated Supply Chain Inventory Cycle Time RS.3.70 – Manage Performance of return Processes Cycle Time RS.3.71 – Manage Performance of Return Processes Cycle Time RS.3.78 – Manage Production CO.1.1 – Total Supply Chain Management Costs

Provide the mechanism to quickly implement corrective actions	sE2	RS.3.2 – Assess Delivery Performance Cycle Time RS.3.3 – Assess Supplier Performance Cycle Time RS.3.65 – Manage Integrated Supply Chain Inventory Cycle Time RS.3.70 – Manage Performance of return Processes Cycle Time RS.3.71 – Manage Performance of Return Processes Cycle Time RS.3.78 – Manage Production CO.1.1 – Total Supply Chain Management Costs
Blockchain's 'super audit trail' can address challenges associated with self-reported data that are provided with supply chain partners	sE3	RS.3.53 – Maintain Source Data Cycle Time RS.3.59 – Manage Deliver Information Cycle Time RS.3.68 – Manage Make Information Cycle Time RS.3.72 – Manage Plan Data Collection Cycle Time RS.3.81 – Manage Return Data Collection Cycle Time CO.3.14 – Order Management Costs
Can provide data that can be used to manage supply chain assets	sE5	RS.3.56 – Manage Capital Assets Cycle Time RS.3.58 – Manage Deliver Capital Assets Cycle Time RS.3.64 – Manage Integrated Supply Chain Capital Assets Cycle Time RS.3.67 – Manage Make Equipment and Facilities Cycle Time RS.3.80 – Manage Return Capital Assets Cycle Time
Simplify machine-to-machine integration	sE5	RS.3.56 – Manage Capital Assets Cycle Time RS.3.58 – Manage Deliver Capital Assets Cycle Time RS.3.64 – Manage Integrated Supply Chain Capital Assets Cycle Time RS.3.67 – Manage Make Equipment and Facilities Cycle Time RS.3.80 – Manage Return Capital Assets Cycle Time
Elimination of paper records while preparing the scheduling documentation and automation of the scheduling administration, including invoicing	sE5	RS.3.56 – Manage Capital Assets Cycle Time RS.3.58 – Manage Deliver Capital Assets Cycle Time RS.3.64 – Manage Integrated Supply Chain Capital Assets Cycle Time RS.3.67 – Manage Make Equipment and Facilities Cycle Time RS.3.80 – Manage Return Capital Assets Cycle Time

(continued)

Table 6.6 (Continued)

Blockchain's roles	Processes	Process metrics affected
Only assets mutually accepted in the network can engage in transactions, facilitating the identification of all assets in need of maintenance	sE5	RS.3.56 – Manage Capital Assets Cycle Time RS.3.58 – Manage Deliver Capital Assets Cycle Time RS.3.64 – Manage Integrated Supply Chain Capital Assets Cycle Time RS.3.67 – Manage Make Equipment and Facilities Cycle Time RS.3.80 – Manage Return Capital Assets Cycle Time
Enable fully automated processing ('straight through processing') of contractual and non-contractual agreements	sE6	RL.3.37 – Forecast Accuracy RS.3.87 – Manage Supplier Agreements Cycle Time CO.2.6 – Mitigation Costs CO.3.15 – Order Delivery and/or Install Costs AM.2.1 – Days Sales Outstanding AM.2.3 – Days Payable Outstanding
Ensure upfront compliance	sE8	RS.3.61 – Manage Import/Export Requirements Cycle Time
Addressing the holistic sources of risk	sE9	The standard metric for quantification of risk is Value at Risk (VaR). VaR = Probability of Occurrence * Monetary Impact of Occurrence
Identifying, collecting, validating, and documenting data on all potential risk events	sE9	AG.2.10 – Value at Risk (Plan) AG.2.11 – Value at Risk (Source) AG.2.12 – Value at Risk (Make) AG.2.13 – Value at Risk (Deliver)
Identifying, collecting, validating, and documenting data beyond the tier-1 supply chain	sE9	AG.2.14 – Value at Risk (Return)
Providing data at the lowest possible level of granularity instead of process	sE9	AG.2.15 – Time to Recovery (TTR)
Crisis involving defective products (eg contaminated food): easily identify the source and engage in strategic removals of affected products instead of recalling the entire product line	sE9	CO.2.6 – Risk/Mitigation Costs

Manage supply chain performance

SCOR defines the process Enable Manage Supply Chain Performance process as the process of defining performance targets for supply chain metrics that align to overall business strategy and goals, and for reporting performance, identifying gaps in performance, performing root cause analysis, and developing and launching corrective actions to close gaps in performance. It is common for organizations to have multiple versions of the process in place, in different parts and levels of the organization.

In terms of the Supply Chain Management Objectives, we can see from Table 6.6 that blockchain is expected to impact:

- responsiveness, through a reduction in the overall cycle time needed to manage supply chain performance;
- agility: through the immediate availability or de-activation of business rules it is possible to quickly develop and launch corrective actions to close gaps in performance;
- system-wide cost reduction, through automating the corrective actions using 'smart contracts'.

Manage data and information

SCOR defines the Enable Manage Data and Information process as the process of collecting, maintaining and publishing data and information required to plan, operate, measure and manage the supply chain (APICS, 2017).

Examples of major data element categories include (APICS, 2017):

- master data: foundational data on for example customers, suppliers, raw materials, bills-of-material, recipes, products, people, processes and assets needed to operate the supply chain;
- transactional data: data associated with, for example, purchasing, receiving, material movements, value add operations, stocking, picking and delivery of materials;
- collaboration data: data from supply chain partners needed to provide the cross-organization supply chain visibility required to plan and execute the supply chain in an integrated end-to-end manner;
- meta data: data that describes and adds information about other data;
- performance data: metrics data and the associated raw input data needed to calculate the metrics;
- sensory/IoT data, data from social networks.

In terms of the supply chain management objectives, we can see from Table 6.6 that blockchain is expected to impact:

- responsiveness, through a reduction in the overall cycle time needed to manage these data categories;
- reliability, through having access to real-time validated data;
- system-wide cost reduction, through having real-time and validated order management data.

Manage supply chain human resources

SCOR defines the Enable Manage Supply Chain Human Resources process as the process of developing, governing and maintaining an organization of permanent, temporary and outsourced staff, with the right qualifications, in support of business objects and supply chain goals (APICS, 2017). This includes identifying required and available skills in the organization, determining gaps in skills and competency levels, identifying training needs, resource gaps and excess resources.

We believe that blockchain technology's role in this process will remain limited in the foreseeble future to providing reliable and validated data, for example about qualifications and professional background, which is already covered in the Enable Manage Data and Information process.

Manage supply chain assets

SCOR defines the Enable Manage Supply Chain Assets process as the process of scheduling, maintaining and dispositioning of supply chain assets developed for supply chain execution. This includes installation, repair, alteration, calibration and other activities necessary to sustain supply chain execution (APICS, 2017).

In terms of the supply chain management objectives, we can see from Table 6.6 that blockchain is expected to impact:

- responsiveness, through a reduction in the overall cycle time needed to manage these supply chain assets.

Manage supply chain contracts/agreements

SCOR defines the Enable Manage Supply Chain Contracts/Agreement process as the management and communication of contractual and non-contractual agreements in support of business objectives and supply chain goals. This includes all agreements related to supply chain operations, such as material and services acquisition, inventory stocking practices and levels, performance targets, planning and decision making, logistics and delivery, and data exchange and visibility (APICS, 2017).

In terms of the supply chain management objectives, we can see from Table 6.6 that blockchain is expected to impact:

- system-wide cost reduction, through lower working capital costs and transactional costs associated with managing supply chain contracts and agreements.
- responsiveness, through a reduction in the overall cycle time needed to manage these contracts and agreements;
- reliability, through increased forecast accuracy.

Manage supply chain network

SCOR defines the Enable Manage Supply Chain Network process as defining and managing the geographic and activity footprint of the supply chain. It defines the location of the facilities and assignment of resources, distribution networks, suppliers, customers, materials, products, capacities, and/or capabilities to those locations.

We believe that blockchain technology's role in this process will remain limited in the forseable future to providing reliable and validated data for the network planning algorithms used in this process, which is already covered in the Enable Manage Data and Information process.

Manage regulatory and voluntary compliance

SCOR defines the Enable Manage Regulatory and Voluntary Compliance process as the process of identifying, collecting, assessing and integrating regulatory compliance requirements in standard supply chain processes, policies and business rules. Regulatory compliance is the term generally used to describe the policies and processes that organizations have in place to ensure that they comply with laws, rules and regulations put in place by external bodies (government). Often, organizations choose to go beyond regulatory compliance to meet voluntary compliance standards and/or pursue voluntary certifications for strategic reasons, such as ISO standards, standards related to sustainability or corporate social responsibility. A key component of Regulatory and Voluntary Compliance is establishing policies, business rules and processes to ensure legislative and regulatory compliance requirements are met (APICS, 2017).

In terms of the supply chain management objectives, we can see from Table 6.6 that blockchain is expected to impact:

- responsiveness, through a reduction in the overall cycle time needed to manage this process.

Manage supply chain risk

SCOR defines the Enable Manage Supply Chain Risk process as the process of identification and assessment of potential disruptions (risks) in the supply chain and developing a plan to mitigate these threats to operating the supply chain. Disruptions can come from within supply chain processes themselves, such as a customer going out of business, or production issues as a result of strikes or fires, or from outside, for example the devaluation of a foreign currency and trade disputes.

In terms of the supply chain management objectives, we can see from Table 6.6 that blockchain is expected to impact:

- supply chain risks, through a reduction in the overall Value at Risk.

Manage supply chain procurement

SCOR defines the procurement cycle as the cyclical process of key steps when procuring goods or services. We believe that the sub-processes where blockchain can play a role, such as sE10.4 (Supplier Selection to Participate in ITT/RFQ/Negotiation), sE10.5 (Issue ITT/RFQ), sE10.6 (Bid/Tender Evaluation and Validation) and sE10.7 (Contract Award and Implementation) have been adequately addressed in the Source process.

Manage supply chain technology

SCOR defines the Enable Manage Supply Chain Technology process as the process of defining, deploying and managing the technology enablement involved in supply chain planning, execution and performance management. While blockchain is part of the technology stack involved in supply chain, planning, execution and performance management, we do not expect blockchain to have a role in this process.

Appendix

Plan processes

SCOR defines the Plan process as the processes associated with determining requirements and corrective actions to achieve supply chain objectives. Table 6.7 provides an overview of the processes and the affected metrics.

Source processes

SCOR defines the Source process as the processes associated with ordering, delivery, receipt and transfer of raw material items, subassemblies, products and/or services. Table 6.8 provides an overview of the processes and the affected metrics.

Make processes

SCOR defines the Make process as the processes associated with adding value to a deliverable through manufacturing or creation of a product or deliverable; or in services industries, creation of service deliverables. Table 6.9 provides an overview of the processes and the affected metrics. It is worth noting that actual applications of blockchain technology in the strictest sense of the Make process are very limited. This is primarily a result of the fact that this process is within the 'four walls' of the focal company. Hence, there's no need for increased trust or to deploy a decentralized application.

Deliver processes

SCOR defines the Deliver process as the processes associated with performing customer-facing order management and order fulfilment activities. Table 6.10 provides an overview of the processes and the affected metrics

Return processes

SCOR defines the Return process as the processes associated with moving material from a customer back through the supply chain to address defects in product, ordering or manufacturing, or to perform upkeep activities. Table 6.11 provides an overview of the processes and the affected metrics.

Table 6.7 Plan process and metrics affected

Process	Description	Blockchain's roles	Mechanisms involved	Process metrics affected
sP1.1 Identify, Prioritize and Aggregate Supply Chain Requirements	The process of identifying, aggregating, and prioritizing all sources of demand for the integrated supply chain of a product or service at the appropriate level, horizon and interval	Only parties mutually accepted in the network can engage in transactions, facilitating the identification of all sources of demand	Validation of the identities of individual entities participating in the supply chain	RL.3.37 Forecast Accuracy
		Integrate data from 2nd tier to n tier distributors	Cryptographic primitives that allow data sharing in a privacy preserving way	RS.3.44 Identify, Prioritize and Aggregate Supply Chain Requirements Cycle Time
		Blockchain's append only ledger can address challenges associated with self-reported data that are provided by distributors	Transaction data can be validated by Oracles before being permanently added to the blockchain	
		Provide a secure, peer-to-peer collaborative planning and forecasting platform without centralized control	Cryptographic primitives that allow data sharing in a secure and, if required, privacy preserving way	

sP1.2	Identify, Prioritize and Aggregate Supply Chain Resources	The process of identifying, prioritizing, and aggregating all sources of supply that are required and add value in the supply chain of a product or service at the appropriate level, horizon and interval	Only parties mutually accepted in the network can engage in transactions, facilitating the identification of all sources of demand	Validation of the identities of individual entities participating in the supply chain.	RS.3.39	Identify, Prioritize and Aggregate Supply Chain Requirements Cycle Time
			Integrate data from 2nd tier to n tier suppliers	Cryptographic primitives that allow data sharing in a secure and, if required, privacy preserving way	AM.2.2	Inventory Days of Supply
			Blockchain's append only ledger can address challenges associated with self-reported data that are provided by suppliers	Transaction data can be validated by Oracles before being permanently added to the blockchain		
			Provide a secure, peer-to-peer collaborative planning and forecasting platform without centralized control	Cryptographic primitives that allow data sharing in a secure and, if required, privacy preserving way		
			Simplify business-to-business integration	Data security and cost-effective transmission of transactions in peer-to-peer networks (Korpela et al 2017)		

(continued)

Table 6.7 *(Continued)*

Process		Description	Blockchain's roles	Mechanisms involved	Process metrics affected	
sP1.3	Balance Supply Chain Resources with Supply Chain Requirements	The process of identifying and measuring the gaps and imbalances between demand and resources in order to determine how to best resolve the variances through marketing, pricing, packaging, warehousing, outsource plans or some other action that will optimize service, flexibility, costs, assets in an iterative and collaborative environment	Provide a secure, peer-to-peer collaborative platform without centralized control	Cryptographic primitives that allow data sharing in a secure and, if required, privacy preserving way	RL.3.36	Fill Rate
			Reward supply chain partners for sharing reliable data	'Atomic swap' type smart contracts allow supply chain partners to transfer data assets in exchange for digital currency such as Ripple's XRP	RS.3.15	Balance Supply Chain Resources with Supply Chain Requirements Cycle Time
			Can provide data that can be used to monitor inventory objects	Detection, measurement and tracking of inventory with IoT	AM.2.2	Inventory Days of Supply

ID	Process	Description			Metric ID	Metric
sP1.4	Establish and Communicate Supply Chain Plans	The establishment and communication of courses of action over the appropriate time-defined (long-term, annual, monthly, weekly) planning horizon and interval, representing a projected appropriation of supply chain resources to meet supply chain requirements	Blockchain's append only ledger, provides a single source of truth for data on which to build the supply chain plan	Once data has been validated by Oracles it can be added to the blockchain and used as the basis on which all supply chain members build their supply chain plan	RS.3.30	Establish Supply Chain Plans Cycle Time
			The outcomes of the supply chain plan are immediately available to those supply chain partners accepted on the network	Point-to-point communication between data silos is replaced by broadcasting the outcomes to all members of the network	AM.2.2	Inventory Days of Supply
sP2.1	Identify, Prioritize and Aggregate Product Requirements	The process of identifying, prioritizing, and considering, as a whole with constituent parts, all sources of demand for a product or service in the supply chain	Only parties mutually accepted in the network can engage in transactions, facilitating the identification of all sources of demand	Validation of the identities of individual entities participating in the supply chain.	RL.3.37	Forecast Accuracy
			Integrate data from 2nd tier to n tier distributors	Cryptographic primitives that allow data sharing in a privacy preserving way	RS.3.41	Identify, Prioritize, and Aggregate Product Requirements Cycle Time

(continued)

Table 6.7 (Continued)

Process	Description	Blockchain's roles	Mechanisms involved	Process metrics affected
		Blockchain's append only ledger can address challenges associated with self-reported data that are provided by distributors Simplify business-to-business integration	Transaction data can be validated by Oracles before being permanently added to the blockchain Data security and cost-effective transmission of transactions in peer-to-peer networks (Korpela et al, 2017)	
sP2.2 Identify, Assess and Aggregate Product Resources	The process of identifying, evaluating, and considering as a whole with constituent parts, all material and other resources used to add value in the supply chain for a product or services	Only parties mutually accepted in the network can engage in transactions, facilitating the identification of all sources of demand Integrate data from 2nd tier to n tier suppliers Blockchain's append only ledger can address challenges associated with self-reported data that are provided by suppliers	Validation of the identities of individual entities participating in the supply chain Cryptographic primitives that allow data sharing in a secure and, if required, privacy preserving way Transaction data can be validated by Oracles before being permanently added to the blockchain	RS.3.38 Identify, Assess, and Aggregate Product Resources Cycle Time

sP2.3	Balance Product Resources with Product Requirements	The process of developing a time-phased course of action that commits resources to meet requirements	Provide a secure, peer-to-peer collaborative platform without centralized control for logistics service providers (LSP)	Cryptographic primitives that allow data sharing in a secure and, if required, privacy preserving way		RS.3.12	Balance Product Resources with Product Requirements Cycle Time
			Reward LSP partners for sharing reliable data	'Atomic swap' type smart contracts allow supply chain partners to transfer data assets in exchange for digital currency such as Ripple's XRP			
			Reputation based vendor selection on the basis of transaction data in the network	Blockchain's 'super audit trail' in combination with privacy preserving cryptographic primitives allows network members to gauge reputation of vendors within the network			
sP2.4	Establish Sourcing Plan	The establishment of courses of action over specified time periods that represent a projected appropriation of supply resources to meet sourcing plan requirements	Provide a secure, peer-to-peer collaborative platform without centralized control for vendors	Cryptographic primitives that allow data sharing in a secure and, if required, privacy preserving way		RS.3.29	Establish Sourcing Plans Cycle Time
			Reward vendors for sharing reliable data	'Atomic swap' type smart contracts allow supply chain partners to transfer data assets in exchange for digital currency such as Ripple's XRP			

(continued)

Table 6.7 *(Continued)*

Process	Description	Blockchain's roles	Mechanisms involved	Process metrics affected	
		Reputation based vendor selection on the basis of transaction data in the network	Blockchain's 'super audit trail' in combination with privacy preserving cryptographic primitives allows network members to gauge reputation of vendors within the network		
		The outcomes of the supply chain plan are immediately available to those supply chain partners accepted on the network	Point-to-point communication between data silos is replaced by broadcasting the outcomes to all members of the network		
sP3.1 Identify, Prioritize and Aggregate Production Requirements	The process of identifying, prioritizing, and considering as a whole with constituent parts, all sources of demand in the creation of a product or service	Only parties mutually accepted in the network can engage in transactions, facilitating the identification of all sources of demand	Validation of the identities of individual entities participating in the supply chain	RL.3.37	Forecast Accuracy
		Integrate data from 2nd tier to n tier distributors	Cryptographic primitives that allow data sharing in a privacy preserving way	RS.3.42	Identify, Prioritize, and Aggregate Production Requirements Cycle Time

		Blockchain's append only ledger can address challenges associated with self-reported data that are provided by distributors	Transaction data can be validated by Oracles before being permanently added to the blockchain		
		Simplify business-to-business integration	Data security and cost-effective transmission of transactions in peer-to-peer networks (Korpela et al, 2017)		
sP3.2	Identify, Assess and Aggregate Production Resources	The process of identifying, evaluating and considering, as a whole with constituent parts, all things that add value in the creation of a product or performance of a service	Only parties mutually accepted in the network can engage in transactions, facilitating the identification of all sources of demand	Validation of the identities of individual entities participating in the supply chain	RS.3.36 — Identify, Assess and Aggregate Production Resources Cycle Time
			Integrate data from 2nd tier to n tier suppliers	Cryptographic primitives that allow data sharing in a secure and, if required, privacy preserving way.	
			Blockchain's append only ledger can address challenges associated with self-reported data that are provided by suppliers	Transaction data can be validated by Oracles before being permanently added to the blockchain	

(continued)

Table 6.7 (*Continued*)

Process	Description	Blockchain's roles	Mechanisms involved	Process metrics affected
		Simplify business-to-business integration	Data security and cost-effective transmission of transactions in peer-to-peer networks (Korpela et al, 2017)	
sP3.3 Balance Production Resources with Production Requirements	The process of developing a time-phased course of action that commits creation and operation resources to meet creation and operation requirements	Provide a secure, peer-to-peer collaborative platform without centralized control Reward supply chain partners for sharing reliable data	Cryptographic primitives that allow data sharing in a secure and, if required, privacy preserving way. 'Atomic swap' type smart contracts allow supply chain partners to transfer data assets in exchange for digital currency such as Ripple's XRP	RS.3.13 Balance Production Resources with Production Requirements Cycle Time
sP3.4 Establish Production Plans	The establishment of courses of action over specified time periods that represent a projected appropriation of supply resources to meet production and operating plan requirements	Provide a secure, peer-to-peer collaborative platform without centralized control for vendors The outcomes of the supply chain plan are immediately available to those supply chain partners accepted on the network	Cryptographic primitives that allow data sharing in a secure and, if required, privacy preserving way Point-to-point communication between data silos is replaced by broadcasting the outcomes to all members of the network	RS.3.28 Establish Production Plans Cycle Time

sP4.1	Identify, Prioritize and Aggregate Delivery Requirements	The process of identifying, prioritizing, and considering, as a whole with constituent parts, all sources of demand in the delivery of a product or service	Only parties mutually accepted in the network can engage in transactions, facilitating the identification of all sources of demand	Validation of the identities of individual entities participating in the supply chain	RL.3.37	Forecast Accuracy
			Integrate data from 2nd tier to n tier distributors	Cryptographic primitives that allow data sharing in a privacy preserving way	RS.3.40	Identify, Prioritize, and Aggregate Delivery Requirements Cycle Time
			Blockchain's append only ledger can address challenges associated with self-reported data that are provided by distributors	Transaction data can be validated by Oracles before being permanently added to the blockchain		
sP4.2	Identify, Assess and Aggregate Delivery Resources	The process of identifying, evaluating, and considering, as a whole with constituent parts, all things that add value in the delivery of a product or service	Only parties mutually accepted in the network can engage in transactions, facilitating the identification of all sources of demand	Validation of the identities of individual entities participating in the supply chain	RL.3.37	Forecast Accuracy
			Integrate data from 2nd tier to n tier suppliers	Crypthographic primitives that allow data sharing in a secure and, if required, privacy preserving way	RS.3.37	Identify, Assess, and Aggregate Delivery Resources Cycle Time

(continued)

Table 6.7 (*Continued*)

Process	Description	Blockchain's roles	Mechanisms involved	Process metrics affected
		Blockchain's append only ledger can address challenges associated with self-reported data that are provided by suppliers	Transaction data can be validated by Oracles before being permanently added to the blockchain	
sP4.3 Balance Delivery Resources and Capabilities with Delivery Requirements	The process of developing a time-phased course of action that commits delivery resources to meet delivery requirements	Provide a secure, peer-to-peer collaborative platform without centralized control for LSP	Cryptographic primitives that allow data sharing in a secure and, if required, privacy preserving way	RL.3.37 Forecast Accuracy
		Reward LSP partners for sharing reliable data	'Atomic swap' type smart contracts allow supply chain partners to transfer data assets in exchange for digital currency such as Ripple's XRP	

| sP4.4 | Establish Delivery Plans | The establishment of courses of action over specified time periods that represent a projected appropriation of delivery resources to meet delivery requirements | Provide a secure, peer-to-peer collaborative platform without centralized control for vendors

Reward vendors for sharing reliable data | Cryptographic primitives that allow data sharing in a secure and, if required, privacy preserving way

'Atomic swap' type smart contracts allow supply chain partners to transfer data assets in exchange for digital currency such as Ripple's XRP | RL.3.36 | Fill Rate |

Table 6.8 Source process and metrics affected

Process		Description	Blockchain's roles	Mechanisms involved	Metrics affected	
sS1.1	Schedule Product Deliveries	Scheduling and managing the execution of the individual deliveries of product against an existing contract or purchase order. The requirements for product releases are determined based on the detailed sourcing plan or other types of product pull signs	Provide a secure, peer-to-peer collaborative platform without centralized control for consignment inventory	Cryptographic primitives that allow data sharing in a secure and, if required, privacy preserving way	RL.3.27	% Schedules Changed Within Supplier's Lead Time
					RS.3.10	Average Days per Schedule Change
					RS.3.122	Schedule Product Deliveries Cycle Time
sS1.2	Receive Product	The process and associated activities of receiving product to contract requirements	Provide lot tracking data	Detection, measurement and tracking of inventory with IoT	RL.3.18	% Orders/Lines Processed Complete
					RL.3.20	% Orders/Lines Received On Time to Demand Requirement
					RL.3.23	% Orders/Lines Received with Correct Shipping Documents
					RS.3.113	Receiving Product Cycle Time

	Supplier Delivery Performance Analysis based vendor selection on the basis of transaction data in the network.	Blockchain's 'super audit trail' in combination with privacy preserving cryptograhic primitives allows network members to gauge reputation of vendors within the network	
	Provide a secure, peer-to-peer collaborative platform without centralized control for consignment inventory	Cryptographic primitives that allow data sharing in a secure and, if required, privacy preserving way	
sS1.3 Verify Product	The process and actions required determining product conformance to requirements and criteria	Enable fully automated processing ('straight through processing') of transfer of ownership and payment of inventory managed or owned by vendors	Event changes, such as the transfer of ownership, trigger 'smart contracts'	RL.3.19 % Orders/Lines Received Defect Free
				RL.3.21 % Orders/Lines Received with Correct Content
				RL.3.24 % Order/Lines Received Damage Free
				RS.3.140 Verify Product Cycle Time

(continued)

Table 6.8 (*Continued*)

Process	Description	Blockchain's roles	Mechanisms involved	Metrics affected
		Elimination of paper records reduces the human interaction and communication	Event changes, such as the transfer of ownership, trigger 'smart contracts'	
		Can provide real time, secure and validated data that can be used to monitor transport conditions of the product	Data related to temperature, humidity, motion, light conditions, chemical composition from IoT devices or sensors	
sS1.4 Transfer Product	The transfer of accepted product to the appropriate stocking location within the supply chain. This includes all of the activities associated with repackaging, staging, transferring and stocking product	Enable fully automated processing ('straight through processing') of transfer of ownership and payment of inventory managed or owned by vendors	Event changes, such as the transfer of ownership, trigger 'smart contracts'	RL.3.25 % Product Transferred On Time to Demand Requirement RL.3.26 % Product Transferred without Transaction Errors RS.3.139 Transfer Product Cycle Time AM.2.2 Inventory Days of Supply

ID	Process	Description	Benefit		Metric ID	Metric
sS1.5	Authorize Supplier Payment	The process of authorizing payments and paying suppliers for product or services	Elimination of paper records reduces the human interaction and communication	Event changes, such as the transfer of ownership, trigger 'smart contracts'.	RS.3.8	Authorize Supplier Payment Cycle Time
			Can provide real time, secure and validated data that can be used to monitor transport conditions of the product	Data related to temperature, humidity, motion, light conditions, chemical composition from IoT devices or sensors		
			Enable fully automated processing ('straight through processing') of the authorization of payments and the payment itself	Event changes, such as the transfer of ownership, trigger 'smart contracts'		
sS2.1	Schedule Product Deliveries	Scheduling and managing the execution of the individual deliveries of product against the contract. The requirements for product deliveries are determined based on the detailed sourcing plan	Provide a secure, peer-to-peer collaborative platform without centralized control for consignment inventory	Cryptographic primitives that allow data sharing in a secure and, if required, privacy preserving way	RL.3.27	% Schedules Changed Within Supplier's Lead Time
					RS.3.10	Average Days per Schedule Change
					RS.3.122	Schedule Product Deliveries Cycle Time

(continued)

Table 6.8 (*Continued*)

Process		Description	Blockchain's roles	Mechanisms involved	Metrics affected	
sS2.2	Receive Product	The process and associated activities of receiving product to contract requirements	Provide lot tracking data	Detection, measurement and tracking of inventory with IoT	RL.3.18	% Orders/Lines Processed Complete
					RL.3.20	% Orders/Lines Received On Time to Demand Requirement
					RL.3.23	% Orders/Lines Received with Correct Shipping Documents
					RS.3.113	Receiving Product Cycle Time
			Supplier delivery performance analysis based vendor selection on the basis of transaction data in the network	Blockchain's 'super audit trail' in combination with privacy preserving cryptographic primitives allows network members to gauge reputation of vendors within the network		

					Metrics
			Provide a secure, peer-to-peer collaborative platform without centralized control for consignment inventory	Cryptographic primitives that allow data sharing in a secure and, if required, privacy preserving way	
sS2.3	Verify product	The process and actions required determining product conformance to requirements and criteria	Enable fully automated processing ('straight through processing') of transfer of ownership and payment of inventory managed or owned by vendors	Event changes, such as the transfer of ownership, trigger 'smart contracts'	RL.3.19 % Orders/Lines Received Defect Free RL.3.21 % Orders/Lines Received with Correct Content RL.3.24 % Order/Lines Received Damage Free RS.3.140 Verify Product Cycle Time
			Elimination of paper records reduces the human interaction and communication	Event changes, such as the transfer of ownership, trigger 'smart contracts'	

(continued)

Table 6.8 (Continued)

Process	Description	Blockchain's roles	Mechanisms involved	Metrics affected	
sS2.3 Verify product	The process and actions required determining product conformance to requirements and criteria	Can provide real time, secure and validated data that can be used to monitor transport conditions of the product	Data related to temperature, humidity, motion, light conditions, chemical composition from IoT devices or sensors	RL.3.19	% Orders/Lines Received Defect Free
				RL.3.21	% Orders/Lines Received with Correct Content
				RL.3.24	% Order/Lines Received Damage Free
				RS.3.140	Verify Product Cycle Time
sS2.4 Transfer Product	The transfer of accepted product to the appropriate stocking location within the supply chain. This includes all of the activities associated with repackaging, staging, transferring and stocking product and or application of service	Enable fully automated processing ('straight through processing') of transfer of ownership and payment of inventory managed or owned by vendors	Event changes, such as the transfer of ownership, trigger 'smart contracts'	RL.3.25	% Product Transferred On Time to Demand Requirement
				RL.3.26	% Product Transferred without Transaction Errors
				RS.3.139	Transfer Product Cycle Time
				AM.2.2	Inventory Days of Supply

ID	Process	Description			Metric ID	Metric
sS2.5	Authorize Supplier Payment	The process of authorizing payments and paying suppliers for product or services. This process included invoice collection, invoice matching and payment	Elimination of paper records reduces the human interaction and communication	Event changes, such as the transfer of ownership, trigger 'smart contracts'		
			Can provide real time, secure and validated data that can be used to monitor transport conditions of the product	Data related to temperature, humidity, motion, light conditions, chemical composition from IoT devices or sensors		
			Enable fully automated processing ('straight through processing') of the authorization of payments and the payment itself	Event changes, such as the transfer of ownership, trigger 'smart contracts'	RS.3.8	Authorize Supplier Payment Cycle Time
sS3.1	Identify Sources of Supply	The identification and qualification of potential suppliers capable of designing and delivering product that will meet all of the required product specifications	Supplier delivery performance analysis based vendor selection on the basis of transaction data in the network		RS.3.35	Identify Sources of Supply Cycle Time
			Blockchain's 'super audit trail' in combination with privacy preserving cryptographic primitives allows network members to gauge reputation of vendors within the network		AM.3.2	% Materials that have a Valid Bill of Materials
					AM.3.3	% Materials that are Recyclable/Reusable

(continued)

Table 6.8 (*Continued*)

Process	Description	Blockchain's roles	Mechanisms involved	Metrics affected
		Reputation based vendor selection on the basis of transaction data in the network	Blockchain's 'super audit trail' in combination with privacy preserving cryptographic primitives allows network members to gauge reputation of vendors within the network	
		Invitation to tender can be made immediately available to those supply chain partners accepted on the network	Point-to-point communication between data silos is replaced by broadcasting the outcomes to all members of the network	
sS3.2 Select Final Supplier and Negotiate	The identification of the final supplier(s) based on the evaluation of RFQs, supplier qualifications and the generation of a contract defining the costs and terms and conditions of product availability	Supplier delivery performance analysis based vendor selection on the basis of transaction data in the network	Blockchain's 'super audit trail' in combination with privacy preserving cryptographic primitives allows network members to gauge reputation of vendors within the network	RL.3.17 % Suppliers with an EMS or ISO 14001 Certification

Process		Description	Blockchain Application	Metric	
		Reputation based vendor selection on the basis of transaction data in the network	Blockchain's 'super audit trail' in combination with privacy preserving cryptographic primitives allows network members to gauge reputation of vendors within the network	RS.3.125	Select Supplier and Negotiate Cycle Time
sS3.3	Schedule Product Deliveries	Scheduling and managing the execution of the individual deliveries of the product against the contract. The requirements for product deliveries are determined based on the detailed sourcing plan	Provide a secure, peer-to-peer collaborative platform without centralized control for consignment inventory	RL.3.27	% Schedules Changed Within Supplier's Lead Time
			Cryptographic primitives that allow data sharing in a secure and, if required, privacy preserving way	RS.3.10	Average Days per Schedule Change
				RS.3.122	Schedule Product Deliveries Cycle Time

(continued)

Table 6.8 (*Continued*)

Process		Description	Blockchain's roles	Mechanisms involved	Metrics affected	
sS3.4	Receive Product	The process and associated activities of receiving product to contract requirements	Elimination of paper records reduces the human interaction and communication	Event changes, such as the transfer of ownership, trigger 'smart contracts'	RL.3.18	% Orders/Lines Processed Complete
			Can provide real time, secure and validated data that can be used to monitor transport conditions of the product	Data related to temperature, humidity, motion, light conditions, chemical composition from IoT devices or sensors	RL.3.20	% Orders/Lines Received On Time to Demand Requirement
					RL.3.23	% Orders/Lines Received with Correct Shipping Documents
					RS.3.113	Receiving Product Cycle Time
sS3.5	Verify product	The process and actions required determining product conformance to requirements and criteria	Can provide real time, secure and validated data that can be used to monitor transport conditions of the product	Data related to temperature, humidity, motion, light conditions, chemical composition from IoT devices or sensors. Event changes, such as the transfer of ownership, trigger 'smart contracts'	RL.3.19	% Orders/Lines Received Defect Free
					RL.3.21	% Orders/Lines Received with Correct Content
					RL.3.24	% Order/Lines Received Damage Free
					RS.3.140	Verify Product Cycle Time

ID	Process	Description			Metric	Metric Name
sS3.6	Transfer Product	The transfer of accepted product to the appropriate stocking location within the supply chain. This includes all of the activities associated with repackaging, staging, transferring and stocking product and or application of service	Provide a secure, peer-to-peer collaborative platform without centralized control for transfer of product	Cryptographic primitives that allow data sharing in a secure and, if required, privacy preserving way	RL.3.25	% Product Transferred on Time to Demand Requirement
					RL.3.26	% Product Transferred without Transaction Errors
					RS.3.139	Transfer Product Cycle Time
					AM.2.2	Inventory Days of Supply
sS3.7	Authorize Supplier Payment	The process of authorizing payments and paying suppliers for product or services. This process included invoice collection, invoice matching and payment	Enable fully automated processing ('straight through processing') of the authorization of payments and the payment itself	Event changes, such as the transfer of ownership, trigger 'smart contracts'	RS.3.8	Authorize Supplier Payment Cycle Time

Table 6.9 Make process and metrics affected

Process		Description	Blockchain's roles	Mechanisms involved	Metrics affected	
sM1.7	Waste / Surplus Management	Activities associated with collecting and managing waste/surplus produced during the value-add and test process including scrap material, unused resources and non-conforming products or deliverables	Elimination of paper records	Enable fully automated processing ('straight through processing') without human communication of interaction	RL.3.57	Waste processing errors
					RS.3.141	Waste accumulation time
					AM.3.15	Hazardous waste as % of total waste
			Provide a decentralized market place for waste/surplus materials	In combination with AI technology find the best possible alternative use for valuable materials contained in waste/surplus materials		
sM2.7	Waste/Surplus Management	Activities associated with collecting and managing waste/surplus produced during the value-add and test process including scrap material, unused resources and non-conforming products or deliverables	Elimination of paper records	Enable fully automated processing ('straight through processing') without human communication of interaction	RL.3.57	Waste processing errors
					RS.3.141	Waste accumulation time
			Provide a decentralized market place for waste/surplus materials	In combination with AI technology find the best possible alternative use for valuable materials contained in waste/surplus materials.	AM.3.15	Hazardous waste as % of total waste

sM3.7	Waste/Surplus Management	Activities associated with collecting and managing waste/surplus produced during the value-add and test process including scrap material, unused resources and non-conforming products or deliverables	Elimination of paper records	Enable fully automated processing ('straight through processing') without human communication of interaction	RL.3.57	Waste processing errors
					RS.3.141	Waste accumulation time
			Provide a decentralized market place for waste / surplus materials.	In combination with AI technology find the best possible alternative use for valuable materials contained in waste/surplus materials	AM.3.15	Hazardous waste as % of total waste

Table 6.10 Deliver process metrics affected

Process		Description	Blockchain's roles	Mechanisms involved	Metrics affected	
sD1.1	Process Inquiry and Quote	Receive and respond to general customer inquiries and requests for quotes	Provide order tracking data	Detection, measurement and tracking of inventory with IoT	RS.3.100	Process Inquiry and Quote Cycle Time
					CO.3.14	Order Management Costs
			Blockchain's serves as a single consensus based source of truth	Transaction data can be validated by Oracles before being permanently added to the blockchain		
sD1.2	Receive, Enter and Validate Order	Receive orders from the customer and enter them into a company's order processing system. 'Technically' examine orders to ensure an orderable configuration and provide accurate price. Check the customer	Elimination of paper records	Cost-effective transmission of transactions in peer-to-peer networks (Korpela et al, 2017)	RL.3.33	Deliver Item Accuracy
					RL.3.34	Delivery Location Accuracy
					RL.3.35	Delivery Quantity Accuracy
					RS.3.94	Order Fulfillment Dwell Time
					RS.3.112	Receive, Enter and Validate Order Cycle Time

sD1.3	Reserve Inventory and Determine Delivery Date	Inventory (both on hand and scheduled) is identified and reserved for specific orders and a delivery date is committed and scheduled	Simplify business-to-business integration	Data security and cost-effective transmission of transactions in peer-to-peer networks (Korpela et al, 2017)
			Enable fully automated order processing ('straight through processing')	Enable fully automated processing ('straight through processing') without human communication of interaction
			Provide inventory tracking data	Real time detection, measurement and tracking of inventory with IoT

RL.2.1	% Orders Delivered in Full
RL.2.2	Delivery Performance to Customer Commit Date
RL.3.36	Fill Rate
RS.3.94	Order Fulfillment Dwell Time
RS.3.116	Reserve Resources and Determine Delivery Date Cycle Time

(continued)

Table 6.10 (*Continued*)

Process		Description	Blockchain's roles	Mechanisms involved	Metrics affected	
sD1.4	Consolidate Orders	The process of analysing orders to determine the groupings that result in least cost/best service fulfilment and transportation	Provide order tracking data	Real time detection, measurement and tracking of inventory with IoT	RL.3.33	Deliver Item Accuracy
					RL.3.34	Delivery Location Accuracy
					RL.3.35	Delivery Quantity Accuracy
					RS.3.18	Consolidate Orders Cycle Time
					CO.3.14	Order Management Costs
					CO.3.15	Order Deliver Costs
			Provide a secure, peer-to-peer collaborative platform without centralized control for order management	Cryptographic primitives that allow data sharing in a secure and, if required, privacy preserving way		
sD1.5	Build Loads	Transportation modes are selected and efficient loads are built	Provide a secure, peer-to-peer collaborative platform without centralized control for order management	Cryptographic primitives that allow data sharing in a secure and, if required, privacy preserving way	RS.3.16	Build Loads Cycle Time
					CO.3.14	Order Management Costs
					CO.3.15	Order Delivery Costs
sD1.6	Route Shipments	Loads are consolidated and routed by mode, lane and location	Provide a secure, peer-to-peer collaborative platform without centralized control for order management	Cryptographic primitives that allow data sharing in a secure and, if required, privacy preserving way	RS.3.16	Build Loads Cycle Time
					CO.3.14	Order Management Costs
					CO.3.15	Order Delivery Costs

sD1.7	Select Carriers and Rate Shipments	Specific carriers are selected by lowest cost per route and shipments are rated and tendered	Provide a secure, peer-to-peer collaborative platform without centralized control for order management and inventory financing	Cryptographic primitives that allow data sharing in a secure and, if required, privacy preserving way	RL.3.16 % Suppliers Meeting Environmental Metrics/Criteria
					CO.3.14 Order Management Costs
					CO.3.15 Order Delivery Costs
sD1.8	Receive Product from Source or Make	The activities such as receiving product, verifying, recording product receipt, determining put-away location, putting away and recording location that a company performs at its own warehouses	Elimination of paper records reduces the human interaction and communication	Digitally signed documents, replacing paper ones, with validated identities of entities, objects and individuals	RS.3.108 Receive Product from Make/Source Cycle Time
			Can provide real time, secure and validated data that can be used to monitor transport conditions of the product	Data related to temperature, humidity, motion, light conditions, chemical composition from IoT devices or sensors	RS.3.110 Receive Product from Source or Make Cycle Time
			Enable fully automated product receipt ('straight through processing')	Cost-effective transmission of transactions in peer-to-peer networks (Korpela et al, 2017)	CO.3.12 Indirect Cost Related to Production

(continued)

Table 6.10 (*Continued*)

Process	Description	Blockchain's roles	Mechanisms involved	Metrics affected	
sD1.11	Load Vehicle and Generate Shipping Documents	The series of tasks including placing/loading product onto modes of transportation, and generating the documentation necessary to meet internal, customer, carrier and government needs	Elimination of paper records reduces the human interaction and communication	Digitally signed documents, replacing paper ones, with validated identities of entities, objects and individuals	RL.2.2	Delivery Performance to Customer Commit Date
					RL.2.3	Documentation Accuracy
					RL.3.31	Compliance Documentation Accuracy
					RL.3.33	Delivery Item Accuracy
					RL.3.34	Delivery Location Accuracy
					RL.3.35	Delivery Quantity Accuracy
					RL.3.43	Other Required Documentation Accuracy
					RL.3.45	Payment Documentation Accuracy
					RL.3.50	Shipping Documentation Accuracy
					RS.3.51	Load Product and Generate Shipping Documentation Cycle Time
					CO.3.12	Indirect Cost Related to Production

sD1.12	Ship Product	The process of shipping the product to the customer site	Provide order tracking data	Real time detection, measurement and tracking of inventory with IoT	RL.2.1	% Orders Delivered in Full
					RL.2.2	Delivery Performance to Customer Commit Date
					RL.3.33	Delivery Item Accuracy
					RL.3.34	Delivery Location Accuracy
					RL.3.35	Delivery Quantity Accuracy
					RS.3.126	Ship Product Cycle Time
					CO.3.15	Order Delivery and/or Install Costs
					CO.3.12	Indirect Cost Related to Production
sD1.13	Receive and Verify Product by Customer	The process of receiving the shipment by the customer (either at customer site or at shipping area in case of self-collection) and verifying that the order was shipped complete and that the product meets delivery terms	Elimination of paper records reduces the human interaction and communication Can provide real time, secure and validated data that can be used to monitor transport conditions of the product	Event changes, such as the transfer of ownership, trigger 'smart contracts' Data related to temperature, humidity, motion, light conditions, chemical composition from IoT devices or sensors	RL.2.2	Delivery Performance to Customer Commit Date
					RL.2.4	Perfect Condition
					RL.3.41	Orders Delivered Damage Free Conformance
					RS.3.102	Receive and Verify Product by Customer Cycle Time

(continued)

Table 6.10 (Continued)

Process	Description	Blockchain's roles	Mechanisms involved	Metrics affected	
sD1.15 Invoice	A signal is sent to the financial organization that the order has been shipped and that the billing process should begin and payment be received or be closed out if payment has already been received	Enable fully automated processing ('straight through processing') of the billing process, including authorization of payments and the payment itself	Event changes, such as the transfer of ownership, trigger 'smart contracts'	RL.2.3	Documentation Accuracy
				RL.3.11	% Faultless Invoices
				RS.3.48	Invoice Cycle Time
				CO.3.14	Order Management Costs
sD2.1 Process Inquiry and Quote	Receive and respond to general customer inquiries and requests for quotes	Provide order tracking data. Blockchain's serves as a single consensus based source of truth.	Detection, measurement and tracking of inventory with IoT Transaction data can be validated by Oracles before being permanently added to the blockchain.	CO.3.14	Order Management Costs

sD2.2	Receive, Enter and Validate Order	Receive orders from the customer and enter them into a company's order processing system. Configure your product to the customer's specific needs, based on standard available parts and options. 'Technically' examine orders to ensure an orderable configuration and provide accurate price. Check the customer	Elimination of paper records.	Cost-effective transmission of transactions in peer-to-peer networks (Korpela et al, 2017)	RL.3.33	Deliver Item Accuracy
					RL.3.34	Delivery Location Accuracy
			Simplify business-to-business integration	Data security and cost-effective transmission of transactions in peer-to-peer networks (Korpela et al, 2017)	RL.3.35	Delivery Quantity Accuracy
					RS.3.94	Order Fulfilment Dwell Time
			Enable fully automated order processing ('straight through processing')	Enable fully automated processing ('straight through processing') without human communication of interaction	RS.3.112	Receive, Enter and Validate Order Cycle Time
					CO.3.14	Order Management Costs
sD2.3	Reserve Inventory and Determine Delivery Date	Inventory (both on hand and scheduled) is identified and reserved for specific orders and a delivery date is committed and scheduled	Provide inventory tracking data	Real time detection, measurement and tracking of inventory with IoT	RL.2.1	% Orders Delivered in Full
					RL.2.2	Delivery Performance to Customer Commit Date
					RS.3.94	Order Fulfilment Dwell Time
					RS.3.115	Reserve Inventory and Determine Delivery Date Cycle Time
					CO.3.14	Order Management Costs

(continued)

Table 6.10 *(Continued)*

Process		Description	Blockchain's roles	Mechanisms involved	Metrics affected	
sD2.4	Consolidate Orders	The process of analysing orders to determine the groupings that result in least cost/best service fulfilment and transportation	Provide a secure, peer-to-peer collaborative platform without centralized control for order management	Cryptographic primitives that allow data sharing in a secure and, if required, privacy preserving way	RL.3.33	Deliver Item Accuracy
					RL.3.34	Delivery Location Accuracy
					RL.3.35	Delivery Quantity Accuracy
			Provide order tracking data	Real time detection, measurement and tracking of inventory with IoT	RS.3.18	Consolidate Orders Cycle Time
					CO.3.14	Order Management Costs
					CO.3.15	Order Deliver Costs
sD2.5	Build Loads	Transportation modes are selected and efficient loads are built	Provide a secure, peer-to-peer collaborative platform without centralized control for order management	Cryptographic primitives that allow data sharing in a secure and, if required, privacy preserving way	RS.3.16	Build Loads Cycle Time
					CO.3.14	Order Management Costs
					CO.3.15	Order Delivery Costs
sD2.6	Route Shipments	Loads are consolidated and routed by mode, lane and location	Provide a secure, peer-to-peer collaborative platform without centralized control for order management	Cryptographic primitives that allow data sharing in a secure and, if required, privacy preserving way	RS.3.117	Route Shipments Cycle Time
					CO.2.4	Cost to Deliver
					CO.3.14	Order Management Costs
					CO.3.15	Order Delivery Costs

Process	Description	Benefit	Detail	Metric	
sD2.7 Select Carriers and Rate Shipments	Specific carriers are selected by lowest cost per route and shipments are rated and tendered	Provide a secure, peer-to-peer collaborative platform without centralized control for order management and inventory financing	Cryptographic primitives that allow data sharing in a secure and, if required, privacy preserving way	RL.3.16	% suppliers meeting environmental metrics/criteria
				CO.2.4	Cost to Deliver
				CO.3.14	Order Management Costs
				CO.3.15	Order Delivery Costs
sD2.8 Receive Product from Source or Make	The activities such as receiving product, verifying, recording product receipt, determining put-away location, putting away and recording location that a company performs at its own warehouses	Elimination of paper records reduces the human interaction and communication	Digitally signed documents, replacing paper ones, with validated identities of entities, objects and individuals	RS.3.108	Receive Product from Make/Source Cycle Time
		Can provide real time, secure and validated data that can be used to monitor transport conditions of the product	Data related to temperature, humidity, motion, light conditions, chemical composition from IoT devices or sensors	RS.3.110	Receive Product from Source or Make Cycle Time
		Enable fully automated product receipt ('straight through processing')	Cost-effective transmission of transactions in peer-to-peer networks (Korpela et al, 2017)	CO.3.12	Indirect Cost Related to Production

(continued)

Table 6.10 *(Continued)*

Process	Description	Blockchain's roles	Mechanisms involved	Metrics affected	
sD2.11	Load Vehicle and Generate Shipping Documents	The series of tasks including placing/ loading product onto modes of transportation, and generating the documentation necessary to meet internal, customer, carrier and government needs	Elimination of paper records reduces the human interaction and communication	Digitally signed documents, replacing paper ones, with validated identities of entities, objects and individuals	RL.2.2	Delivery Performance to Customer Commit Date
					RL.2.3	Documentation Accuracy
					RL.3.31	Compliance Documentation Accuracy
					RL.3.33	Delivery Item Accuracy
					RL.3.34	Delivery Location Accuracy
					RL.3.35	Delivery Quantity Accuracy
					RL.3.43	Other Required Documentation Accuracy
					RL.3.45	Payment Documentation Accuracy
					RL.3.50	Shipping Documentation Accuracy
					RS.3.51	Load Product and Generate Shipping Documentation Cycle Time
					CO.3.12	Indirect Cost Related to Production

sD2.12	Ship Product	The process of shipping the product to the customer site	Provide order tracking data	Real time detection, measurement and tracking of inventory with IoT	RL.2.1 % Orders Delivered in Full
					RL.2.2 Delivery Performance to Customer Commit Date
					RL.3.33 Delivery Item Accuracy
					RL.3.34 Delivery Location Accuracy
					RL.3.35 Delivery Quantity Accuracy
					RS.3.126 Ship Product Cycle Time
					CO.2.4 Cost to Deliver
					CO.3.14 Order Management Cost
					CO.3.15 Order Delivery Costs
sD2.13	Receive and Verify Product by Customer	The process of receiving the shipment at the customer and verifying that the order was shipped complete and that the product meets delivery terms	Can provide real time, secure and validated data that can be used to monitor transport conditions of the product	Data related to temperature, humidity, motion, light conditions, chemical composition from IoT devices or sensors	RL.2.2 Delivery Performance to Customer Commit Date
					RL.2.4 Perfect Condition
					RL.3.32 Customer Commit Date Achievement Time Customer Receiving
					RL.3.33 Delivery Item Accuracy
					RL.3.34 Delivery Location Accuracy

(continued)

Table 6.10 (Continued)

Process	Description	Blockchain's roles	Mechanisms involved	Metrics affected
		Elimination of paper records reduces the human interaction and communication	Event changes, such as the transfer of ownership, trigger 'smart contracts'	RL.3.35 Delivery Quantity Accuracy RL.3.41 Orders Delivered Damage Free Conformance RL.3.42 Orders Delivered Defect Free Conformance RS.3.102 Receive and Verify Product by Customer Cycle Time RS.3.103 Receive and Verify Product Cycle Time
sD2.15 Invoice	A signal is sent to the financial organization that the order has been shipped and that the billing process should begin and payment be received or be closed out if payment has already been received	Enable fully automated processing ('straight through processing') of the billing process, including authorization of payments and the payment itself	Event changes, such as the transfer of ownership, trigger 'smart contracts'	RL.2.3 Documentation Accuracy RL.3.11 % Faultless Invoices CO.3.14 Order Management Costs AM.2.1 Days Sales Outstanding

sD3.1	Obtain and Respond to RFP/RFQ	The process of receiving a request for proposal or request for quote, evaluating the request (estimating the schedule, developing costs estimates, establishing price), and responding to the potential customer	Provide order tracking data	Detection, measurement and tracking of inventory with IoT	CO.3.14	Order Management Costs
			Blockchain's serves as a single consensus based source of truth	Transaction data can be validated by Oracles before being permanently added to the blockchain	RS.3.93	Obtain and Respond to Request for Quote/Request for Proposal Cycle Time
sD3.2	Negotiate and Receive Contract	The process of negotiating order details with customer (eg price, schedule, and product performance) and finalizing the contract	Elimination of paper records	Cost-effective transmission of transactions in peer-to-peer networks (Korpela et al, 2017)	RS.3.92	Negotiate and Receive Contract Cycle Time
			Simplify business-to-business integration	Data security and cost-effective transmission of transactions in peer-to-peer networks (Korpela et al, 2017)	CO.3.14	Order Management Costs

(continued)

Table 6.10 (Continued)

Process		Description	Blockchain's roles	Mechanisms involved	Metrics affected	
			Enable fully automated order processing ('straight through processing')	Enable fully automated processing ('straight through processing') without human communication of interaction	RL.2.1	% Orders Delivered in Full
					RL.2.2	Delivery Performance to Customer Commit Date
					RL.3.33	Deliver Item Accuracy
					RL.3.34	Deliver Location Accuracy
					RL.3.35	Deliver Quantity Accuracy
sD3.3	Enter Order, Commit Resources and Launch Program	The process of entering/finalizing the customer's order, approving the planned resources (eg engineering, manufacturing, etc) and officially launching the program	Provide inventory tracking data	Real time detection, measurement and tracking of inventory with IoT	RS.3.25	Enter Order, Commit Resources and Launch Program Cycle Time
					RS.3.94	Order Fulfilment Dwell Time
					CO.3.14	Order Management Costs

sD3.5	Build Loads	Transportation modes are selected and efficient loads are built	Provide a secure, peer-to-peer collaborative platform without centralized control for order management	Cryptographic primitives that allow data sharing in a secure and, if required, privacy preserving way	RS.3.16 Build Loads Cycle Time CO.3.14 Order Management Costs CO.3.15 Order Delivery Costs
sD3.6	Route Shipments	Loads are consolidated and routed by mode, lane and location	Provide a secure, peer-to-peer collaborative platform without centralized control for order management	Cryptographic primitives that allow data sharing in a secure and, if required, privacy preserving way	RL.3.33 Delivery Item Accuracy RL.3.34 Delivery Location Accuracy RL.3.35 Delivery Quantity Accuracy RS.3.117 Route Shipments Cycle Time CO.3.14 Order Management Costs CO.3.15 Order Delivery Costs
sD3.7	Select Carriers and Rate Shipments	Specific carriers are selected by lowest cost per route and shipments are rated and tendered	Provide a secure, peer-to-peer collaborative platform without centralized control for order management and inventory financing	Cryptographic primitives that allow data sharing in a secure and, if required, privacy preserving way	RS.3.124 Select Carriers and Rate Shipments Cycle Time CO.3.14 Order Management Costs CO.3.15 Order Delivery Costs

(continued)

Table 6.10 (*Continued*)

Process		Description	Blockchain's roles	Mechanisms involved	Metrics affected	
sD3.8	Receive Product from Source or Make	The activities such as receiving product, verifying, recording product receipt, determining put-away location, putting away and recording location that a company performs at its own warehouses	Elimination of paper records reduces the human interaction and communication	Digitally signed documents, replacing paper ones, with validated identities of entities, objects and individuals	RS.3.108	Receive Product from Make/Source Cycle Time
			Can provide real time, secure and validated data that can be used to monitor transport conditions of the product	Data related to temperature, humidity, motion, light conditions, chemical composition from IoT devices or sensors		
			Enable fully automated product receipt ('straight through processing')	Cost-effective transmission of transactions in peer-to-peer networks (Korpela et al, 2017)		

sD3.11	Load Vehicle and Generate Shipping Documents	The series of tasks including placing/ loading product onto modes of transportation, and generating the documentation necessary to meet internal, customer, carrier and government needs	Elimination of paper records reduces the human interaction and communication	Digitally signed documents, replacing paper ones, with validated identities of entities, objects and individuals	RL.2.2	Delivery Performance to Customer Commit Date
					RL.2.3	Documentation Accuracy
					RL.3.31	Compliance Documentation Accuracy
					RL.3.33	Delivery Item Accuracy
					RL.3.34	Delivery Location Accuracy
			Can provide real time, secure and validated data that can be used to monitor transport conditions of the product	Data related to temperature, humidity, motion, light conditions, chemical composition from IoT devices or sensors	RL.3.35	Delivery Quantity Accuracy
					RL.3.43	Other Required Documentation Accuracy
					RL.3.45	Payment Documentation Accuracy
					RL.3.50	Shipping Documentation Accuracy
					RS.3.51	Load Product and Generate Shipping Documentation Cycle Time
					CO.3.12	Indirect Cost Related to Production

(continued)

Table 6.10 (Continued)

Process	Description	Blockchain's roles	Mechanisms involved	Metrics affected	
sD3.12 Ship Product	The process of shipping the product to the customer site	Provide order tracking data	Real time detection, measurement and tracking of inventory with IoT	RL.2.1	% Orders Delivered in Full
				RL.2.2	Delivery Performance to Customer Commit Date
				RL.3.33	Delivery Item Accuracy
				RL.3.34	Delivery Location Accuracy
				RL.3.35	Delivery Quantity Accuracy
				RS.3.126	Ship Product Cycle Time
				CO.2.4	Cost to Deliver
				CO.3.14	Order Management Cost
				CO.3.15	Order Delivery Costs
sD3.13 Receive and Verify Product by Customer	The process of receiving the shipment at the customer and verifying that the order was shipped complete and that the product meets delivery terms	Can provide real time, secure and validated data that can be used to monitor transport conditions of the product	Data related to temperature, humidity, motion, light conditions, chemical composition from IoT devices or sensors	RL.2.2	Delivery Performance to Customer Commit Date
				RL.2.4	Perfect Condition
				RL.3.32	Customer Commit Date Achievement Time Customer Receiving
				RL.3.33	Delivery Item Accuracy
				RL.3.34	Delivery Location Accuracy

			Metrics
	Elimination of paper records reduces the human interaction and communication	Event changes, such as the transfer of ownership, trigger 'smart contracts'	RL.3.35 Delivery Quantity Accuracy RL.3.41 Orders Delivered Damage Free Conformance RL.3.42 Orders Delivered Defect Free Conformance RS.3.102 Receive and Verify Product by Customer Cycle Time RS.3.103 Receive and Verify Product Cycle Time
sD3.15 Invoice	A signal is sent to the financial organization that the order has been shipped and that the billing process should begin and payment be received or be closed out if payment has already been received	Enable fully automated processing ('straight through processing') of the billing process, including authorization of payments and the payment itself	Event changes, such as the transfer of ownership, trigger 'smart contracts'
			RL.2.3 Documentation Accuracy

Table 6.11 Return process and metrics affected

Process		Description	Blockchain's roles	Mechanisms involved	Metrics affected	
sSR2.1	Identify MRO Product Condition	The process where the customer utilizes pre-determined MRO policies, business rules and product operating conditions such as criteria to identify and confirm that an item requires maintenance, repair, overhaul or disposal	Blockchain's 'super audit trail' can address challenges associated with self-reported data that are provided with supply chain partners	Identifying and collecting data on product operating conditions within key SCM processes using IoT. Access to this data would speed up the identification process	AM.3.42	% Unserviceable MRO Inventory in Identification
			Business rules implemented on the blockchain using smart contracts	Reduce or eliminate the needs of physical interactions and communications can reduce the time needed to identify the product's condition		

sSR2.3	Request MRO Return Authorization	The process of a customer requesting and obtaining authorization, from a service provider, for the return of an MRO product. In addition to discussing the MRO issue, the customer and service provider would discuss enabling conditions such as return replacement or credit, packaging, handling, transportation and import/ export requirements to facilitate the efficient return of the MRO product to the service provider	Business rules implemented on the blockchain using smart-contracts Elimination of paper records	Reduce or eliminate the needs of physical interactions and communications can reduce the time needed to identify the product's condition Reduce or eliminate the time needed for requesting return authorization by removing 'machine-to-paper-to-machine' processes	AM.3.41	% Unserviceable MRO Inventory in Return Authorization
sSR2.4	Schedule MRO Shipment	The process where the customer develops the schedule for a carrier to pick-up and deliver the MRO product. Activities include selecting the carrier and rates, preparing the item for transfer, preparing scheduling documentation and managing overall scheduling administration	Elimination of paper records while preparing the scheduling documentation and automation of the scheduling administration	Reduce or eliminate the time needed for requesting return authorization by removing 'machine-to-paper-to-machine' processes	RL.3.28	% Shipping Schedules that Support Customer Required Return by Date
					AM.3.43	% Unserviceable MRO Inventory in Scheduling

(continued)

Table 6.11 (Continued)

Process		Description	Blockchain's roles	Mechanisms involved	Metrics affected	
sSR2.5	Return MRO Product	The process where the customer packages and handles the MRO product in preparation for shipping in accord with pre-determined conditions. The product is then provided by the customer to the carrier who physically transports the product and its associated documentation to the service provider	Provide order tracking data	Real time detection, measurement and tracking of inventory with IoT	RL.3.5	% Error-free Returns Shipped
					RL.3.47	Return Shipments Shipped on Time
					AM.3.40	% Unserviceable MRO Inventory in Transportation
sDR1.1	Authorize Defective Product Return	The process where the last known holder or designated return centre receives a defective product return authorization request from a customer, determines if the item can be accepted and communicates decision to the customer	Business rules implemented on the blockchain using smart-contracts	Reduce or eliminate the needs of physical interactions and communications can reduce the time needed to authorize the return	RS.3.5	Authorized Defective Return Cycle Time

sDR1.2	Schedule Defective Return Receipt	The process where the last known holder or designated return centre evaluates the defective product handling requirements including negotiated conditions and develops a schedule that tells the customer when to ship the product. The scheduling activity would also inform receiving when to expect the shipment and where to send the product, for disposition, upon receipt	Provide a secure, peer-to-peer collaborative platform without centralized control for scheduling of the return	Cryptographic primitives that allow data sharing in a secure and, if required, privacy preserving way	CO.2.5 Cost to Return
sDR1.3	Receive Defective Product (includes Verify)	The process where the last known holder or designated return centre receives and verifies the returned defective product against the return authorization and other documentation and prepares the item for transfer	Elimination of paper records reduces the human interaction and communication. Can provide real time, secure and validated data that can be used to monitor transport conditions of the product	Digitally signed documents, replacing paper ones, with validated identities of entities, objects and individuals. Data related to temperature, humidity, motion, light conditions, chemical composition from IoT devices or sensors	RS.3.118 Schedule Defective Return Receipt Cycle Time; RS.3.104 Receive Defective Product Cycle Time

(continued)

Table 6.11 (*Continued*)

Process	Description	Blockchain's roles	Mechanisms involved	Metrics affected
		Enable fully automated product receipt ('straight through processing')	Cost-effective transmission of transactions in peer-to-peer networks (Korpela *et al*, 2017)	
		Elimination of paper records reduces the human interaction and communication	Digitally signed documents, replacing paper ones, with validated identities of entities, objects and individuals	
sDR1.4	Transfer Defective Product	The process where the last known holder or designated return centre transfers the defective product to the appropriate process to implement the disposition decision	Provide order tracking data	Real time detection, measurement and tracking of inventory with IoT	RS.3.104 Receive Defective Product Cycle Time
			Provide a decentralized market place for waste/surplus materials	In combination with AI technology find the best possible alternative use for valuable materials contained in waste/surplus materials	

sDR2.1	Authorize MRO Product Return	The process where a service provider receives an MRO product return authorization request from a customer, determines if the item can be accepted for MRO and communicates their decision to the customer. Accepting the request would include negotiating the conditions of the return with the customer, including authorizing return replacement or credit. Rejecting the request would include providing a reason for the rejection to the customer	Business rules implemented on the blockchain using smart-contracts	Reducing or eliminating the need for physical interactions and communications can reduce the time needed to authorize the return	RS.3.7	Authorize MRO Product Return Cycle Time
sDR2.2	Schedule MRO return Receipt	The process where the service provider evaluates the MRO service requirements including negotiated conditions and develops a schedule that tells the customer when to ship the part. The scheduling activity would also inform Receiving when to expect the shipment and where to send the part	Provide a secure, peer-to-peer collaborative platform without centralized control for scheduling of the return	Cryptographic primitives that allow data sharing in a secure and, if required, privacy preserving way	RS.3.121	Schedule MRO Return Receipt Cycle Time

(continued)

Table 6.11 (*Continued*)

Process		Description	Blockchain's roles	Mechanisms involved	Metrics affected
sDR2.3	Receive MRO Product	The process where the service provider receives and verifies the returned MRO item against the return authorization and other documentation and prepares the item for transfer	Elimination of paper records reduces the human interaction and communication	Digitally signed documents, replacing paper ones, with validated identities of entities, objects and individuals	RS.3.106 Receive MRO Product Cycle Time
			Can provide real time, secure and validated data that can be used to monitor transport conditions of the product	Data related to temperature, humidity, motion, light conditions, chemical composition from IoT devices or sensors	
			Enable fully automated product receipt ('straight through processing')	Cost-effective transmission of transactions in peer-to-peer networks (Korpela *et al*, 2017)	

sDR2.4	Transfer MRO Product	The process where the service provider transfers the MRO product to the appropriate process to implement the disposition decision	Provide order tracking data	Real time detection, measurement and tracking of inventory with IoT	RS.3.138	Transfer MRO Product Cycle Time
			Provide a decentralized market place for waste/surplus materials	In combination with AI technology find the best possible alternative use for valuable materials contained in waste/surplus materials		
sDR3.1	Authorize Excess Product Return	The process where a service provider receives an Excess product return authorization request from a customer, determines if the item can be accepted for MRO and communicates their decision to the customer. Accepting the request would include negotiating the conditions of the return with the customer, including authorizing credit or cash discount. Rejecting the request would include providing a reason for the rejection to the customer	Business rules implemented on the blockchain using smart-contracts	Reduce or eliminate the needs of physical interactions and communications can reduce the time needed to authorize the return	RS.3.6	Authorize Excess Product Return Cycle Time

(continued)

Table 6.11 (*Continued*)

Process		Description	Blockchain's roles	Mechanisms involved	Metrics affected
sDR3.2	Schedule Excess Return Receipt	The process where the designated return centre evaluates an authorized excess material return to determine packaging and handling requirements. This assessment will lead to the development of a return disposition decision and a return schedule with terms and conditions that will tell the customer how and when to ship the product. The scheduling activity would also inform the return centre's receiving department when to expect the shipment and where to send the product, for disposition, upon receipt	Provide a secure, peer-to-peer collaborative platform without centralized control for scheduling of the return	Cryptographic primitives that allow data sharing in a secure and, if required, privacy preserving way	RS.3.119 Schedule Excess Return Receipt Cycle Time

sDR3.3	Receive Excess Product	The process where the designated return centre receives and verifies the returned excess product and associated documentation against the return authorization and other documentation and prepares the item for transfer. Administer any discrepancies that arise	Elimination of paper records reduces the human interaction and communication Can provide real time, secure and validated data that can be used to monitor transport conditions of the product	Digitally signed documents, replacing paper ones, with validated identities of entities, objects and individuals Data related to temperature, humidity, motion, light conditions, chemical composition from IoT devices or sensors	RS.3.105	Receive Excess Product Cycle Time
			Enable fully automated product receipt ('straight through processing')	Cost-effective transmission of transactions in peer-to-peer networks (Korpela et al, 2017)		
			Elimination of paper records reduces the human interaction and communication	Digitally signed documents, replacing paper ones, with validated identities of entities, objects and individuals		

(continued)

Table 6.11 (*Continued*)

Process		Description	Blockchain's roles	Mechanisms involved	Metrics affected	
sDR3.4	Transfer Excess Product	The process where the designated return centre transfers the excess product to the appropriate process to implement the disposition decision	Provide order tracking data	Real time detection, measurement and tracking of inventory with IoT	RS.3.137	Transfer Excess Product Cycle Time
			Provide a decentralized market place for waste/surplus materials	In combination with AI technology find the best possible alternative use for valuable materials contained in waste/surplus materials		
sSR1.1	Identify Defective Product Condition	The process where the customer utilizes planned policies, business rules and product operating conditions inspections as criteria to identify and confirm that material is excess	Blockchain's 'super audit trail' can address challenges associated with self-reported data that are provided with supply chain partners	Identifying and collecting data on product operating conditions within key SCM processes using IoT. Access to this data would speed up the identification process	AM.3.29	% Defective Inventory in Disposition

sSR1.2	Disposition Defective Product	The process of the customer determining whether to return the defective item and the appropriate source contact for a return authorization	Business rules implemented on the blockchain using smart contracts	Reduce or eliminate the needs of physical interactions and communications can reduce the time needed to identify the product's condition	
			Provide order tracking data	Real time detection, measurement and tracking of inventory with IoT	AM.3.29 % Defective Inventory in Disposition
sSR1.3	Request Defective Product Return Authorization	The process of a customer requesting and obtaining authorization, from last known holder or designated return centre, for the return of the defective product. Additionally, the customer and last known holder or designated return centre would discuss enabling conditions such as return replacement or credit, packaging, handling, transportation and import/export requirements to facilitate the efficient return of the defective product	Business rules implemented on the blockchain using smart contracts	Reduce or eliminate the needs of physical interactions and communications can reduce the time needed to identify the product's condition	AM.3.30 % Defective Inventory in Return Authorization

(continued)

Table 6.11 (Continued)

Process	Description	Blockchain's roles	Mechanisms involved	Metrics affected
		Elimination of paper records	Reduce or eliminate the time needed for requesting return authorization by removing 'machine-to-paper-to-machine' processes	
sSR1.4	Schedule Defective Product Shipment	The process where the customer develops the schedule for a carrier to pick-up for delivery of the defective product. Activities include selecting the carrier and rates, preparing the item for transfer, preparing scheduling documentation and managing overall scheduling administration	Elimination of paper records while preparing the scheduling documentation and automation of the scheduling administration	Reduce or eliminate the time needed for requesting return authorization by removing 'machine-to-paper-to-machine' processes	RL.3.28 % Shipping Schedules that Support Customer Required

AM.3.32 Percentage Defective Product Inventory in Scheduling |

| sSR1.5 | Return Defective | The process where the customer packages, and handles the defective product in preparation for shipping in accordance with the pre-determined conditions. The product is then provided by the customer to the carrier who physically transports the product and its associated documentation to the last known holder or designated return centre | Provide order tracking data | Real time detection, measurement and tracking of inventory with IoT. | RL.3.5 | % Error-free Returns Shipped |

Table 6.12 Enable process and metrics affected

Process	Description	Blockchain's roles	Mechanisms involved	Metrics affected
sE1 Manage Supply Chain Business Rules	The process of establishing, documenting, communicating and publishing supply chain business rules	Document business rules at the transactional level to enable 'straight through processing' Business rules are immediately available to those supply chain partners accepted on the network Business rules on the network can be immediately de-activated	'Smart contracts' enabled machine-to-machine transactions Business rules are broadcasted immediately to all relevant parties in the network Retirement of business rules can be broadcasted immediately to all relevant parties in the network	RS.3.54 RS.3.55 RS.3.57 RS.3.79 RS.3.86	Manage Business Rules for Plan Processes Cycle Time Manage Business Rules for Return Processes Cycle Time Manage Deliver Business Rules Cycle Time Manage Production Rules Cycle Time Manage Sourcing Business Rules Cycle Time

| sE2 | Manage Supply Chain Performance | The process of defining performance targets for supply chain metrics that align to overall business strategy and goals, and for reporting performance, identifying gaps in performance, performing root cause analysis, and developing and launching corrective actions to close gaps in performance | Provide data that can be used to assess useful, meaningful and representative indicators for performance

Provide the mechanism to quickly implement changes in business rules throughout the network

Provide the mechanism to quickly approve and launch changes in business rules throughout the network | Detection, measurement and tracking of key SCM processes with IoT

Business rules in the form of 'smart contracts' are broadcast immediately to all relevant parties in the network

Business rules in the form of 'smart contracts' are broadcast immediately to all relevant parties in the network and network partners can approve these changes autonomously | RS.3.2

RS.3.3

RS.3.65

RS.3.70

RS.3.71

RS.3.78

CO.1.1 | Assess Delivery Performance Cycle Time

Assess Supplier Performance Cycle Time

Manage Integrated Supply Chain Inventory Cycle Time

Manage Performance of return Processes Cycle Time

Manage Performance of Return Processes Cycle Time

Manage Production

Total Supply Chain Management Costs |

(continued)

Table 6.12 *(Continued)*

Process		Description	Blockchain's roles	Mechanisms involved	Metrics affected	
sE3	Manage Data and Information	The process of collecting, maintaining and publishing data and information required to plan, operate, measure and manage the supply chain	Provide data from key SCM processes	Real-time detection, measurement and tracking using IoT	RS.3.53	Maintain Source Data Cycle Time
			Blockchain's 'super audit trail' can address challenges associated with self-reported data that are provided with supply chain partners	Identifying and collecting data on product operating conditions within key SCM processes using IoT. Access to this data would speed up the identification process	RS.3.59	Manage Deliver Information Cycle Time
			Blockchain's append only ledger can address challenges associated with self-reported data that are provided by distributors		RS.3.68	Manage Make Information Cycle Time
					RS.3.72	Manage Plan Data Collection Cycle Time
					RS.3.81	Manage Return Data Collection Cycle Time
				Transaction data can be validated by Oracles before being permanently added to the blockchain	CO.3.14	Order Management Costs

sE5	Manage Supply Chain Assets	The process of scheduling, maintaining and dispositioning of supply chain assets developed for supply chain execution	Can provide data that can be used to manage supply chain assets	Detection, measurement and tracking of assets' maintenance needs with IoT	RS.3.56	Manage Capital Assets Cycle Time
				Simplify machine-to-machine integration		
				Elimination of paper records while preparing the scheduling documentation and automation of the scheduling administration, including invoicing	Data security and cost-effective transmission of transactions between IoT devices in a peer-to-peer network	RS.3.58	Manage Deliver Capital Assets Cycle Time
					Only assets mutually accepted in the network can engage in transactions, facilitating the identification of all assets in need of maintenance	RS.3.64	Manage Integrated Supply Chain Capital Assets Cycle Time
					Reduce or eliminante the time needed for the administrative processes related to the management of supply chain assets, by removing 'machine-to-paper-to-machine' processes	RS.3.67	Manage Make Equipment and Facilities Cycle Time
					Validation of the identities of individual entities participating in the supply chain	RS.3.80	Manage Return Capital Assets Cycle Time

(continued)

Table 6.12 (Continued)

Process	Description	Blockchain's roles	Mechanisms involved	Metrics affected	
sE6 Manage Supply Chain Contracts/ Agreements	The management and communication of contractual and non-contractual agreements in support of business objectives and supply chain goals	Enable fully automated processing ('straight through processing') of contractual and non-contractual agreements	Event changes, such as the transfer of ownership, trigger 'smart contracts'	RL.3.37	Forecast Accuracy
				RS.3.87	Manage Supplier Agreements Cycle Time
				CO.2.6	Mitigation Costs
				CO.3.15	Order Delivery and/or Install Costs
				AM.2.1	Days Sales Outstanding
				AM.2.3	Days Payable Outstanding
sE7 Manage Supply Chain Network	The process of defining and managing the geographic and activity footprint of the supply chain	Obtain accurate date to model the supply chain	Identifying and collecting data on product operating conditions within key SCM processes using IoT Transaction data can be validated by Oracles before being permanently added to the blockchain	RL.3.37	Forecast Accuracy
				RS.3.66	Manage Integrated Supply Chain Transportation Cycle Time
				RS.3.74	Manage Planning Configuration Cycle Time
				RS.3.77	Manage Production Network Cycle Time
				RS.3.83	Manage Return Network Configuration Cycle Time

				RS.3.85	Manage Return Transportation Cycle Time
				RS.3.88	Manage Supplier Network Cycle Time
				RS.3.89	Manage Transportation (WIP) Cycle Time
				RS.3.90	Manage Transportation Cycle Time
				CO.1.1	Total SCM Costs
				CO.1.2	Cost of Goods Sold
				AM.2.2	Inventory Days of Supply
sE8	Manage Regulatory and Voluntary Compliance	The process of identifying, collecting, assessing and integrating regulatory compliance requirements in standard supply chain processes, policies and business rules	Ensure upfront compliance	'Smart contracts' ensure that transactions can only be executed if all conditions are met ('atomic swap')	RS.3.61 Manage Import/Export Requirements Cycle Time

(continued)

Table 6.12 (Continued)

Process	Description	Blockchain's roles	Mechanisms involved		Metrics affected
sE9 Manage Supply Chain Risks	The process of identification and assessment of potential disruptions (risks) in the supply chain and developing a plan to mitigate these threats to operating the supply chain	Addressing the holistic sources of risk	Blockchain's ability to validate identities can be used to verify the provenance of items such as diamonds		The standard metric for quantification of risk is value at risk (VaR). VaR = Probability of Occurrence * Monetary Impact of Occurrence
		Identifying, collecting, validating and documenting data on all potential risk events	Detection, measurement, and tracking of key SCM processes with IoT	AG.2.10	Value at Risk (Plan)
				AG.2.11	Value at Risk (Source)
				AG.2.12	Value at Risk (Make)
				AG.2.13	Value at Risk (Deliver)
		Identying, collecting, validating and documenting data beyond the tier 1 supply chain	Preservation of privacy while allowing traceability through a single tracking key and validation of the authenticity of transactions (El Maouchi, 2018)	AG.2.14	Value at Risk (Return)

Providing data at the lowest possible level of granularity instead of process	AG.2.15	Time to Recovery (TTR)
Crisis involving defective products (eg contaminated food): easily identify the source and engage in strategic removals of affected products instead of recalling the entire product line	Detection, measurement, and tracking of key SCM processes with IoT	CO.2.6	Risk/Mitigation Costs

Enable processes

SCOR defines the Enable process as the processes associated with establishing, maintaining and monitoring information, relationships, resources, assets, business rules, compliance and contracts required to operate the supply chain as well as monitoring and managing the overall performance of the supply chain. Table 6.12 provides an overview of the processes and the affected metrics.

Notes

1 TCP/IP is a collection of protocols that work together to allow for end-to-end communication between systems and how the data that is being interchanged should be packetized, addressed, transmitted, routed and received (https://en.wikipedia.org/wiki/Internet_protocol_suite).
2 Only for the sE5 'Manage Supply Chain Assets' and sE9 'Manage Supply Chain Risk' were the metrics defined at the process element level.
3 http://excessmaterialsexchange.com/

References

APICS (2017) [Online] https://www.apics.org/docs/default-source/scc-non-research/apicsscc_scor_quick_reference_guide.pdf

Blackstone Jr, JH (2010) *APICS Dictionary*, American Production & Inventory Control Society

BSR (2014) [Online] https://www.bsr.org/reports/BSR_UNGC_Guide_to_Traceability.pdf

El Maouchi, M (2018) Decouples: a privacy-preserving solution for traceability in supply chains, Masters Thesis, Technical University, Delft

Higgins, P, Le Roy, P and Tierney, L (1996) *Manufacturing Planning and Control Beyond MRP II*, Chapman & Hall, London

Iansiti, M and Lakhani, KM (2017) [Online] https://hbr.org/2017/01/the-truth-about-blockchain

Korpela, K, Hallikas, J and Dahlberg, T (2017) Digital supply chain transformation toward blockchain integration, Hawaii International Conference on System Sciences, volume 50

Ksehtri, N (2017a) Blockchain's roles in strengthening cybersecurity and protecting privacy, *Telecommunications Policy*, **41** (10), pp 1027–38

Kshetri, N (2017b) Blockchain's roles in meeting key supply chain management objectives, *International Journal of Information Management.*

Martinez de Andino, JM (2014) Counterfeits in the supply chain: A big problem and it's getting worse. [Online] http://www.industryweek.com/inventory-management/counterfeits-supply-chain-big-problem-and-its-getting-worse

Risius, M and Spohrer, K (2017) A blockchain research framework: What we (don't) know, where we go from here, and how we will get there? *Business and Information Systems Engineering*, pp 385–409

Setboonsarng, S, Sakai, J and Vancura, L (2009) *Food Safety and ICT Traceability Systems: Lessons from Japan for developing countries*, Technical Report, ADBI working Paper Series

Simchi-Levi, D, Kaminsky, P and Simchi-Levi, E (2000) *Designing and Managing the Supply Chain*, McGraw-Hill

Simchi-Levi, D, Schmidt, W and Wei, Y (2014) [Online] https://hbr.org/2014/01/from-superstorms-to-factory-fires-managing-unpredictable-supply-chain-disruptions

Williamson, OE (1985) *The Economic Insitutions of Capitalism*, Free Press, New York

Blockchain projects in practice

07

Case study: Deliver

Introduction

In this chapter we address the question of how to approach a blockchain project. We have chosen to do this in the form of a case study that centres around a blockchain project that involves the Port of Rotterdam (PoR), Samsung Digital Solutions (SDS) and ABN-AMRO Bank (AAB). While not presenting a standard methodology or best practices, this chapter will provide practitioners with practical insights about the specificities of a blockchain project, such as its governance, the platform ecosystem and its architecture.

On 19 October 2018 these three companies signed a memorandum of understanding to jointly conduct a pilot with the aim of making two, up to now, independent blockchain ecosystems interoperable and provide an open development environment for Distributed Applications (Dapps) that work on the validated transactional data available in the two ecosystems.

Together, the two ecosystems represent close to 100 large multinational companies from the Netherlands and South Korea. As such, the pilot is more than just simply connecting supply chains of individual companies; it has the potential to connect the trade lane between the Netherlands and South Korea.

This use case description provides insight into the journey embarked upon by the PoR, AAB and SDS over a 10-month period, the challenges faced and some of the solutions developed. To our knowledge, this is the first detailed description of a blockchain use case in supply chain management that is publicly available. As such, it provides the reader with valuable insight on the 'how?' part, or the implementation of blockchain.

The companies

The PoR is the number one port in Europe and 10th largest port in the world. In 2017 over 13 million twenty foot equivalent units (TEU) and 467 million tons of cargo flowed through the port's infrastructure, which was named 'best Dutch infrastructure' for six years in a row by the World Economic Forum. The interest in blockchain is driven by a clear strategy on port digitization, which incorporates various other technologies such as machine learning and artificial intelligence, 3-D printing and the Internet of Things. The core of this strategy is that, next to a physical infrastructure, a port has a digital infrastructure, or a so-called digital twin of the port. Together with the Municipality of Rotterdam, the PoR founded a separate entity, Blocklab,[1] to boost blockchain research and development within the Rotterdam region.

AAB is the second largest bank of the Netherlands and ranked in the top 15 of European banks with approximately €394 billion of total assets. It employed close to 20,000 full-time equivalent employees as per the end of 2017 and has offices in Brazil, Europe, the United States of America, the Middle East and Asia Pacific. The interest in blockchain is driven by a clear strategy on innovation and sustainable growth. As such, AAB is a consortium member in Komgo,[2] a trade finance venture between some of the world's largest institutions, including international banks like the AAB, Citibank, and Crédit Agricole, a number of trading companies, like Gunvor and Mercuria and oil giant Shell.

Samsung Digital Solutions is a global software solutions and IT provider with its headquarters in Seoul, South Korea and offices in the USA, Europe, the Middle East, Africa and Asia Pacific. Annual turnover in 2017 was $8.2 billion. Established in 1985, SDS is of particular importance for Samsung as an organization. The reason is that it is the subsidiary capable of rapidly adopting unique creative digital business models that are based on contemporary and emerging digital technologies. In August 2018 it was awarded the contract by Korean Customs to develop the Korean Blockchain Platform for Global Trade. Furthermore, SDS developed the Cello platform.[3] Cello was launched in 2012 as an integrated supply chain management suite to power Samsung's own logistics network and has culminated in a dedicated SCM division that caters to both internal and external clients and had an annual global turnover in 2017 of $5 billion.

While impressive companies on their own, with all three of them having been involved in a number of blockchain developments, they all shared a common understanding – to successfully transform their operations by using blockchain technology required (international) cross-industry collaboration. This common understanding brought together a combination of organizational capabilities that is unique in the supply chain industry.

A brief history

Next to the common understanding that blockchain is in fact a team activity other factors contributed to the collaboration between PoR, AAB and SDS. One of those factors was that SDS on its own and AAB together with PoR developed blockchain proof-of-concepts (PoCs) that were complementary in terms of their functionality.

In 2017 SDS ran two supply chain related blockchain PoCs. The first one centred on the shipment of goods from their factories in China to Korea and 'chained together' those parties involved in the physical flow of goods, such as LSP, Ocean Carrier, Customs and the importer and exporter. The emphasis was therefore on the digitization of various export-related shipping documents, such as the booking request and confirmation and the bill of lading and integration with IoT devices. The second one expanded not only the number of destinations, so that now also non-Korean ports of discharge (PoD), such as Cat Lai in Vietnam and Dubai, were included as well as those parties involved in the financial flow in the supply chain, such as an insurance company and banks. Therefore the emphasis of the second PoC was on the digitization of various trade finance documents such as the letter of credit, purchase order and insurance policy. Both PoCs were built on the Hyperledger Fabric blockchain framework, which is one of the Hyperledger projects hosted by the Linux Foundation.[4]

SIF is basically a development of the classic factoring arrangement, which has been around for a long time. SIF is referred to when a firm independently sells an invoice to a financial institution against a premium. Factoring differs from ordinary balance sheet lending or bank overdrafts, because it takes into account the risk profile and value of the receivable instead of only relying on the general financial health of the supplier (Boer *et al*, 2015).

The basic principle of SIF is that an investment-grade buyer cooperates with a financial institution to facilitate cheaper short-term financing for its suppliers, based on the buyer's creditworthiness. The buyer's suppliers discount confirmed invoices towards a financial institution and can obtain liquidity that was previously not available (Boer *et al*, 2015).

Roughly around the same time, PoR and AAB conducted, together with Transfollow,[5] a Dutch company specialized in paperless transport, a PoC that involved single invoice factoring (SIF) for logistics service providers (LSPs) and tracking and tracing from pick-up to delivery of a container with road transport in the Netherlands. After the digital consignment note is signed by the receiver and trucker, this note provides incontestable proof that the actual transport has taken place. The consignment note is then uploaded together with the invoice to the SIF platform. As financiers now have proof that the invoice is for a transport that actually took place, they can offer a lower discount margin. Given the strong emphasis on the financial flow, the experiment was built on the Corda platform, a distributed ledger technology platform rooted in the financial services industry that is actively being developed by R3 and over 200 technology and industry partners.

The idea for the pilot started after SDS presented the results of their first and second PoCs to the PoR in February 2018. As SDS was interested in extending the PoCs with the hinterland transport to their European distribution centres in Breda and Oosterhout, PoR proposed combining the SDS PoC with the PoC the PoR had performed with AAB. For PoR and AAB the collaboration with SDS would allow them to further develop the initial PoC beyond SIF and tracking and tracing of the import process. After initial discussions and two workshops the participants concluded that there was indeed enough common ground to pursue a pilot. The pilot was pitched to the respective investment boards and at the end of July 2018 the project received the green light to proceed.

Based on the experience from the previous PoCs, the consortia members all shared a common vision about how best to realize blockchain's potential; and that is the tight integration of the financial and the physical flow, through digital assets and data. This is in sharp contrast with how these flows currently operate in supply chains; not only do we have silos in terms of systems, but also in flows, as depicted in Figure 7.1.

This integrated approach, addressing all the three flows in the supply chain, is a unique aspect of the Deliver consortium, and is the guiding principle for the system's architecture and business proposition.

Figure 7.1 Organizational and flow silos

The problem   DELIVER

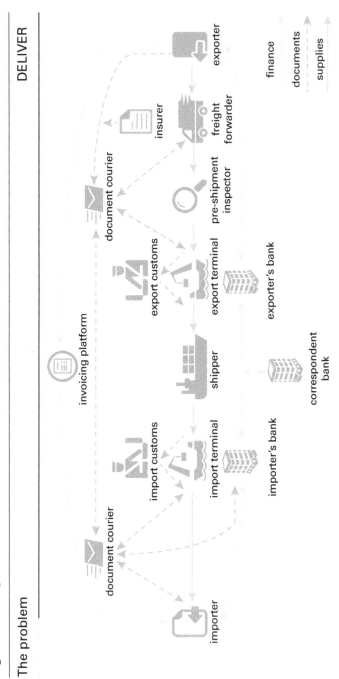

The pilot goals

In August 2018 a two-day workshop was organized to finalize the goals of the pilot. While the 'quick and dirty' solution would have been to 'simply' bolt the two blockchain ecosystems together, this was deemed too easy a solution because the end result would not result in a scalable solution and would leave the participants not much wiser about the business case for the solution, in particular because it would result in a technology driven project instead of a business one. For a more detailed description of the architecture, see page 220.

At the end of the workshop the participants identified the following pilot goals:

- End-to-end visibility of the physical movement of goods from pick-up at the origin to delivery at the destination. The owner of the goods is provided access to the data, using a portal on the web, for tracking (ie where are my goods now?) and tracing (ie what has the flow of the goods been up to now?) purposes. Data for tracking and tracing would come from a combination of (predictive) event data, digitized documents and data streams provided by IoT devices. Visibility is provided at the voyage, shipment, container and goods level.

- Straight though processing of the data. The pilot will create an end-to-end decentralized data repository that will allow pre-filling of transport documentation, such as the master bill of lading and the CMR,[6] with validated data. The CMR is a consignment note that is digitally signed by the receiver of the goods and has, in the Netherlands, the same legal status as the paper version of the document. As such it provides an undisputable proof of delivery of these goods and can be thought of as an Oracle. The undisputable PoD will be used for SIF, as discussed in the next bullet.

- Single invoice factoring based on a signed proof of delivery. By including a digitally signed proof of delivery with the invoice, the financier knows that the transaction underlying the invoice actually took place and was accepted by the receiver of the goods, who contracted the LSP. The LSP, who is normally paid in, say, 30 days now can decide whether he wants to be paid immediately, or for example in 15 days, by selling his invoice to the financier, with a small discount. The financier assumes the credit risk on the invoice and collects the invoice on the originally agreed open payment due date.

- Validate the concept of an Oracle platform. Combining data from various sources and turning it into a 'consensus-based source of the truth' is bound to result in conflicts for a number of reasons, ranging from technical challenges such as latency of a network, to data and identity standardization issues, and mutually agreed upon validation and consensus rules. In the pilot we use estimated time of arrival (ETA) data coming from Pronto, a port-call optimization application, developed by the Digital Business Solutions department of the PoR as an ETA Oracle, for all the members currently connected to the two platforms.

- As stated by Buterin (2016), one of the advantages of using platforms where cryptographic authentication is naturally baked into every single operation is that we can actually provide much tighter and more secure coupling than is possible with previously existing systems. In order to preserve that cryptographic integrity, we needed to work out a strategy to make the two blockchain protocols involved in the pilot truly interoperable, as opposed to interconnective.

Interoperability versus interconnectivity

Just as blockchain and distributed ledger technology (DLT) are often used interchangeably, this appears also to be the case with interoperability and interconnectivity. While interconnectivity is a necessary condition to reach interoperability, as decentralized data needs to be made available across multiple blockchain platforms, it is not a sufficient condition.

In essence, interconnectivity is concerned with data, while interoperability is about moving digital assets in a way that secures their cryptographic authenticity. These digital asset do contain data, but having the data alone will not allow you to recreate the exact digital asset and that is the whole point of cryptographic integrity. Further to data, these assets might represent smart contracts. In those cases we can also ensure that the cryptographic integrity of the behaviour.

- Record data from an IoT device inside a container on the blockchain. This provides an immutable record of the conditions under which the goods were transported, eg humidity, temperature and the location, and can be created for each and every shipment. Not only can this data be used for end-to-end visibility, but also to assess and in a later phase even predict product quality risks associated with the transport.

Consortium creation and alignment

Aligning three different parties, from three very distinctive industries and cultures, is by no means an easy process. What united the three parties from day one was that they realized the potential of blockchain technology within their own industry and, most importantly, realized they couldn't do it on their own. This common understanding led to a number of conference calls, primarily to get a better understanding of each other's (technical) capabilities, results from past pilots and ecosystems in which these pilots were done, and a non-disclosure agreement was drawn up. During these discussions it quickly became evident that the three consortium members brought unique technical, network and domain specific capabilities to the table and that there was potential to do more than just a pilot together.

To further explore this, a one-day workshop was organized, involving senior management of the three consortium members. This workshop was not about the technology; it was business-centred. Hence the discussions that day revolved around identifying the expected and observed pains in the supply chain, the size of the pain and who were most affected by it. This provided valuable insight into the potential users of the platform and the value proposition we needed to provide to them. One of the major challenges identified was the need to develop a governance model that satisfactorily answers the questions of control and ownership of the platform, including the intellectual property rights. Closely related to this was the development of a business model that fosters further development of the platform and related standards, ensures platform neutrality and fair sharing of the gains and pains. While a detailed description of the resulting governance and business model would be a single use-case by itself, two of the building blocks will be discussed in some detail in the next two paragraphs; first, how the architecture of Deliver ensures that data remains owned by the producer of that data (page 220), and second how the Deliver platform provides value for the various roles within the ecosystem (page 218).

As a result of the outcomes of the business workshop, the pilot's scope had to be extended, to include non-technical work packages. The technical and other work packages are described in some detail on page 224. Also, a second workshop was initiated to identify, amongst other things the customer journey for the pilot, the parties that needed to get involved in the pilot and high-level planning. The outcome of this workshop provided the input for initial design of the overall architecture of the solution. This design was further fine-tuned in a two-day technical workshop at the headquarters of Samsung SDS in Seoul, South Korea. The business workshop also laid the groundwork for what later would become the memorandum of understanding (MoU) between the consortium members. Despite the complexity of some of the topics, such as intellectual property rights and the governance of the project, and the relatively short time that was available (slightly less than two months), the MoU was ready to be signed at Blocklab's first annual event.

The Deliver ecosystem

An important conclusion from the first business workshop was that thinking in terms of traditional 'client–supplier' relationships within a platform ecosystem will most likely result in a broken business model. Within a platform, entities can take up various roles over time, change their role or even have multiple roles at the same time. In other words, there's not such a thing as *the ecosystem* but only *a snapshot*, representing an instance of that particular ecosystem at a given point in time. Therefore Figure 7.2 should be considered a snapshot of the ecosystem and not an end-state.

As can be seen from Figure 7.2 we identify the following entities or roles within the Deliver ecosystem. These are:

1 Producers are entities interested in *providing value* on the supply side of the ecosystem/marketplace, seeking opportunities to improve their capabilities in order to become more efficient or increase their performance.

2 Consumers are entities interested in *consuming, utilizing and accessing the value* that is created by the platform.

3 Super users are entities that *create additional value* and collaborate with platform owners. They tend to specialize in a certain niche product or service.

Not shown in Figure 7.2 are so-called stakeholders. These are entities that have a specific interest in the platform success or failure, in controlling platform externalities and outcomes, in regulating it, or in exercising rights in the platform governance.

Each role within the ecosystem has its own reasons to join. For example, super users are primarily interested in the value created by being part of the ecosystem or, in case of co-creation of Dapps with the platform owners, in developing joined IP or some form of revenue sharing. For consumers, the value is in the available services provided by the producers or super users, in

Figure 7.2 Snapshot of the Deliver ecosystem

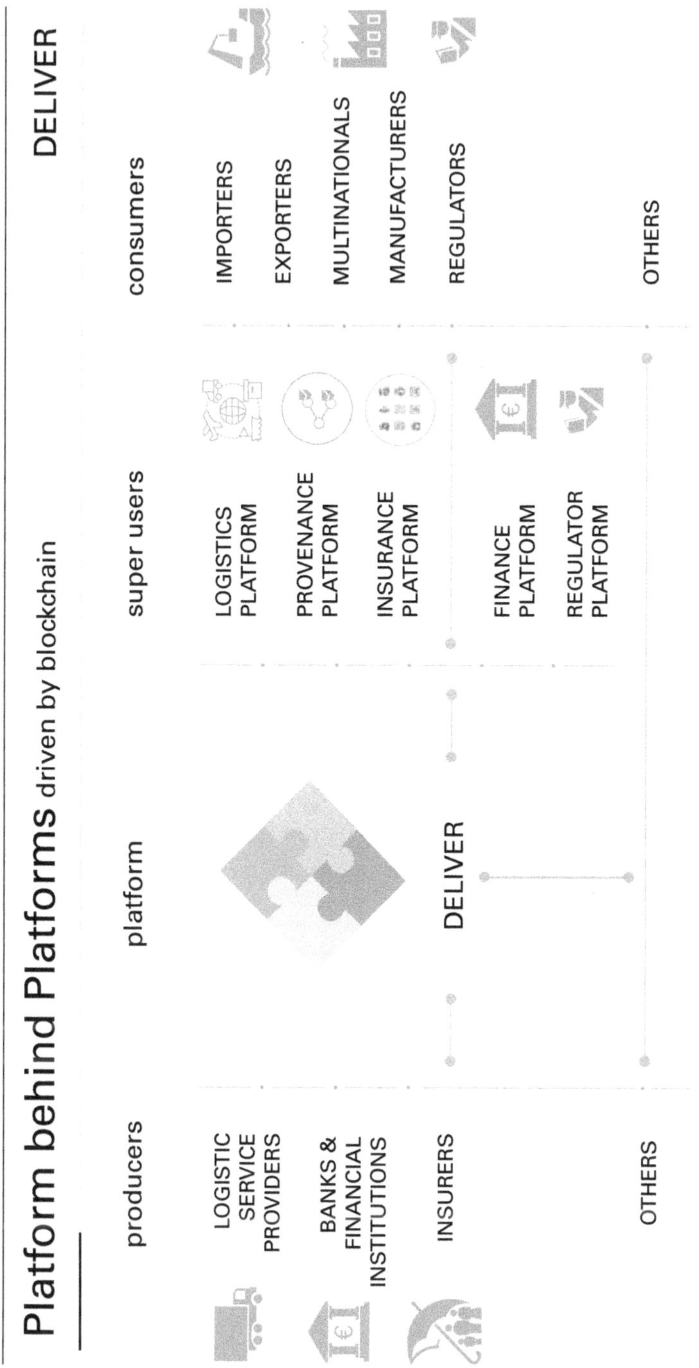

Platform behind Platforms driven by blockchain

producers	platform	super users	consumers	DELIVER
LOGISTIC SERVICE PROVIDERS		LOGISTICS PLATFORM	IMPORTERS	
BANKS & FINANCIAL INSTITUTIONS		PROVENANCE PLATFORM	EXPORTERS	
INSURERS	DELIVER	INSURANCE PLATFORM	MULTINATIONALS	
		FINANCE PLATFORM	MANUFACTURERS	
OTHERS		REGULATOR PLATFORM	REGULATORS	
			OTHERS	

the form of Dapps or even physical services offered on the platform and the access to validated data. For producers, being part of the Deliver ecosystem allows them to provide their services to a wide ranging number of consumers while simultaneously having access to services they currently cannot provide themselves. Platform owners derive the value from micro transaction fees as a reward for maintaining the integrity of the notary blockchain and specific licensing agreements with super users and producers.

Architecture

As the Deliver pilot's architecture is very much a result of the requirements set out at the start of the pilot, the technical work stream faced the challenge of somehow assessing this architecture against a reference architecture, if the pilot architecture wanted to provide a meaningful contribution to the creation of open standards. Fortunately, more or less parallel to the Deliver pilot in terms of timeline, the United Nations Centre for Trade Facilitation and Electronic Business (UN/CEFACT) established a number of working groups to develop technical specifications for the implementation of blockchain technology in international trade, with one of the working groups focusing on ledger interoperability/notary specification. To put technologies such as blockchain, IoT and cloud platforms into the context of the international supply chain, UN/CEFACT developed a draft conceptual model of the international supply chain with relevant technologies.

UN/CEFACT characterizes the international supply chain as a set of three flows: of goods, data and funds. These three flows are supplemented by a layer of trust. It is in this layer that UN/CEFACT expects blockchain technology will deliver significant improvements and automation (UN/CEFACT, 2018). In essence, the UN/CEFACT contextual model is very close to the integrated approach as discussed in this chapter.

As we can see in Figure 7.3, the end state architecture explicitly includes trade ecosystems at both the import (the Netherlands) and export (South Korean) side as well as allowing data coming from various sources, such as ERP, cloud platforms, IoT devices, stand-alone solutions and both private and public blockchains. One important note is that the lines between the objects in the diagram represent dependency relationships so should be read as 'uses' or 'depends on'. They do not represent flows of information, which of course are between various platforms and ledgers.

Figure 7.3 Deliver end state architecture

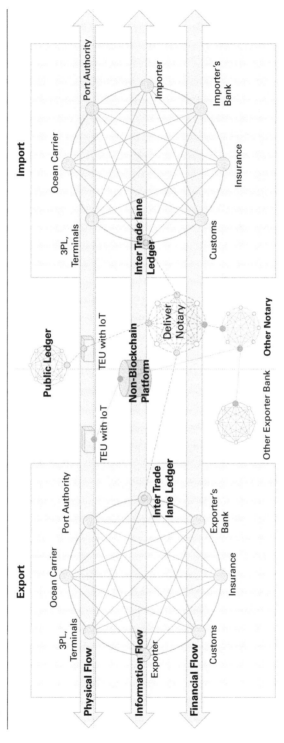

Interoperability and interconnectivity

Although interoperability is not a goal in itself, but a means to the above described ends, it was considered by all the consortia members to be the single most critical technical aspect that was validated in the pilot. To make things practical, two particular interoperability use-cases were defined. These were:

1 Portability of assets, generally speaking, involves transferring a digital asset from its 'home ledger' that is ultimately authoritative on its ownership, securely move it to another chain, trade, use it as collateral or otherwise take advantage of it on that chain, and be confident that the option to move the asset back to its home ledger is always available if desired (Buterin, 2016). For the pilot we decided to ensure portability of the bill of lading, as title of ownership of the goods changes when the goods are made available to the buyer. In the caseof the pilot, this transaction occurs when the goods are ready for unloading from the arriving conveyance and cleared for import and all applicable taxes and duties are paid. For the BoL this was practically implemented by registering the BoL on the Deliver blockchain with the Cello blockchain as the initial owner. The owner's address is based on the public key of the particular node that owns the asset, in this case Cello. Transfer of ownership is triggered through a smart contract that sends a message to the new owner upon meeting the conditions as set out in the smart contract. This new owner has to sign the message with his private key in order to take possession of the digital asset.

2 Cross-chain Oracles involves a node on one chain that acts as an Oracle service for an asset or data provided from a certain source, and a smart contract on another chain that validates the asset or data from the Oracle service, and accepts it, and in case of positive validation registers the asset or data. For the pilot, various Oracle services were set up for Pronto (ETA and actual time of arrival (ATA) data), Transfollow (CMR asset and data, including event data), automatic identification system (AIS)[7] data and IoT data. In contrast with portability of an asset, cross-chain Oracles is a form of interoperability that doesn't involve changes on the chain that is being read.

While there exist various strategies (Buterin, 2016) to ensure interoperability,[8] we opted for a multi-signature notary scheme in which the role of the notary is to ensure the secure transfer of the asset from its 'home chain' and the registration of the asset on the other chain. In the case of the pilot it involved the transfer of the master bill of lading from the South Korean Blockchain Platform for Global Trade onto the Deliver platform. This notary scheme also registers the asset and allows authorized parties to authenticate the asset they have fetched, by comparing the hash of the fetched asset with the one on the notary. Another role of the notary is to ensure that there's an incontestable audit trail of the various versions of the digital asset. This audit trial can be used to resolve conflicts between supply chain members. Note that the data remains decentralized and is not stored somewhere on a centralized location.

The Deliver notary is built on the Ethereum protocol, a public ledger. As such, it provides the highest level of integrity, as the hash of any asset or dataset that has ever been registered by the notary can be viewed by everybody who has access to the network. This doesn't mean that everybody can just access the data; only those addresses that have a subscription on the Oracle service can do so. This is done through the issuance of a digital token to the subscriber of that service by the Oracle.

While the use of IoT and blockchain is a very powerful one (Christidis and Devetsikiotis, 2016; Kshetri, 2017), it also possesses a number of unique challenges related to, amongst other things, security, storage capacity and data privacy (Reyna *et al*, 2018). Solving these challenges would have been beyond the scope of this pilot.

As with other forms of interconnectivity, such as electronic data interchange (EDI), the biggest challenge the consortium faced was the lack or imperfect implementation of data exchange standards. Developing standards or even making a decision on which standard to adopt was beyond the scope of the project, but we did discuss this in some detail with various representatives of the Blockchain Platform Ecosystem. The general consensus is that there's a distinct need for standardization at both the protocol (interoperability) and data (interconnectivity) level and that consortia such as Deliver, provide important stimuli for this. Not by reinventing the wheel, but by linking trade lanes, as the one between South Korea and the Netherlands and the inclusion of trusted and neutral parties, such as ports, customs and other regulatory authorities involved in international trade. Furthermore, consortia such as Deliver involve multiple parties from various industries, which further facilitates setting cross-industry standards, together with standard bodies such as UN/CEFACT, GS1 and the World Economic Forum.

The governance of the pilot

The ground rules for the governance of the projects were laid down in the MoU and included a wide ranging number of topics, ranging from scope to dispute resolution. While it goes beyond the scope of this case description to cover all items included in the MoU, we have selected two of them based on their relevance or their specificity for blockchain. These are:

1 Project governance.

2 GDPR compliance.

Project governance

Based on the deliverables of the pilot, a number of work packages were identified. These were:

- Commercial work package. This work package was responsible for the commercial validations for the various producers and consumers (see page 218) on the platform. Activities included giving presentations and participating in panel discussions at relevant industry summits, meeting prospective producers and consumers and creating a business model that would meet the internal business case of the platform as well as the external business case for consumers and producers. Members of this work package came from the business development and sales and marketing departments of the three consortium partners.

- Technical work package. This work package was responsible for the overall technical development of the pilot solution. Members of this work package were in-house IT architects, developers and analysts of the three consortium partners; with Blocklab added as subcontractor for PoR.

- Communication work package. This work package was responsible for the development of materials for internal/external communication, including sales pitch, name and press releases. Members of this work package came from the communication departments of the consortium members, with regular input from the commercial and technical work packages.

- Legal work package. This work package provided legal counselling for the project and developed various legal deliverables, such as the memorandum of understanding between the three consortium members, the template for the letter of intent for the various consumers and producers and the legal framework for the prospective joint venture.

Members of this work package came from the legal departments of the consortium members, with regular input from the commercial and technical work packages.

- Validation work package. This work package was added later on, as it became clear that the validation of the solution, originally part of the commercial work package, was too expansive a task; in particular, because the validation would have to be done at both the export and import side, which required a unified approach that would cover both processes and could be implemented easily. The approach implemented typical business process modelling, value stream mapping and similar techniques to get a clear picture of the difference in transaction costs between the 'as-is' and 'to-be' situations. The approach is discussed in more detail in the 'Deliver and the SCOR processes' paragraph. Members of this work package came from the commercial and technical work packages.

In terms of project management structure, each work package had its own team leader. With the various constituting parts of the solution early agreed upon during a two-day workshop, the Scrum software development methodology was used throughout the development of the pilot solution, with a functional review at the end of every two weeks. These functional reviews were conducted by a panel of three people, each one representing one of the consortia members. While this might seem excessive at first, the rationale behind this was to ensure the tight integration of the physical, financial and information flows; ie the guiding principle in the development of the pilot. The actual development was done in three different locations (Rotterdam, Amsterdam and Seoul). To coordinate development, Slack, a cloud-based team collaboration tool and Github, a web-based service for version control, were used. Both the commercial and validation work packages decided to meet weekly in order to align their activities.

The other two work packages' meetings were on a less regular basis as they were linked to certain deliverables, such as the MoU or the communication around a certain event.

The team leaders reported directly to the steering committee as the risk of team managers inundating the steering committee members with issues was deemed, and indeed turned out to be, small. This was primarily due to the experience level of the key members and team leaders within the various work packages. Practical support was provided by a project support officer, who took care of minutes, preparing the project plan and keeping track on the actionable items.

GDPR compliancy

The European General Data Protection Regulation (GDPR) was adopted by the European Parliament on 4 April 2016 and came into effect on 25 May 2018. The focus lies on harmonizing privacy regulation, strengthening the protection of natural persons and enabling free flow of data within the European Economic Area (Moser, 2017). Parallel to this, the European Parliament issued another, less well-publicized regulation, the ePrivacy Regulation, which deals with privacy in electronic communications and has implications for everything from online media, to the IoT industry as well as blockchain technology. While the ePrivacy Regulation was intended to become effective on the same date as the GDPR, it is still very much work-in-progress, as the Council of the European Union intends to produce no more than a status update on the regulation's progress by the end of the year. Therefore it is not expected that the ePrivacy Regulation will become effective before 2020. Because of this we will limit our discussions in this paragraph to the GDPR. It is important to note that companies not established in the European Union must abide by the GDPR as well, if they offer goods (free or paid) to EU citizens, or monitor their behaviour in the EU.

The GDPR applies only to processing of 'personal data' (Art 1 par 1 GDPR), or personally identifiable information (PII). PII is all data that is not anonymous, such as names, postal addresses, email addresses, complete IP addresses, user IDs or pseudonymous, such as cookie IDs, device IDs, MAC addresses etc. In other words, only truly anonymous data is exempted from the GDPR. Hashing of data, such as discussed in Chapter 3 of this book, is mostly considered an insufficient method of anonymization, because of the increasing computing capabilities, that allow deductions to be made about your identity through observing your transactions or simply decrypting the hash through 'brute-force' computing. Furthermore, somewhere down the line, a natural person, either directly or within an entity, authorizes a transaction either by signing it with his or her private key or through invoking a contract. Therefore, data on the blockchain, be it public, consortium or private, is mostly considered to be pseudonymous data to which the GDPR applies. As a full discussion of the GDPR is beyond the scope of this case, we will address only two elements of the regulation that are of particular relevance for this project. The first element is the need for parties within the consortium to enter into a data processing agreement before any personal data is made available, and the second one is 'the right to be forgotten'.

First and foremost, many of the GDPR challenges encountered in IT projects based on more traditional technology apply to blockchain technology projects as well. For example, in cases where a party processes PII ('processor') on behalf of another party ('controller') on a blockchain, a data processing agreement needs to be in place that defines how the controller will comply with various obligations under the GDPR. Such obligations include, at a minimum, agreeing on and memorializing (a) the types of personal data being processed, (b) the purposes and means relevant to the personal data being processed, (c) the role of each relevant party (as controller, processor or sub-processor), (d) the technical and organizational measures that must be adhered to in order to prevent the loss or misuse of personal data, (e) the obligations and responsibility towards subcontractors, (f) a comprehensive procedure for personal data breaches, (g) a comprehensive procedure for assistance, (h) international data transfers, (i) audit rights, (j) the retention of personal data, and (k) business continuity measures.

All blockchains, be they private, consortium or public, have to deal with 'the right to be forgotten' (Art. 17 (1) GDPR). This GDPR requirement is very much at odds with the blockchain ledger's 'append only' nature. However, as there's no general exemption under the GDPR that allows the controller to keep the data in a blockchain because it is technically unfeasible to delete it (Moser, 2017), blockchain controllers have to find a way to comply with this part of the GDPR. Fortunately, the Deliver notary only needs to store the hashes of the digital assets, not the data contained in the digital asset. So, although these assets themselves might contain PII, for example a personal mail address on a CMR, the hash stored on the notary blockchain of the digital asset is the message digest of the asset itself, not of the PII data of the asset. Furthermore, as the data itself is not stored on the blockchain but remains decentralized, the individual who wants to have their mail address removed from this particular CMR would simply contact the processor and have the data removed there.

Deliver and the SCOR processes

In this section we will have a closer look at how the various blockchain roles we have identified in Chapter 6 are being implemented in the SCOR processes covered by the Deliver pilot. For obvious reasons, the Make and Return processes will not be covered, as they are not part of the scope of the pilot. Therefore our focus will be on:

- Plan process;
- Source process;
- Deliver process (no pun intended);
- Enable process.

As we are covering both the export and import sides and we have various consumer, producer and even super user roles in the pilot, we continuously have to shift between these various roles when assessing the implementation of the blockchain roles and the mechanisms involved.

The Plan process

Table 7.1 provides an overview of the Plan processes implemented by the Deliver pilot. As the starting point for the pilot is the shipping instruction of a full-load container, the planning processes related to supply chain, source and production (Make) were not implemented (SCOR Plan Processes sP1 to sP3).

The Source process

Table 7.2 provides an overview of the Source processes implemented by the Deliver pilot. The products (LCD televisions) being shipped are make-to-stock products. Therefore, (a number of) processes that are part of the source process covering stocked products (sS1) were implemented.

The Deliver process

Table 7.3 provides an overview of the Deliver processes implemented by the Deliver pilot. The products (LCD televisions) being shipped are make-to-stock products. Therefore, (a number of) processes that are part of the deliver process covering stocked products (sS1) were implemented.

Table 7.1 Deliver – Plan processes

Process	Description	Blockchain's roles	Mechanisms involved	Examples
sP4.3 Balance delivery resources and capabilities with delivery requirements	The process of developing a time-phased course of action that commits delivery resources to meet delivery requirements	Provide a secure, peer-to-peer collaborative platform without centralized control for logistics service providers (LSP)	Cryptographic primitives that allow data sharing in a secure and, if required, privacy preserving way	Deliver in its essence is a peer-to-peer collaborative platform without centralized control. The notary only registers the ownership of digital assets and ensures the integrity of the blockchain. Balancing of delivery resources with capabilities takes place at arrival of the container at the port of discharge, where availability of various hinterland modes of transport (road, barge, train) is balanced with the inflow of containers. A similar process is in place at the export side on the Cello blockchain

(continued)

Table 7.1 *(Continued)*

Process	Description	Blockchain's roles	Mechanisms involved	Examples
sP4.4	Establish delivery plans	The establishment of courses of action over specified time periods that represent a projected appropriation of delivery resources to meet delivery requirements	Provide a secure, peer-to-peer collaborative platform without centralized control for LSP	Cryptographic primitives that allow data sharing in a secure and, if required, privacy preserving way	Deliver in its essence is a peer-to-peer collaborative platform without centralized control. The notary only registers the ownership of digital assets and ensures the integrity of the blockchain. Input from sP4.3 is used to provide delivery plans to the various LSPs responsible for the hinterland transport. A similar process is in place at the export side on the Cello network

Table 7.2 Deliver – Source processes

Process	Description	Blockchain's roles	Mechanisms involved	Examples
sS12 Receive product	The process and associated activities of receiving product to contract requirements	Provide lot tracking data	Detection, measurement and tracking of inventory with IoT	Provide real time data about temperature, humidity and the location of the container that can be verified on the notary blockchain
sS12 Receive product	The process and associated activities of receiving product to contract requirements	Blockchain's append only ledger can address challenges associated with self-reported data that are provided by LSPs	Transaction data can be validated by Oracles before being permanently added to the blockchain	The use of Pronto and Transfollow as Oracles for providing respectively uncontestable ETA/ATA and proof of delivery data
sS15 Authorize supplier payment	The process of authorizing payments and paying suppliers for product or services	Enable fully automated processing ('straight through processing') of the authorization of payments and the payment itself	Event changes, such as the transfer of ownership, trigger 'smart contracts'	Straight through processing of the transport invoice, together with the uncontestable CMR (proof of delivery), to the single invoice factoring solution, allows for near real time approval and payment of the invoice

(continued)

Table 7.3 Deliver – Deliver processes

Process	Description	Blockchain's roles	Mechanisms involved	Examples
sD1.4	Consolidate orders	The process of analysing orders to determine the groupings that result in least cost/best service fulfilment and transportation	Provide order tracking data	Real time detection, measurement and tracking of inventory with IoT	Real time and validated data with regard to the discharge of the container at the terminal allows for better grouping of orders (containers) for the hinterland transport. Similar process is in place at the export side on the Cello blockchain.
			Blockchain's append only ledger can address challenges associated with self-reported data that are provided by LSPs.	Transaction data can be validated by Oracles before being permanently added to the blockchain.	The use of Pronto and Transfollow as Oracles for providing respectively incontestable ETA/ATA and proof of delivery data

			Provide a secure, peer-to-peer collaborative platform without centralized control for order management	Cryptographic primitives that allow data sharing in a secure and, if required, privacy preserving way	Deliver in its essence is a peer-to-peer collaborative platform without centralized control. The notary only registers the ownership of digital assets and ensures the integrity of the blockchain.
					
					    Consolidation of orders takes place on arrival of the container at the port of discharge, where availability of various hinterland modes of transport (road, barge, train) is balanced with the inflow of containers.
					
					    A similar process is in place at the export side on the Cello blockchain

sD1.5	Build loads	Transportation modes are selected and efficient loads are built	Provide a secure, peer-to-peer collaborative platform without centralized control for order management	Cryptographic primitives that allow data sharing in a secure and, if required, privacy preserving way	Deliver in its essence is a peer-to-peer collaborative platform without centralized control. The notary only registers the ownership of digital assets and ensures the integrity of the blockchain. Input from sD1.4 is used to build the loads for the various LSPs responsible for the hinterland transport. Similar process is in place at the export side on the Cello blockchain
sD1.6	Route shipments	Loads are consolidated and routed by mode, lane and location	Provide a secure, peer-to-peer collaborative platform without centralized control for order management	Cryptographic primitives that allow data sharing in a secure and, if required, privacy preserving way	Deliver in its essence is a peer-to-peer collaborative platform without centralized control. The notary only registers the ownership of digital assets and ensures the integrity of the blockchain. Input from sD1.5 is used to instruct the various LSPs responsible for the hinterland transport. Similar process is in place at the export side on the Cello blockchain

(continued)

Table 7.3 (Continued)

Process	Description	Blockchain's roles	Mechanisms involved	Examples
sD1.8	Receive product from Source or Make	The activities such as receiving product, verifying, recording product receipt, determining put-away location, putting away and recording location that a company performs at its own warehouses	Elimination of paper records reduces the human interaction and communication	Digitally signed documents, replacing paper ones, with validated identities of entities	Use of an incontestable digital proof of delivery Oracle (Transfollow) removes the need for paper copies
			Can provide real time, secure and validated data that can be used to monitor transport conditions of the product	Data related to temperature, humidity, motion, light conditions, chemical composition from IoT devices or sensors	Provide real time data about temperature, humidity and the location of the container that can be verified on the notary blockchain
sD1.12	Ship product	The process of shipping the product to the customer site	Provide order tracking data	Real time detection, measurement and tracking of inventory with IoT	Real time and validated data throughout the whole transport of the container using IoT devices and Oracles allows for superior tracking and tracing

| sD1.13 | Receive and verify product by customer | The process of receiving the shipment by the customer (either at customer site or at shipping area in case of self-collection) and verifying that the order was shipped complete and that the product meets delivery terms | Elimination of paper records reduces the human interaction and communication | Digitally signed documents, replacing paper ones, with validated identities of entities, objects and individuals | Use of an incontestable digital proof of delivery Oracle (Transfollow) removes the need for paper copies |
| | | | Can provide real time, secure and validated data that can be used to monitor transport conditions of the product | Data related to temperature, humidity, motion, light conditions, chemical composition from IoT devices or sensors | Provide real time data about temperature, humidity and the location of the container that can be verified on the notary blockchain |

(continued)

Table 7.3 (Continued)

Process		Description	Blockchain's roles	Mechanisms involved	Examples
sD1.15	Invoice	A signal is sent to the financial organization that the order has been shipped and that the billing process should begin and payment be received or be closed out if payment has already been received	Enable fully automated processing ('straight through processing') of the billing process, including authorization of payments and the payment itself	Event changes, such as the transfer of ownership, trigger 'smart contracts'	Straight through processing of the transport invoice, together with the incontestable CMR, to the single invoice factoring solution, allows for near real-time approval and payment of the invoice

Table 7.4 Deliver – Enable processes

Process	Description	Blockchain's roles	Mechanisms involved	Examples
sE1 Manage supply chain business rules	The process of establishing, documenting, communicating and publishing supply chain business rules	Document business rules at the transactional level to enable 'straight through processing'	'Smart contracts' enabled machine-to-machine transactions	Various smart contracts have been implemented to ensure straight through processing, both for digital assets such as the BL and CMR and for data (eg transport order and IoT)
sE2 Manage supply chain performance	The process of defining performance targets for supply chain metrics that align to overall business strategy and goals, and for reporting performance, identifying gaps in performance, performing root cause analysis, and developing and launching corrective actions to close gaps in performance	Provide data that can be used to assess useful, meaningful and representative indicators for performance	Detection, measurement and tracking of key SCM processes with IoT	Extensive management-by-exception based on real time and validated data

(continued)

Table 7.4 (*Continued*)

Process	Description	Blockchain's roles	Mechanisms involved	Examples
sE3 Manage data and information	The process of collecting, maintaining and publishing data and information required to plan, operate, measure and manage the supply chain	Provide data from key SCM processes	Real-time detection, measurement and tracking using IoT	Real time and validated data throughout the whole transport of the container using IoT devices and Oracles allows for superior tracking and tracing
		Blockchain's 'super audit trail' can address challenges associated with self-reported data that are provided with supply chain partners	Transaction data can be validated by Oracles before being permanently added to the blockchain	The use of Pronto and Transfollow as Oracles for providing respectively uncontestable ETA/ATA and proof of delivery data
sE6 Manage supply chain contracts/ agreements	The management and communication of contractual and non-contractual agreements in support of business objectives and supply chain goals	Enable fully automated processing ('straight through processing') of contractual and non-contractual agreements	Event changes, such as the transfer of ownership, trigger 'smart contracts'	Transfer of BoL and CMR from one owner to the other, based upon mutually agreed business rules

sE8	Manage regulatory and voluntary compliance	The process of identifying, collecting, assessing and integrating regulatory compliance requirements in standard supply chain processes, policies and business rules	Ensure upfront compliance	'Smart contracts' ensure that transactions can only be executed if all conditions are met	Various regulatory compliance requirements have been incorporated into smart contracts, such as the necessary export documentation and the expiration dates of digital assets such as the CMR (proof of delivery)
sE9	Manage supply chain risks	The process of identification and assessment of potential disruptions (risks) in the supply chain and developing a plan to mitigate these threats to operating the supply chain	Identifying, collecting, validating and documenting data on all potential risk events	Detection, measurement, and tracking of key SCM processes with IoT	Real time and validated data throughout the whole transport of the container using IoT devices and Oracles allows for superior tracking and tracing

The Enable process

Table 7.4 provides an overview of the Enable processes implemented by the Deliver pilot. These processes apply to all the SCOR processes, independent of the strategies used to fill the orders (make-to-stock, make-to-order etc).

Pilot outcomes

At the time of writing, the preparations for the pilot were still in full swing and the outcome wasn't yet known. Because of this, the pilot outcomes will made available as an addendum on the book's website.

Notes

1 www.blocklab.nl
2 www.komgo.io
3 https://www.samsungsds.com/global/en/solutions/off/cello/cello.html
4 https://www.hyperledger.org/projects/fabric
5 https://www.transfollow.org/en
6 CMR stands for *Convention relative au Contrat de transport international de Marchandises par Route*
7 AIS is a transponder based system that provides data about the location of vessels operating at sea, in the port and inland waterways.
8 For an overview of the primary strategies of chain interoperation we refer to Buterin (2016).

References

Boer, RD, Steeman, M and Bergen, MV (2015) *Supply Chain Finance, its Practical Relevance and Strategic Value*, 2nd edn, Supply Chain Finance Community

Buterin, V (2016) [Online] https://static1.squarespace.com/static/55f73743e4b051cfcc0b02cf/t/5886800ecd0f68de303349b1/1485209617040/Chain+Interoperability.pdf

Christidis, Kand Devetsikiotis, M (2016) Blockchains and smart contracts for the internet of things, *IEEE Access* 4, pp 2292–303

Kshetri, N (2017). Blockchain's roles in meeting key supply chain management objectives, *International Journal of Information Management*

Moser, J (2017) GDPR Blockchains R3. [Online] https://www.r3.com/wp-content/uploads/2018/04/GDPR_Blockchains_R3.pdf

Reyna, A, Martin, C, Chen, J, Soler, E and Diaz, M (2018) On blockchain and its integration with IoT: Challenges and opportunities, *Future Generation Computer Systems*, pp 173–90.

UN/CEFACT (2018) [Online] https://uncefact.unece.org/download/attachments/17832710/180522%203b%20eGOV%20Blockchain%20WP%20for%20Public%20Review.pdf?api=v2

Blockchain use cases in supply chain 08

Container shipping: IBM and Maersk

The last innovation

On 26 April 1956 SS Ideal X, a retrofitted Second World War oil tanker, set sail from Newark harbour for Houston. The ship carried 58 trailer-sized steel containers weighing 15,000 tons on a customized deck – that single event heralding a new era in shipping.

Ideal X was the brainchild of Malcolm P McLean (1914–2001), a North Carolina businessman who sought to do away with the cumbersome practice of longshoremen loading and unloading bags of cotton bales or coffee onto ships and back onto trucks, all of which consumed a lot of labour, time and money. Intermodal container shipping changed all that. Before Ideal X, loading break bulk on a cargo ship cost $5.83 per ton. McLean's experts calculated that the cost of loading the Ideal X was 15.7 cents per ton (Jeroen de Haas, 2016).

Standardize containers notion is accepted globally. A standard shipping container is 8 feet wide, either 20 or 40, 45, 53 feet long, with heights of 8, 8½ or 9½ feet. Thanks to containerization, the average cost for a shipper is incredibly low. Today, a product can be shipped via sea at less than 1 per cent of its retail value – a single container can hold 10,000 iPads at the cost of 5 cents each from Shanghai to Hamburg. The average TV travelling from China to the USA costs less than $2 to ship.

Container shipping not only brought down the costs of transportation, it also made the industry much more organized, leading to the rise of global shipping giants like Maersk Line, CMA CGM and Cosco Shipping. It also increased the share of sea trade in global commerce. Out of over $4 trillion of goods shipped in 2017, 80 percent of them were carried through ocean vessels.

Figure 8.1   Container steamship Ideal X, built in 1944 as the tanker Potrero Hills

SOURCE Karsten Kunibert, licensed under CC BY-SA 3.0
(https://commons.wikimedia.org/wiki/File:Ideal_X.jpg)

Build more, sell cheaper

Fuelled by globalization with an ever-rising consumer demand, container shipping enjoyed an uninterrupted run of growth right up to the economic crisis of 2009. Primarily, it was hit harder than most industries because of the inherent inefficiencies built up during the period of fast growth, the biggest of them being the carriers' insatiable desire to build capacity, which resulted in a downward trend of freight prices. The industry has not been able to find its feet ever since.

The worst, however, was yet to come. Despite a double-digit drop in the growth rate in 2009, major container liners continued to build capacities at an even faster pace than before. The average size of newly built container vessels had been hovering around 3,400 twenty-foot equivalent unit (TEU) between 2001 and 2008. Between 2009 and 2013 it grew to 5,800 TEU and soared to 8,000 TEU in 2015, the year in which top carriers like Maersk and MSC launched ultra-large container vessels (UCLV) of 18,000-plus TEU and planned to go bigger. The aim was not to acquire bragging rights; it made business sense. The construction cost of ultra-large ships of 18,000 TEU and above was $7,500 per TEU in 2015, a good 20–30 per cent lower compared with one of 14,000 TEU. Also, larger ships carry more boxes per ship, which means lower operating costs and competitive freight rates. What's more, ULCVs consume less fuel than smaller vessels. Cheaply available finance added grist to the mill, and the trend continued, prompting Nick Cutmore, Secretary General of the International Maritime Pilots Association to comment, 'These ships are the largest moving objects on the planet.'

Caught in the prisoners' dilemma

The combined effect of overcapacity and slowing of consumer demand in the years following the downturn precipitated the worst-ever global crisis in container shipping in 2016. The Altman Z is a statistical tool that predicts the probability of bankruptcy. A Z-score of 2.99 or more indicates that the entity is safe from bankruptcy and 1.81 or less predicts a considerable risk of bankruptcy. The Z-score for container shipping hit a historic low of 1.10 in 2016. Sure enough, on 31 August 2016, Hanjin Shipping, the world's then-sixth largest container carrier, declared bankruptcy, throwing the shipping industry into chaos. During the same year, the world's largest container shipping company, AP Moller-Maersk Group (aka Maersk), posted its second-ever loss since the Second World War and its first-ever loss since 2009. The top 20 ocean carriers ended 2016 with a cumulative loss of about $5 billion. The widespread financial distress caused a wave of consolidation, eventually seeing the top 20 carriers shrink to 11. Edwin Lopez and Elizabeth Rogan summed up the woes of the industry in an excellent article published in 2017 titled 'Big ship chronicles: How overcapacity disrupted the production':

> The shipping industry's current struggles, then, are self-imposed. It was due to a race to the top; a desire to undercut competition; a prisoners' dilemma that ended, even, in bankruptcy for one major carrier. While low rates were beneficial for shippers, the instability and drop in service that came with them were not.

Often used by game theorists to analyse non-cooperative behaviour, the prisoner's dilemma is a theory that demonstrates why two prisoners choose the worst choice (maximum sentence for two) instead of the best one (least punishment for two) because they don't trust each other. In other words, individual rationality is collectively self-destructive in the absence of mutual trust and cooperation. The tendency of ocean carriers to undercut and gain market share at the expense of the other was pointed out by analysts to be a textbook case of the prisoner's dilemma. A 2015 *Financial Review* article noted: 'An industry, such as container shipping, plagued by falling prices and overcapacity should reduce capacity. The biggest players, stuck in a prisoner's dilemma, do the reverse.'

Not that the shipping industry did not know this issue. As early as the 1990s, the industry had formed alliances to improve service standards and keep oversupply in check. In 1998 six ocean carrier alliances represented 50 per cent of the worldwide fleet. In 2017 the number consolidated into three big ones: 2M, comprising Maersk and MSC; Ocean Alliance, which includes CMA-CGM, Cosco Group, OOCL and Evergreen;, and The Alliance, comprising Hapag Lloyd, Yang Ming Line, and Ocean Network Express. The three alliances represented nearly 80 per cent of global container trade and roughly 90 per cent of container capacity on major trade routes.

However, alliances haven't helped solve the twin problems of oversupply and falling freight rates, which continue to have a telling effect on the industry even as the global economy has begun to show signs of recovery. In the first quarter of 2018, the three major container lines, Maersk, Hapag Lloyd and Yang Ming Line reported losses. Average operating margins of container carriers fell from negative 3.1 per cent in the first quarter to negative 3.8 per cent in the second quarter of the year as surplus capacity pushed down the freight rates across the board, while fuel costs continued to increase. An AlixPartners report, published in April 2018, entitled *2018 Global Container Shipping Outlook: Though challenges remain, opportunities exist for carriers*, said that freight rates would remain 'squeezed' with supply continuing to outpace demand for services, with total demand needing a minimum of 4–5 per cent growth to provide a real opportunity for margin growth.

Why haven't the alliances worked? Because they haven't made operations more transparent and less complicated; instead they have had the opposite effect. Steve Saxon, Expert Partner, McKinsey & Company Shangai, pointed out at a 2016 TPM Asia Conference:

> If the new alliances have any impact, it could be to increase complexity. Larger alliances create hardships for both lines and shippers: the new Ocean Alliance, for example, could mean that a shipper's box gets delivered to any one of seven terminals in the Los Angeles–Long Beach area. The need to organize trucks and separate chassis to meet them complicates life for lines and shippers alike.

Simply put, not only have alliances not found any solution to the liners' problems, they haven't made it easy for the shipper either, who has traditionally gained from the price war. Saxon quoted a shipper who expressed frustration with the still-existing 'communication gaps and inefficient coordination among shippers, terminals, ocean carriers, and land-transport companies in the scheduling and movement of containers in and out of the ports'.

Create transparency, reduce complexity, enable sharing of relevant information among people who don't trust each other (an antidote to the prisoner's dilemma) without creating an oligopoly or reducing competition, facilitate coordination among all the stakeholders of the container shipping industry – the solution lies in blockchain, which, to twist the old phrase, kills all the birds with one stone. But these are all the benefits that could only be accrued in the long term, whereas for any technology to be adopted in any industry it needs to offer immediate gains. For shipping, blockchain extends two quick gains – reduced administrative costs and protection from fraud.

Figure 8.2   Shipping alliances have had no impact on rate fluctuations. The figure shows average time charter rates for bulk carriers from December 2001 to May 2012 (weekly data in US dollars per day)

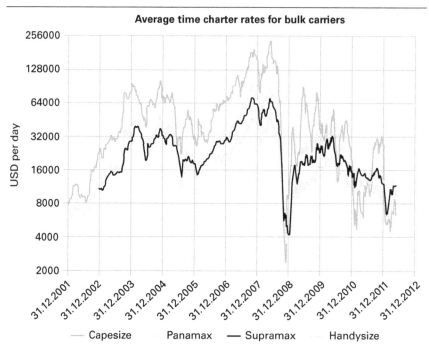

SOURCE Jashuah; data from Essence Securities, Shipping Risk Manager and Optima Shipbrokers. Licensed under CC BY-SA 3.0 (https://commons.wikimedia.org/wiki/File:Baltic_Shipping_Rates.png)

How IBM and Maersk found common cause in blockchain

In 2016, still smarting under the crisis, Maersk was looking for a better way to reduce operational costs and the immediate way to do it was to reduce the paperwork that goes with each container. Two years before, Maersk had found that a single shipment of frozen goods from East Africa to Europe went through nearly 30 people and organizations, entailing more than 200 different interactions and communications among them.

In the autumn of 2016 Maersk participated in a proof of concept with the IT University of Copenhagen to apply blockchain to bills of lading (BoL), a traditional, paper-based system of documentation particularly vulnerable to frauds. A BoL is a crucial paper-based document used in international trade to ensure that exporters receive payment and importers receive merchandise. BoL is the weakest spot and the most significant pain point in the shipping and trade finance chain because of a big loophole: once a container is closed,

Figure 8.3 Alliance shuffles

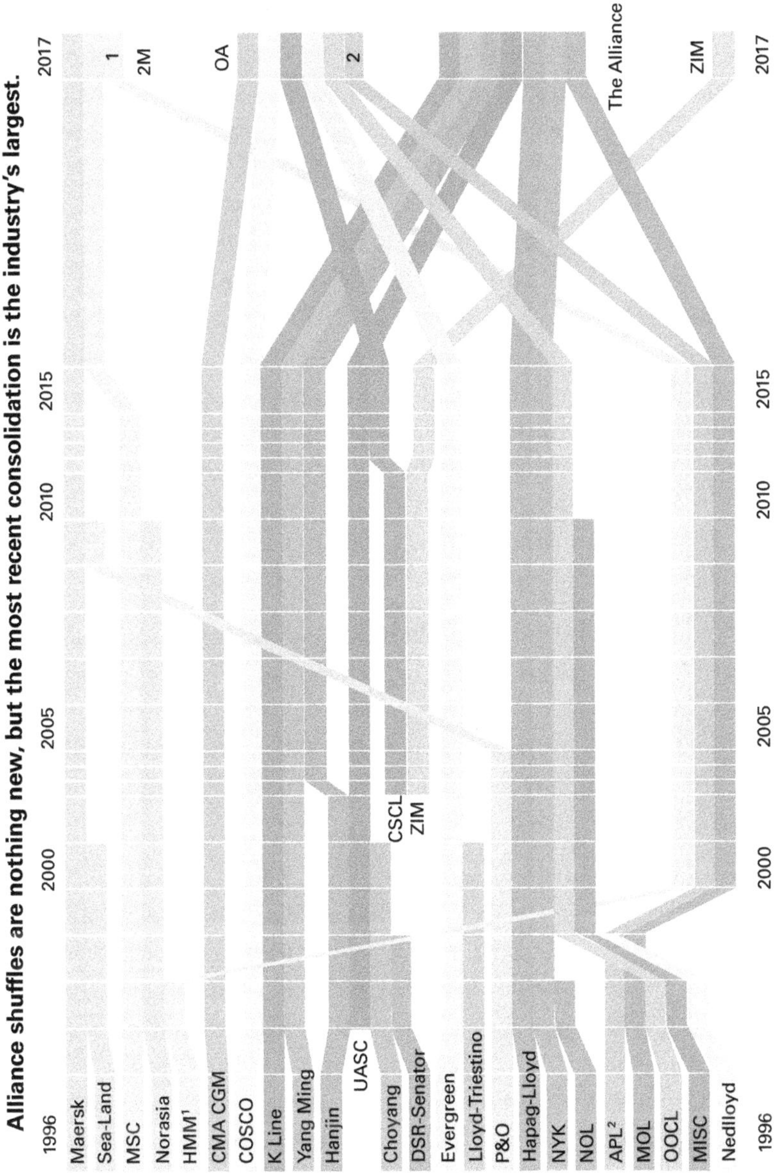

Alliance shuffles are nothing new, but the most recent consolidation is the industry's largest.

[1] HMM not yet confirmed.
[2] APL to merge with CMA CGM.

it is practically impossible to match all the items listed in the BoL with the actual contents of the container. Every year, fraudulent BoLs cause shipowners, carriers, banks and brand owners to suffer losses ranging from a few thousand dollars from under-reported freight to billions of dollars in fines, pilferages and counterfeit products. One option is to switch to electronic BoLs, which have been around since the 1980s, but their adoption been limited for the same reasons that necessitate the presence of the mountains of paperwork that accompanies each container: humans can still manipulate different laws and regulations and the eBOLs. Maersk's 2016 blockchain-enabled BoL proof of concept optimized information flow management involved in shipping a consignment of roses from Kenya to Rotterdam.

Meanwhile, IBM had been working on its own version of blockchain since 2014. The *New York Times*, in a 2017 article, detailed how IBM's research director Arvind Krishna lent his support to an exploratory project within IBM. Mr Krishna recognized the potential of the technology, dubbed Openchain by the team. He recounted this moment, 'This was not really about digital payments, but establishing trust in transactions in general.' He saw this as 'a technology that can change the world'.

Recently, IBM's Blockchain Leader, Indian and South Asia, Jitan S Chandanani spoke about the benefits that IBM realized with its own vendors:

> When we at IBM started to use Blockchain for our vendor management, I think the amount that we had in [invoice payment] disputes on any given date was about $100 million and the average time to solve these disputes was 21 to 40 days. [The use of Blockchain] brought down the amount to under $10 million and the dispute time is under 5 days. Blockchain users can expect about 30–40 percent gains in cost efficiencies.

It was Erich Clementi, Chairman of IBM Europe, who took the idea of working with blockchain technology to a senior Maersk executive. IBM and Maersk tested the blockchain solution in the summer of 2016 where they tracked a shipment of flowers from Mombasa Port, Kenya to Rotterdam, the Netherlands. The success of the project encouraged them to follow it up with several more projects, including an EU research project. The project focused on goods from Schneider Electric that were transported from the Port of Rotterdam to the Port of Newark in a pilot with the Customs Administration of the Netherlands, the US Department of Homeland Security Science and Technology Directorate, and US Customs and Border Protection. Similarly, oranges from California and pineapples from Colombia were transported to Rotterdam to validate the blockchain solution for shipments. Maersk involved its renowned customers, including DuPont, Dow Chemical, Tetra Pak, and many others in the pilot programmes.

Their success convinced Maersk that blockchain could help them track all the shipments on a highly secure, shared network, providing complete transparency to all essential players.

In August 2018 Maersk IBM jointly announced the creation of TradeLens, a global trade blockchain platform. They informed the press that TradeLens built on IBM's blockchain technology, which is based on the open-source Hyperledger Fabric 1.0 specification created by the Linux Foundation. Maersk and IBM jointly own the IP and market, sell and contract TradeLens through their own respective sales channels.

Unlike Bitcoin, which is an open blockchain where all participants can see every data entry, IBM and Maersk's solution is centrally administered. Thus, industry stakeholders including, manufacturers, freight forwarders, terminal operators and customs authorities can have access to the platform's virtual dashboard on a permission basis. Participants can interact through real-time access to shipping data and shipping documents, including IoT and sensor data ranging from temperature control to container weight.

At the time of the launch, TradeLens had enlisted participation from 94 organizations, including more than 20 port and terminal operators across the globe such as PSA Singapore, International Container Terminal Services Inc, Patrick Terminals, Modern Terminals in Hong Kong, Port of Halifax, Port of Rotterdam, Port of Bilbao, PortConnect, PortBase and terminal operators Holt Logistics at the Port of Philadelphia. As importantly, two global container carriers, Pacific International Lines and Hamburg Süd, had joined the platform.

Forbes reported, 'Collectively, the shipping companies account for more than 20 per cent of the global supply chain market share, with 20 port and terminal operators in Singapore, the US, Holland and more, serving 235 marine gateways around the world.'

A good start

Among all the innovations that have come up in shipping since the invention of containerization, TradeLens offers the most significant promise of them all. With all the cited benefits, it can provide the much-needed solution to the problems that plague the shipping industry. However, for it to truly make a difference, it must see participation from a majority of the liners, if not all of them. Currently, it has only two other than Maersk, and understandably so because TradeLens in its current form (at the time of writing) is an

IBM-Maersk-owned centralized system. It will be interesting to see whether it will evolve into a pan-industry platform that will finally stem the problems of overcapacity and price wars, or the industry puts forth an agnostic platform that brings together all the liners. It looks certain, however, that blockchain could be the panacea the industry has long been waiting for.

The palm oil supply chain

Growing disquiet

There is a 50 per cent chance that the packaged product you bought in a supermarket has palm oil in it. Palm oil is a versatile vegetable oil used in foods, cleaning products and fuels. Its ability to lock in flavours and create creamy texture makes it a favourite constituent for food products like mayonnaise, pizza, chocolate and ice cream brands. Its ability to bind products and work as a stabilizing agent makes it ideal for shampoos, moisturizing lotions, soaps, body oils and many other personal care products. It serves a similar function in household cleaners and a host of other home care products.

Commercial palm oil is extracted from the fruit of the oil palm tree (Elaeis guineensis), also called the African oil palm because it is native to the rainforests of South-West Africa.

Humans may have been using palm oil for more than 5,000 years. In the late 1800s, archaeologists found palm oil in an early tomb at Abydos, Egypt, dating back to 3000 BC. Palm oil became a global commodity in the late 19th century after its production took off in Indonesia and Malaysia due to favourable climatic and socio-economic conditions. Not only does a single palm tree produce fruit for more than 30 years, but it also yields more oil per hectare than any significant oilseed crop. Naturally, it is a valuable source of sustenance and employment for poor rural communities. Presently, over 85 per cent of the $62-billion global palm oil industry comes from Indonesia and Malaysia.

Complex and environmentally unsustainable

Palm oil supply chains are incredibly complex. The product is often mixed with other sources. Also, the biggest palm oil producing countries have little or no regulations on palm oil production, thanks to its contribution to the countries' exports earning.

The journey of palm oil starts when fresh fruit bunches (FFB) from planta-tions are supplied to a mill, from where they are taken by various intermediaries to refineries for processing before the palm oil enters a company's supply chain.

Palm oil companies source FFB supplies from two primary channels. The first channel comprises the plantations the companies own directly or man-age for smallholder farmers. The direct channel, controlled by companies, is relatively transparent, where companies ensure compliance with global reg-ulations. The second channel comprises third-party suppliers, who collect FFB from different sources including independent farmers, which makes it difficult to regulate.

In March 2018 Hermawati Widyapratami and Bukti Bagja of the re-search organization WRI Indonesia conducted field research at PPTN V, a plantation company located in Rokan Hulu, Riau, Indonesia. The research-ers found that the agents who collected FFB directly from farmers usually mixed the bunches and sorted them based on quality before they were trans-ported to mill. The mixing and sorting made it difficult to track the origin of the FFB since the transaction between smallholder farmers and intermediar-ies did not have a record. The researchers noted that the middlemen were unregulated actors since no system is currently present to control their busi-ness despite their significant role in palm oil supply chain.

Not only are the palm oil chains complex, but they also cause many envi-ronmental and social issues. Farmers burn forests to clear areas where they can grow oil palms. The rapid intensification and expansion of palm oil pro-duction have caused widespread destruction of rainforests in the producer countries. Palm oil production is said to have been responsible for about 8 per cent of the world's deforestation between 1990 and 2008. A recent Scientific American article noted that palm oil production has been the most significant cause of deforestation in Indonesia and other equatorial countries.

Deforestation not only causes flooding and soil depletion, but it also con-tributes to global warming because cutting of trees reduces the Earth's capac-ity to absorb carbon dioxide (CO_2). Besides, deforestation poses a clear and present danger to wildlife in these regions. In July 2017 a *Guardian* article reported that Pepsico, Unilever and Nestlé have been accused of complicity in the destruction of Sumatra's last tract of rainforest shared by elephants, orangutans, rhinos and tigers together in one ecosystem. Indonesia's endan-gered orangutan population, which depends upon the rainforest, has been reduced by as much as 50 per cent in recent years (Neslen, 2017).

The report cited a Rainforest Action Network field investigation that found evidence of active, illegal clearance of critically endangered Sumatran elephant habitat within the rainforests of the Leuser ecosystem. Leuser is Sumatra's

Figure 8.4   The palm oil supply chain

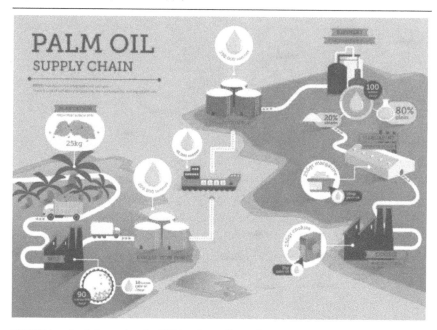

largest rainforest and a UNESCO world heritage site. The alleged culprit was a company called PT Agra Bumi Niaga (PT denotes a limited liability company in Indonesia), which reached major brands via a complex supply chain through some of the world's largest traders. The fragmentation of animal habitats due to the expansion of palm oil plantations leads to an increase in human–animal conflicts – between 2012 and 2015, at least 35 elephants were killed in Leuser. The vanishing rainforest ecosystem has made many species such as tigers, clouded leopards and sun bears more vulnerable to poachers in these areas. 'If more immediate action is not taken to enforce "no deforestation" policies, these brands will be remembered as the corporate giants responsible for the destruction of the last place on earth where Sumatran elephants, orangutans, rhinos and tigers roamed side by side,' said the RAN study.

Palm oil sourced from plantations in these areas finds its way to products made by well-known brands such as McDonald's, Kellogg's, Mars, Unilever, Nestlé and Procter & Gamble. In 2010 Nestlé was accused by Greenpeace of abetting deforestation in tropical countries by using unsustainable palm oil in its products. Public outcry over deforestation due to palm oil and the alleged complicity of major brands has urged industry stakeholders to launch and pursue major initiatives and campaigns over the years.

Toward a transparent, sustainable supply chain

Various initiatives have been launched over the years to streamline the production of palm oil and mitigate its impact on the environment, but most of them have not made much difference.

Roundtable on Sustainable Palm Oil (RSPO), the world's most significant and most influential palm oil industry association, has led the most effective drive for sustainability in the palm oil supply chain. An RSPO certification assures the buyers of palm oil products that the standards of production are socially and environmentally sustainable. To obtain the certificate, the oil producers must fulfil the principles and criteria, a set of conditions that mandate best agricultural practices, fair treatment of workers, proper acquisition of the land, care for the environment, biodiversity and other similar guidelines.

Consumer goods companies such as Nestlé and PepsiCo and major palm oil traders such as Cargill also make commitments for achieving sustainability in their supply chains. In 2010 Nestlé made a 'no deforestation commitment', stating that all its products globally will not be associated with deforestation by 2020. It has made good progress – in 2017 the company reported that 58 per cent of its total palm oil purchased in 2017 was responsibly sourced, while 48 per cent was traceable to its source. In September 2018 Nestlé took a big step toward meeting its 2020 goal by implementing Starling, a satellite-based service to monitor the entirety of its global palm oil supply chains.

Unilever, on its part, laid bare in 2018 its entire palm oil supply chain, including all the suppliers and mills it sources from, to boost transparency in a rare industry initiative. The fast-moving consumer goods (FMCG) behemoth disclosed the location of more than 1,400 mills and over 300 direct suppliers of the oil used in products from snacks and soaps to cosmetics and biofuels.

Marc Engel, Unilever's Chief Supply Chain Officer, said the company hoped sharing the information would be the start of a new industry-wide movement toward supply chain transparency. 'This is a big step toward greater transparency, but we know there is more work to be done to achieve a truly sustainable palm oil industry, and we will continue our efforts to make this a reality,' Engel said in a statement posted on Unilever's website. Unilever noted that transparency and the ability to trace palm oil are vital in addressing deforestation and human rights abuses.

Finding an ally in blockchain

In 2017 sales from global palm oil exports totalled $33.3 billion, to which the world's largest exporter Indonesia contributed 55.5 per cent followed by Malaysia at 29 per cent. Initiatives such as RSPO and the individual initiatives of leading brands like Nestlé and Unilever have not helped stop and reduce the environmental impact of palm oil production, particularly in these two countries. An industry-wide survey done by the World Wide Fund for Nature (WWF) in 2016 found out that only 17 per cent of global oil production was certified sustainable. In the last couple of years, the industry has begun to realize that blockchain could be just the technology to help solve the significant supply chain challenges, and would also provide additional benefits.

In a November 2017 article written for Linux Foundation's Hyperledger, a collaborative platform for blockchain, Jesus Oregui and Kiran Kumar N of Bengaluru, India-based IT consulting firm Wipro Limited, illustrated how blockchain could 'close current gaps in transparency', creating a sustainable supply chain with an audit trail.

The authors proposed that blockchain would not only provide unprecedented transparency, but also improve working conditions of field workers, and provide rich data on crop harvesting to the producers. Also, blockchain could help minimize the spoilage of oil in the supply chain. Furthermore, noted the authors,

> With Blockchain and IoT-backed sensors, transportation companies can monitor temperature and humidity during processing, storage, and transport, and integrate the data on a Blockchain to record out-of-range instances, thus efficiently identifying poor batches. Blockchain's smart contracts can then enforce rules that automatically grade products in a way that only those that meet the highest standards enter the market for human consumption.

Meanwhile, other industries with similar supply chains had begun to recognize the benefits. In January 2018 WWF teamed up with US-based tech companies ConsenSys and TraSeable and tuna fishing and processing company Sea Quest Fiji Ltd to launch a pilot project in the Pacific Islands tuna industry to use blockchain for the tracking of the journey of tuna from 'bait to plate'.

Lately, the palm oil industry appears to be following suit. In September 2018 the Malaysian Government created a task force, Malaysian Industry–Government Group for High Technology, that will use blockchain to improve

Figure 8.5 Local Nigerian women from Osun State carrying out the process of extracting palm oil from the palm seeds

transparency and sustainability in its palm oil supply chain. Blockchain will be used to help sellers and consumers track the source of palm oil, monitor transactions and overall help the Government move the industry toward sustainability. During the same month, the World Bank invited bids from parties to do a PoC which leads to a prototype for a blockchain use-case on the traceability of smallholder palm oil supply chains in Indonesia.

Also in September 2018 a group of oil palm producers, consumer goods manufacturers, not-for-profit organizations and technology companies gathered in Singapore to form the Sustainability Assurance and Innovation Alliance (SUSTAIN). The alliance, which aimed to initiate a blockchain solution to improve traceability and sustainability in palm oil supply chains, includes: palm oil companies Apical and Asian Agri; renewable diesel producer Neste; consumer goods manufacturer KAO; facilitation team CORE; and technology partner SAP. Additional collaborators from across the palm oil supply chain are expected to join the new alliance. SUSTAIN's blockchain platform will provide open access to palm oil industry stakeholders such as dealers and smallholders who could use downloadable tools to establish traceability, monitor policy compliance, efficiently trade FFBs, obtain best practice guides and avail themselves of micro-financing. Media reports say that SAP, the alliance's technology partner, has been working with more than 60 companies across industries to create blockchain use cases in the supply chain, manufacturing, transportation and pharmaceuticals.

Unilever's appetite for palm oil

Unilever, the British–Dutch consumer goods company, is the world's largest in its league by revenue – in 2017 it earned $62.6 billion. Every day, one-third of the world's population uses Unilever's products.

The supply chain is Unilever's primary sphere of activity. Over half of its 165,000 employees work in the supply chain. In 2017 the company spent $29 billion in the supply chain with over 76,000 suppliers.

In Asia and Africa alone Unilever products are sold at over 10 million outlets for which the cumulative logistics distance travelled is 500 million kilometres. It has over 380 manufacturing sites, and 12 per cent of total supply chain costs are to third-party manufacturers.

Two-thirds of Unilever's raw materials are sourced from more than 100,000 small farmers. One of the most widely used raw materials for Unilever's product range of more than 400 brands is palm oil.

Expectedly, Unilever is the single largest buyer of palm oil in the world. The company buys around one million tonnes of crude palm oil and around 0.5 million tonnes of palm kernel oil and other derivatives every year.

Unilever has not disclosed the technologies that it is using to track its palm oil supply chain, but the company has been a proponent of the use of blockchain for supply chain transparency. In August 2017 Unilever joined a group of 10 large food and retail companies, including Nestlé and Tyson Foods, to run a project with IBM to study how blockchain systems can help track food supply chains and improve safety. One of the goals of the project was to generate secure digital records and improve traceability of foods within seconds rather than weeks.

Leveraging blockchain for the tea supply chain

In December 2017 Unilever launched a one-year pilot project that leveraged blockchain technology to track supply chains for tea sold by consumer goods giant Unilever and the British supermarket Sainsbury's. The company partnered with big banks and technology start-ups to track tea farmers in Malawi, who supply tea for Unilever brands. The project used technology to maintain transparency on the supply chain, so both the company and the consumer knew the origins of their tea. 'Malawian tea is the start, not the end,' said Andrew Voysey, Director of Sustainable Finance at the University of Cambridge Institute for Sustainability Leadership. Up to 10,000 farmers in Malawi were eligible to join the pilot, which aimed to reward those who produced a fairer, more sustainable brew, with financial incentives such as preferential loans and access to credit. There is a reasonable probability that Unilever's blockchain use-case of the tea supply chain could encourage the FMCG giant to extend it to its palm oil supply chain.

Blockchain for the automotive industry

Imagine a world without traffic jams. What would one not give to live in a world where you could enjoy a quick drive to work and, better still, a safe and peaceful drive back home? Ford Motors already has some ideas as to how to achieve this through the capabilites of cryptocurrency.

Early in 2018 the United States Patent and Trademark Office granted a patent to Ford Global Technologies, a Ford Motors subsidiary, for a vehicle communication platform called Cooperatively Managed Merge and Pass (CMMP). It's well understood that traffic jams are caused by an over-capacity of individual car drivers urgently following the course to their destination. However, cars magically make way when they act on a standard protocol, such as letting an ambulance or a fire truck pass. CMMP improves upon the same principle. It works on a 'cooperative adaptive cruise control' module that allows car drivers to buy or sell preferential lane access in exchange for a few trade units of cryptocurrency.

According to the patent, 'The CMMP system operates with individual token-based transactions, where the merchant vehicles and the consumers' vehicles agree to trade units of cryptocurrency. [Seller] vehicles voluntarily occupy slower lanes of traffic to facilitate the consumer vehicle to merge into their lanes and pass as needed.'

The benefits of the blockchain-powered CMMP, however, would be limited at present to a few megacities such as New York and London where drivers observe, or are made to observe, lane discipline; CMMP has no use in the newer metropolises such as Bengaluru or Beijing where motorists switch lanes with the zeal of a Kamikaze pilot.

On a global scale, car-makers have found immediate applications of blockchain to help them address some of their biggest challenges. The critical problems of the auto industry – one of the world's most complex, dynamic and globally networked sectors – can be broadly classified into three categories: increasing complexity; customer service, safety and aftermarket-related challenges; and keeping up with tectonic shifts. Car-makers are finding use cases for blockchain in all these areas.

The future of car-making: unpredictable

A direct consequence of slow growth has been the growing pressure on original equipment manufacturers' (OEMs') bottom line, as evidenced by their latest financial reports. It has prompted among them a rush to look for cost savings and market consolidation.

The most obvious upshot of this trend was the recent birth of the unique car-making alliance of three automakers – Renault, Nissan and Mitsubishi. In 2016 the coalition declared annual savings of $6.2 billion, which it promised to double by 2022. Regarding market presence, the three car-makers brought together the lucrative markets of Europe, China and America. In 2017, with total sales of 10.61 million, the alliance moved past Volkswagen to become the world's largest car-maker.

The auto industry's lacklustre growth has made it vulnerable to the emerging challenges, most prominently the ongoing global trade war. It does not help that the industry likely stands at the cusp of its most significant shift since the discovery of assembly line: the rise of electric and autonomous cars.

When you can't change the external factors that affect your growth, the next natural step is to effect change within, to home in on the areas that are holding you back, and become more responsive to the ebb and flow of the market. For automakers, the answer is obvious. The Achilles heel of the auto industry is the increasingly complex supplier ecosystem, which, despite the process improvements and technological advancements of more than a century, impacts car companies dearly on the three crucial measures of performance: cost, quality and delivery. As recently as 2018 the order-to-delivery time of a factory-order car was calculated to be anywhere from four to eight months, and the number of problems experienced per 100 vehicles in the USA was 142, as per JD Power's 2018 US vehicle dependability study. These facts are hardly the hallmarks of a well-oiled manufacturing machine.

Fortunately, blockchain offers a glimmer of hope to the industry in the many unique ways it can address the problem of supply chain complexity. But first, how did auto manufacturing get so complicated?

Status: it's complicated

Cars have come a long way, figuratively speaking, regarding the number and efficiency of auto parts since the day when the solid rubber tyres of the world's fastest automobile, Benz Patent Motorwagen, first met the road on New Year's Eve 1879.

Benz Motorwagen's parts included a single-cylinder four-stroke engine with an electrical vibrator ignition with a spark plug, a chassis made of bent and welded steel tube, and a small number of drive components, all of which could be detailed in a pocket-sized service manual.

In comparison, today's car-makers deal with a dizzying array of components. A single car is made of more than 30,000 parts (Figure 8.7) brought together through the logistics and assembly of a host of inputs including steel, glass, rubber, plastic and semi-assembled components sourced from a global network of suppliers.

Figure 8.6   Benz Patent Motorwagen: the first automobile (1885–86), by DaimlerChrysler AG

SOURCE Mediaseite der DaimlerChrysler AG. Licensed under CC BY-SA 3.0 (https://commons. wikimedia.org/wiki/File:Patent-Motorwagen_Nr.1_Benz_2.jpg)

Figure 8.7   Today's standard car is an assembly of more than 30,000 parts (representative image)

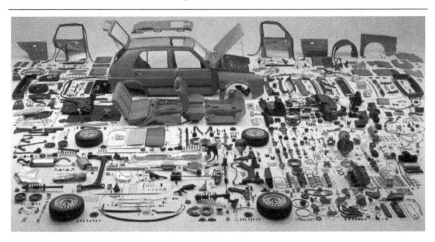

SOURCE Aaron 'Tango' Tang. Licensed under CC BY 2.0 (https://www.flickr.com/photos/hahatango/2161518548)

Accurate data on the number of systems and sub-systems of an OEM's supply network is surprisingly hard to come by. Manufacturers closely guard their supplier-related information for many valid reasons, competition being the primary one. Arguably the closest researchers came to an understanding the size and scale of an OEM's supply network was in 2010 when scholars from the Universities of Oxford and Cranfield examined Toyota Motor Company's supply keiretsu, (ie the hierarchal structure of Toyota's supply network). The report, published in a 2014 research paper titled *The Structure of the Toyota Supply Network: An empirical analysis*, identified 2,192 firms that supplied components directly or indirectly to Toyota. Researchers noted that the supplier network was so little-studied that it took severe supply chain disruptions in the wake of the 2011 Tohoku earthquake and tsunami disasters for Toyota to realize the actual shape of its supplier network structure. A 2011 *Japan Times* report quoted a Toyota official as saying, 'We thought it was pyramid-shaped, but it turned out to be barrel-shaped.' Have a look at the report's 'diagram of the Toyota supply network' to marvel at its complexity.

Extended enterprise

The process of car-making was not always so complex. A quick look at the history of car production will reveal that the Ford Model T, the world's first affordable car, relied on a vertically integrated and centralized manufacturing process. Ford's assembly-line innovation of the early 1900s revolutionized production to such an extent that it brought down the production time of a single car from 12 hours to 90 minutes. The vastly reduced assembly time also necessitated that car-makers produce most of the critical components themselves. For example, in 1926 car-makers purchased only 26 per cent of the number of components used in a car from outside suppliers. However, tenacious competitors such as General Motors soon realized that a decentralized manufacturing paradigm was more conducive to product innovation. The final blow to centralized production was dealt by the Toyota-led lean production revolution of the 1950s, and the accompanying just-in-time production technique, which not only transformed global auto manufacturing but also introduced the sweeping organizational reform termed 'the extended enterprise' system.

Extended enterprise was a term first used by Chrysler in the 1990s to describe its partnership with its suppliers [James B. Ayers, 2006]. The company, which considered the system important enough to trademark it in 1999, defined extended enterprise thus: 'Extending business relationships by providing process management consultations and workshops to… suppliers and supplier tiers in order to reduce cycle time, to minimize system cost and to improve the quality of the goods or services provided by the suppliers.'

The extended enterprise approach to supply chain management worked very well for Chrysler and other auto and auto-component manufacturers. Chrysler, under its president Thomas Stallkamp – widely regarded as the father of the extended enterprise approach – used it along with Supplier Cost Reduction Effort (SCORE) to achieve cost savings of $5.5 billion in about ten years. TRW's similar implementation of SCORE generated savings of $6.3 billion within the first five months (Dyer, 2000). Inspired by these successes, car-makers have expanded the enterprise system to engage all the parties along the supply chain, right from procurement to delivery to aftermarket services.

However, much like any hierarchical system, the extended enterprise-system has become rigid over time. To further accentuate the challenge, the industry is facing at present slow growth and long lead times. There are several other problems that the extended enterprise is not able to provide a fast response to anymore. Even more, facts indicate that it could be contributing to some of the issues. Americans are paying more than ever for new cars and trucks. The average transaction price of cars hit a record high of $36,270 in January 2018. The main reason for this is the soaring cost of auto parts. Chicago-based consumer automotive journalist Jim Gorzelany noted in a February 2018 Forbes article that car components have become too prohibitively costly to be replaced. Furthermore, the skyrocketing costs have helped fuel a rise in car thefts.

Extended enterprise has worked very well to make the auto industry one of the most sophisticated and resilient industries in history. It only needs to be improved to make the system more agile and responsive. The ongoing buzz around the use of blockchain in automotive is precisely about that – about how useful blockchain is in helping make the system agile enough to respond to the growing challenges.

Managing complexity: making extended enterprise great again

The solution to the problem of systemic rigidity is to improve the way in which information is exchanged and acted upon in among the enterprise system partners. The information systems that connect OEMs with suppliers are based on electronic data interchange (EDI), a 50-year-old, internally focused technology. It was the automotive industry that implemented the EDI standards that are followed globally (ANSI ASC is the standard for the US, EDIFACT for Europe and beyond). EDI-based documents cover all types of transactional communication, including purchase orders to invoices to advance shipping notification, other than, of course, monetary instruments.

Companies capture (or relay) the EDI documents through the back-end business systems called enterprise resource planning (ERP) systems for further processing. Warehouse management solutions, transport management solutions, and distribution process management are some examples of ERP modules.

Despite the advancements in technology, the existing EDI-to-ERP communication, interpretation and execution system presents a number of challenges that limit its responsiveness. Integrating blockchain with enterprise systems not only solves these issues, but will also create a highly agile, automated system that will help transform the industry. Let's look at the systemic challenges, how blockchain can help, and the use cases where the technology is being put to use for the purpose.

First, a quick recap of blockchain's distinct advantages. Blockchain is a shared, immutable, scalable, cryptographically secure document that ensures traceability and authenticity, offers peer-to-peer trust without middlemen, and enables real-time purchase of assets using smart contracts, thus reducing costs, lead times and risk. Now, let us consider the challenges of the existing system and the applicable use cases of blockchain.

Say no to errors

Suppliers and OEMs operate on their custom ERP systems, which means that the information has to flow through myriad points of integration, often leading to issues with stock reconciliation. Each position of integration requires ERP users to collect data from different sources and make timely and accurate entries. This process is prone to errors and consumes time. Manufacturers, for example, often complain about receiving poor quality data from suppliers. Further, an issue affecting the quality of data at any of the nodes is mostly discovered during the accounting processes, and that can have significant financial implications.

Blockchain-based records don't need to be entered manually more than once, and they are tamper-proof. In simple terms, when a company puts a record on its blockchain ledger, the blockchain software replicates the record across the dashboards of all the peers in the network. Even more, you can seamlessly transfer EDI and ERP data to blockchain with zero errors – removing the need for manual entries at any point of integration. For example, one of blockchain's use cases in the supply chain is that the procurement information like purchase orders and purchase agreements held in the ERP system can be converted to blockchain-powered digital formats that can work across incompatible ERP systems. The integrity of data throughout the supply chain thus ensured reduces erroneous orders, improves just-in-time logistics and raises inventory turns.

It's no surprise that IT vendors have begun to launch blockchain–ERP integrators. In January 2017 financial service provider Finlync's created the world's first blockchain-agnostic integrator for ERP systems. During the same year, Norway-based Skye Consulting developed integrations of SAP with blockchain offering solutions for finance, HR, and supply chain. Today, we have blockchain integrators available in the market for types of ERP solutions.

For a seamless and transparent supply chain

According to a global survey of 623 companies in 2017 by logistics firm Geodis, supply chain visibility rose to become the third most important strategic priority in 2017. However, 77 per cent of the firms surveyed had either no visibility or a restricted view. Only 6 per cent had complete visibility!

Consulting firm KPMG says that demand for supply chain transparency is not just coming from just the manufacturing OEMs; regulatory bodies are insisting on it. In 2016 the European automakers and their suppliers were asked to harmonize the different assessment and certification systems in the automotive supply chain by publishing a new set of standards. KPMG's Erich Gampenreider noted that 'All EU carmakers have agreed to ensure that every auto part can be monitored so that every company knows where the part comes from and how it was produced.'

Supply chain visibility has become more critical to companies because it offers a bevy of competitive advantages, including better control over processes, reduction in disputes, improved risk anticipation, agility, better customer satisfaction and, above all, profitability.

At a LinuxCon Conference held in Toronto, Canada in 2016, IBM Fellow (Enterprise Solutions) Donna Dillenberger presented a blockchain use-case that gave the audience an insight into something incredible happening at IBM over the previous two years. Ms Dillenberger told the audience that IBM had integrated the supply chain of its computer-making division on blockchain. The results were astonishing. IBM makes mainframe-class computers, enterprise servers and storage-area network hardware. IBM has 4,000 suppliers and partners all over the world that generated (at the time of the conference) about 25,000 disputes every year. Typically, a conflict between IBM and a supplier would arise when one of them would not acknowledge any particular invoice or payment made against a shipment of goods. Until 2015 IBM had close to a hundred million dollars tied up in its supply chain at a given point of time, with the disputed invoice amount averaging at $31,000. It took about a month and a half for a dispute to be resolved. With the implementation of blockchain, both IBM and its suppliers could verify the entire life of a transaction from purchase order through remittance, bringing the average dispute resolution down to under ten days. Encouraged by its success, IBM launched a proof of concept in 2016 with half a dozen members of IBM Global Finance, its supplier and partner financing arm that manages over $50 billion in IT hardware and software annually.

In the same vein, improved transparency in a blockchain-enabled automotive supply chain can enable faster processing of documents, such as a letter of credit from the purchaser's bank and a bill of lading by the manufacturer, thus dramatically reducing the settlement period between suppliers, banks, export and import authorities and the OEMs.

As importantly, it will help OEMs receive payments faster from the end-user via the distributors and dealers for cars delivered. Blockchain's self-executable smart contracts, already empowering IBM's computer supply chain, will even automate the entire process. Smart contracts ensure that what is committed is delivered and what is delivered is paid.

Of course, a welcome by-product of on-time settlements will be improved supplier performance. As an extension, connected IoT sensors and smart devices could measure the condition of containers and other information that can be recorded on the blockchain and inform final settlements if, for example, goods have been damaged.

For example, Deloitte's TraceChain solution creates digital identities for physical goods in the supply chain and enables the tracking and tracing of finished goods and materials.

Creating trust

During the same speech, Ms Dillenberger shared with the audience that the companies IBM is working with to implement blockchain demanded some additional features.

First of all, companies wanted to set permissions for who can see their data. Second, they also wanted every record on the blockchain to be digitally signed so that they know who keyed in a particular record. Today's blockchain solutions, such as the Linux Foundation's Hyperledger, which technology leaders like IBM, SAP and Intel use, have both these features built in. Hyperledger's blockchain solution and related tools are permission-based or 'permission', to use industry-speak, and every entry has a digital signature that follows the established protocol.

The companies' fears were not unfounded. Supply chain partners are justified in withholding sensitive cost data, such as production yields or parts pricing, because such information could compromise their competitive advantage. Recalls to correct defects in auto parts have grown a staggering 30 per cent a year in recent years, said an AlixPartners study released in 2018. In 2016, a record year for auto recalls, 52 million vehicles were recalled in the US alone. The study said that, during the year, US automakers and suppliers paid almost $11.8 billion in claims and recorded $10.3 billion in warranty accruals, totalling $22.1 billion, a 26 per cent increase over the previous year.

Overall, almost 400 million vehicles have been recalled in the US since 1966, says a *Fortune* magazine report. Most common reasons for recall are exploding airbag inflators, axle or steering components, brakes, tyres, wheels, defective seat belts and engine parts.

It signals one of the two likelihoods: either car companies and their suppliers value cost reductions and innovation over consumer safety, or they are unable to solve a growing crisis due to inherent, systemic problems. By all accounts, the problem seems to be the latter, as pointed out earlier in the chapter. The automotive industry's supply chain has become far too complicated to be able to deliver the expected level of consumer safety.

Rising complexity and a lack of supply-chain visibility also impact the $740-billion global automotive aftermarket industry, which struggles to meet rising inventory demands, therefore leaving enough room for counterfeit parts to flourish.

The European Union Intellectual Property Office (EUIPO) has estimated that more than €2 billion ($2.26 billion) is lost every year due to counterfeit tyres and batteries alone. In the US, Customs seized 31,560 shipments with a combined retail value of $1.4 billion in 2016 fiscal.

The most common fake auto parts worldwide include clutch housings, brake pads, lights, ignition coils, wheel rims, windshields and airbags – many of these parts have direct safety implications and, if they fail, can lead to severe accidents.

A blockchain-based solution connected with IoT sensors can correct these problems. It can help mitigate the number of auto recalls by enabling the permission OEMs, and suppliers get a real-time, end-to-end view of the supply chain. OEMs and contract manufacturers can rely on smart contracts to reorder the damaged or defective parts identifiable through breaches of set thresholds, for example continuous vibration for a certain amount of time. These applications can issue specific recalls or service bulletins for these vehicles, reducing disruptions to customers as well as the recall costs for the process. They will also track the status of the recall, which can be used for regulatory reporting to the authorities.

At the customers' end, service centres and car owners can detect counterfeit aftermarket parts by tracing their provenance through every step in the supply chain right to its original manufacturing date and location.

Solutions such as Deloitte's ArtTracktive (a proof of concept which provides a distributed ledger for tracking the provenance and locations of items), SmartID (a digital ID for entities to be used for digital assets, contracts and workflows on the blockchain), and TraceChain are being used to address the problems of auto recall and fake parts.

After-sales and resale services

Consumer auto finance is a big area of application for blockchain use cases. A finance provider can view the driving, selling and servicing history of cars to finance resale and lease of vehicles appropriately. Such applications can help automate the process of leasing a vehicle to a customer, by performing know your customer checks, recording a leasing contract and automating payment upon the returns of the vehicle. For example, in June 2017 Daimler AG and Landesbank Baden-Württemberg (LBBW) jointly used blockchain technology to execute a financial transaction. Through LBBW, Daimler launched a €100 million ($126 million) one-year corporate Schuldschein (a German debt instrument). The entire operation – from the origination, distribution, allocation, and execution of the Schuldschein loan agreement to the confirmation of repayment and of interest payments – was digitally carried out via blockchain technology in cooperation with the IT subsidiaries TSS (Daimler) and Targens (LBBW).

Presently, mileage is the most critical parameter for determining the return value of a vehicle. Top-of-the-line car brands like BMW and Audi make a lot of money from financing and leasing cars, which is why they put a lot of efforts into maintaining residual values of the vehicles that come back to the market after a lease or fleet assignment. In May 2018 BMW and Alphabet did the first pilot with crypto startup DOVU with a blockchain use-case to automate the mileage gathering process.

Similarly, insurance companies can use blockchain to pay users for car repairs as well as sharing of data that can then be used for actuarial valuations and reporting of warranty claims.

Toyota's telematics car insurance arm is developing a proof of concept for a similar application, Toyota Insurance Management Solutions, in collaboration with the Japanese insurance company Aioi Nissay Dowa Insurance Services and the blockchain platform Gem. The three partners are building a usage-based insurance platform that can use a vehicle's usage information to set insurance rates. Likewise, carVertical's blockchain tools gather information about a car's history from different sources, including national and private registries, and helps users spot way to spot mileage fraud and accidents.

Car brands can also use blockchain to issue loyalty points to customers and dealers based on purchase history. The loyalty points can be used as a currency within the OEM's loyalty network that could include parts suppliers and service centres. Loyyal, a loyalty and rewards platform, leverages blockchain and smart contract technology to enhance loyalty programmes.

Blockchain for the automotive industry 4.0

Catching investors and customers unawares, General Motors made a stunning announcement on 26 November 2018, that it would lay off more than 14,000 workers and close five plants in the US and Canada that will result in cash savings of $6 billion by 2020. The company said it aims to shift focus to producing electric and autonomous vehicles in line with its new motto, 'Zero Crashes, Zero Emissions, Zero Congestion.'

In April 2018 Ford announced it would stop all production of sedans in North America. Instead, the car-maker wants to launch a fleet of thousands of self-driving cars in 2021. New-age companies such as Alphabet, Apple, Tesla, and Uber are investing billions of dollars in building the cars of the future.

As per Encyclopedia.com's meticulously-researched treatise on the automotive industry's evolution, the industry has passed through three stages: (1) craft production (1890–1908), in which a number of small automakers vied to establish a standard product and process; (2) mass production (1908–73), initiated by Henry Ford's moving assembly lines; and (3) lean manufacturing (1973–present), led by Toyota, which introduced a revolutionary management process of product development and production. Sector onlookers believe that the automotive industry has entered the fourth stage of evolution, which is being driven by the resurgence of electric vehicles (EV), the rise of autonomous vehicles, connected cars, and shared mobility services. Industry leaders seem to concur – GM, Toyota, Porsche and Daimler AG have all put their might behind integrating emerging tech like blockchain, AI, and IoT to develop newer vehicle and fleet management solutions, which includes routing, payment systems, digital content, and access services for shared mobility. Let's look at some use cases where blockchain, in combination with other technologies, is to be deployed for auto industry 4.0.

Germany-based blockchain and IoT startup Slock are developing a peer-to-peer EV charging station. It is collaborating with the German energy company RWE that will allow users to automate the process of charging their EV.

To improve ride sharing and hailing services, blockchain-based applications can enable service providers like Lyft and Uber to offer subscribing customers access to vehicles that suit their mobility preferences, such as seat settings, climate and the choice of infotainment.

A car eWallet platform developed by ZF in cooperation with UBS and IBM will enable users to pay for tolls, parking fees, infotainment services or car sharing. The first pilot projects of Car eWallet is up for launch anytime soon, as per a company press release.

Another mobility payment solution has been developed by Toyota Research Institute and Oaken Innovations to support car sharing, vehicle access and interconnect autonomous cars.

Oaken Innovation (formerly Project Oaken), an IoT and blockchain start-up, is also a part of the largest and most talked-about blockchain consortium of major automakers and tech startups: Mobility Open Blockchain Initiative (MOBI). Launched in mid-2018, MOBI's partners include carmakers of the likes of BMW, Bosch, Ford, General Motors and Renault that account for over 70 per cent of global vehicle production. MOBI aims to accelerate adoption and to promote standards in blockchain and related technologies for the benefit of the mobility industry and consumers. The consortium recently launched the MOBI Grand Challenge (MGC) contest. A press statement announced that the winners of MGC will be expected to demonstrate how blockchains and related technologies – distributed ledgers, cryptography, tokens and consensus mechanisms – can leverage the connections and computing power of vehicles to extend the 'effective range of perception' of autonomous vehicles to make mobility safer, cleaner, faster, more efficient and accessible.

Time and again, the automobile industry has been a pioneer (assembly lines, lean and JIT production) as well as an early adopter (interchangeable parts) of revolutionary technologies and processes. It has shown the same readiness and fast pace of adoption of distributed ledger technologies, which is a good indication of their potential for transforming all industries.

Blockchain and other technologies in context: considerations and challenges

In this chapter we have explored a wide range of use cases where blockchain can play a role in the context of the supply chain. One for container shipping highlighting the IBM–Maersk initiative and the TradeLens multinational consortium that involves more than 94 parties. One for establishing a blockchain-based palm oil supply chain that is sustainable and environment-friendly. And one for the automotive structure, particularly the contract manufacturing supply chain. The sheer diversity of these use cases points to the significant potential that blockchain could have as a transformative technology.

It is clear from these case studies and the previous chapters that blockchain brings some fundamentally new capabilities to creating greater trust and reducing frictions of data-based interactions between supply chain partners. It creates a way to have shared knowledge, not only globally across all companies in a supply chain, but also, where needed for business reasons, shared among particular sub-groups of companies. The data that is shared is more trustworthy because of the immutable properties of blockchain technologies. All parties that receive some information can be assured that they receive the same information in the same order as others that receive that information. It allows for the use of autonomous, transparent and fair computations that cannot easily be tampered with by malicious or selfish parties without detection. It enables the creation and execution of smart contracts that can be triggered by business logic to do everything from placing orders to actuating the movement of supplies between partners to making payments.

There are several technology-related questions that are worth considering in the context of these use cases and others like them:

- Public versus permissioned blockchains: As we have discussed, there are essentially two classes of blockchain technologies that can be adopted for supply chain applications and so a decision must be made on which type of technology to use. Public chains such as Ethereum or EOS offer greater security because they run on more nodes and are inherently more open, allowing for more flexible participation; however, today they are relatively slow and scale poorly for business applications with significant transaction rates. On the other hand, permissioned systems such as Hyperledger Fabric are in principle faster but have some element of centralized permissioning that is required before allowing participants to interact with each other. New hybrid systems that will enable permissions on public blockchains are being developed but may be some years away from meeting the performance requirements for many applications.

- Consortium governance: In onboarding business networks on to a blockchain, they have to come together in the context of a consortium such as the one organized by TradeLens for container shipping. However, the rules for the governance of such a consortium need to be carefully considered and agreed upon by all parties in a way that the whole ecosystem is seen as fair and trustworthy. These are relatively early days even for determining best practices for the formation and operation of such blockchain-based supply chain consortia.

- Standards and interoperability: Industries in different sectors, and even different companies within the same industry, may be using different software for data and operations management such as ERP and CRM systems and common data standards are needed for them to be able to upload and download data shared using blockchain. While there are examples of common data standards adopted previously for certain aspects of the supply chain, such as GS1 standards, the future adoption of blockchain technologies will require even more standardization efforts. Existing software tools will need to be enhanced or integrated with new gateway software to connect them to blockchain. Further, new developments in the adoption of IoT systems in the supply chain will pose challenges; for example, temperature sensors in containers to monitor temperature-sensitive goods in transit may need to be connected to blockchain-based verification or smart contracts to trigger pertinent actions such as payment or rejection of a batch of delivered goods in an automated fashion.

- Device integrity: While blockchain can guarantee that the data on the ledger is tamper proof, it cannot guarantee that the data came from a legitimate source (only that the source that entered the data possessed a specific key) or that the source of data itself has not been tampered with at the hardware level.

- Identity and access management: Likewise, a key but challenging aspect of developing a permissioned blockchain for the various supply chain uses cases is the management of identities at many levels, from device identity to individual identities (and corresponding access permissions) to organizational identities.

- Privacy: With the emergence of new laws such as the GDPR that pose strict requirements on the retention of privacy-sensitive data belonging to other entities, including the possibility of revoking data access, the systems that are designed to share data have to be designed extremely carefully so that the privacy-sensitive data is managed in a regulation-compliant manner so that data assets do not become data liabilities.

As blockchain technology evolves and starts to become adopted in the supply chain for uses cases such as those covered in this chapter, the above challenges will have to be addressed by the community.

References

Ayers, JB (2006) [Online] https://trove.nla.gov.au/work/20348325?q&versionId= 24048397

bbc.co.uk (2018) Iceland Christmas advert: What is palm oil? CBBC Newsround. [Online] https://www.bbc.co.uk/newsround/39492207

de Haas, J (2016) [Online] http://climatesavers.org/wp-content/uploads/2016/03/ENECO-Factsheet.pdf

Dyer (2000) [Online] https://dspace.mit.edu/bitstream/handle/1721.1/1441/147b.pdf?sequence=1

Neslen, A (2017) Pepsico, Unilever and Nestlé accused of complicity in illegal rainforest destruction, *Guardian*. [Online] https://www.theguardian.com/environment/2017/jul/21/pepsico-unilever-and-nestle-accused-of-complicity-in-illegal-rainforest-destruction

Rainforest Action Network (2018) Leuser watch: Rainforest Action Network. [Online] https://www.ran.org/leuser_watch_ptabn

Statista (2017) Total number of Unilever employees worldwide 2003–2017 statistic. [Online] https://www.statista.com/statistics/254366/total-number-of-unilever-employees-worldwide/

Supply Chain Dive (2018) Unilever taps into blockchain to manage tea supply chain. [Online] https://www.supplychaindive.com/news/unilever-blockchain-tea/513365/

Reuters (2018) Can blockchain ensure Unilever's tea farmers produce a fairer brew? [Online] https://www.reuters.com/article/us-malawi-tea-technology/can-blockchain-ensure-unilevers-tea-farmers-produce-a-fairer-brew-idUSK-BN1E729G

Transparency, U (nd) Unilever releases locations of palm oil mills in a bid for supply chain transparency, Space Intelligence. [Online] https://www.space-intelligence.com/2018/04/12/unilever-releases-locations-of-palm-oil-mills-in-a-bid-for-supply-chain-transparency/

Unilever (2011) [video] YouTube: Our Unilever.

Unilever (2018a) Transforming the palm oil industry. [Online] https://www.unilever.com/sustainable-living/reducing-environmental-impact/sustainable-sourcing/transforming-the-palm-oil-industry/

Unilever (2018b) Unilever supply chain overview. [Online] https://www.unilever.com/Images/unilever-supply-chain-overview—may-2018_tcm244-523172_1_en.pdf

Economic impact and future outlook

In the previous chapters of the book we tracked the evolution of trade and commerce over thousands of years, starting from the first wave of migrations of humans out of Africa, to the development of modern cities of today and tomorrow. We looked at the evolution of the supply chain that enabled man to exchange ideas across continents in the form of goods and services. We examined the foundation of blockchain and how other technologies, such as the Internet of Things, artificial intelligence, machine learning and robotic process automation can support the evolving ecosystems. Our aim is that the premise built through these chapters will help future supply chain leaders to see how blockchain integrated with emerging technologies can help transform the supply chain. However, organizations continue to struggle with the notion of when, why and how they should participate in integrating their legacy supply chain network with emerging technologies.

The economics of blockchain

The question still arises, when should you implement blockchain in your organization? How much should you invest into it? Do you have a clear case for a sound return on investment (ROI)? Does it exceed the internal hurdle rate? Should we wait for the market to mature and then catch up? Why should I be among the first to go in? Are there first mover advantages, and if so, what are they? There are many more questions about blockchain technology and its implementations, and all of them would be fair. However, in today's disruptive world, an organization has to make a paradigm shift – from the conventional approach of focusing strictly on ROI to focusing instead on return on investment on innovation (ROI^2), a potential buzzword that we may have just coined, to articulate the need of the times.

Speaking of return on investment in traditional terms, the ROI clock starts ticking when we allocate the capital and then hope to produce a return, counting years in 0, 1 and so on. Naturally, organizations become fixated on getting the returns faster. ROI^2, on the other hand, is a different concept. It can best be understood from the perspective of a farmer who would take \$100, buy 100 seeds, and sow them, knowing quite well that not all 100 will come to fruition. The farmer will have the insight to put their energy and resources into nurturing only those that sprout, a strategy that will yield greater return on limited resources. The innovative organizations of today follow that simple strategy. This ROI^2 strategy works under the philosophy of distributing your investments amongst a variety of potential opportunities, but only nurturing the ones that are deemed most fruitful, rather than focusing on only one investment at a time. ROI^2 leaders look for the feasibility of all the innovative undertakings, and move on from those that won't work to the next ones. In fact, a skilled ROI^2 leader tries multiple things at the same time. Our aim is to appeal to such future leaders – through the use cases articulated in the chapters and by pointing out many more that will follow – in order to provide a concrete justification for creating an internal thought leadership that identifies all the possible areas of implementation.

Organizations must realize the urgent need for creating the ROI^2 paradigm to be able to survive as well as leverage a number of strong forces that are shaping the world. In fact, the reason behind the rapid evolution and the

Figure 9.1   ROI versus ROI_2 argument

Tradition ROI **(Return on Investment)**	=	$\dfrac{\text{Return (Year = 0)} - \text{Investment (N = 1)}}{\text{Investment (N = 1)}}$
New paradigm of ROI^2 **(Return on Investment on** **innovation)**	=	$\dfrac{\text{Return (Year > 3)} - \text{Investment (N > 1)}}{\text{Investment *(N > 1)}}$

* N > 1, in many cases, it is 10 to 20 small projects in a portfolio of innovation bucket providing yield for ROI^2.

SOURCE NVyas

race for adoption of blockchain is that the technology enmeshes well with these forces. Let's look at some of these forces and how blockchain could prove to be just the application to hasten their progress.

Globalization's backwash

Three major developments in the last three years may indicate to an observer that the first wave of globalization, in the form that we have seen it rise over the past three decades, could be ebbing. In 2019 the UK plans to leave the European Union, marking a potential end to the two-year Brexit period. On 23 January 2017 President Trump signed a 'Presidential Memorandum' in which he directed the United States Trade Representative to 'withdraw the United States as a signatory to the Trans-Pacific Partnership (TPP), and begin pursuing, wherever possible, bilateral trade negotiations to promote American industry, protect American workers, and raise American wages'. The TPP was a proposed trade agreement between 12 countries including the US that aimed to lower tariff barriers among the signatories, and establish an investor-state dispute settlement mechanism. This followed a series of tariff impositions on China (and counter-imposition) that have continued subsequently.

What do these recent developments portend for the future of international trade? Is this the beginning of the end of globalization – are we going back to the pre-1950s era of economic nationalism? And what does it mean for global supply chains? The answer is, globalization is irreversible. In the future, it may not have the active support of major economies, but international trade will continue its forward march. After all, the world's top multinationals are far too expansive – and deeply invested into making their supply chains diverse for cost, competitiveness and quality. For example, Apple has suppliers in more than 30 countries across the globe. About 30 per cent of a Boeing aircraft's parts come from suppliers outside the USA.

In all likelihood, future trade agreements and multilateral negotiations will take place between organizations, empowered by the deployment of technologies like blockchain. Therefore, trade negotiations will not involve thousands of pages of documents detailing rules and regulations, but it will be process-driven, blockchain-based track and trace capabilities that will validate and execute mutually agreed-upon terms. This will create a level playing field in the emerging and underdeveloped countries so that they are able to put the right focus on their economic growth.

Figure 9.2   Boeing's parts come from across the world

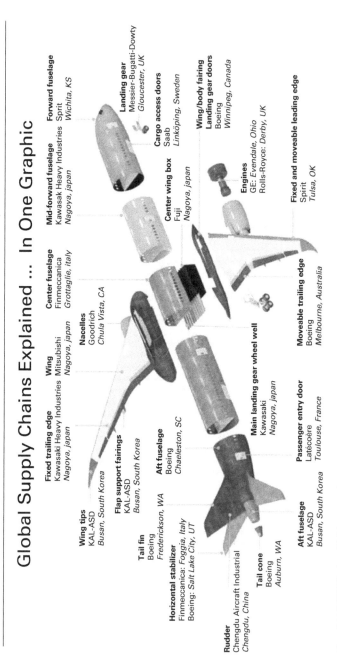

Global Supply Chains Explained ... In One Graphic

Fixed trailing edge
Kawasaki Heavy Industries
Nagoya, Japan

Wing
Mitsubishi
Nagoya, Japan

Center fuselage
Finmeccanica
Grottaglie, Italy

Mid-forward fuselage
Kawasak Heavy Industries
Nagoya, Japan

Forward fuselage
Sprit
Wichita, KS

Nacelles
Goodrich
Chula Vista, CA

Wing tips
KAL-ASD
Busan, South Korea

Flap support fairings
KAL-ASD
Busan, South Korea

Tail fin
Boeing
Frederickson, WA

Aft fuselage
Boeing
Chaeleston, SC

Horizontal stabilizer
Finmeccanica: *Foggia, Italy*
Boeing: *Salt Lake City, UT*

Rudder
Chengdu Aircraft Industrial
Chengdu, China

Tail cone
Boeing
Auburn, WA

Aft fuselage
KAL-ASD
Busan, South Korea

Main landing gear wheel well
Kawasaki
Nagoya, Japan

Passenger entry door
Latécoère
Toulouse, France

Center wing box
Fuji
Nagoya, Japan

Landing gear
Messier-Bugatti-Dowty
Gloucester, UK

Cargo access doors
Saab
Linköping, Sweden

Wing/body fairing
Landing gear doors
Boeing
Winnipeg, Canada

Engines
GE: *Evendale, Ohio*
Rolls-Royce: *Derby, UK*

Moveable trailing edge
Boeing
Melbourne, Australia

Fixed and moveable leading edge
Spirit
Tulsa, OK

SOURCE Boeing

Online marketplaces

Recent years have witnessed the emergence of 'sharing economy' successes like Airbnb, Uber, and Lyft, or to use Silicon Valley's preferred phrase, start-ups that enable 'underused asset utilization'.

Airbnb, an online marketplace for short-term lodging, has had a disruptive impact on the hospitality services industry. In 2017 three million people in over 80,000 cities worldwide spent their New Year's Eve in Airbnb apartments. A recent Morningstar Equity Research report says that Airbnb is worth about $55 billion, more than any other hotel company, including the $46 billion Marriott International, the world's biggest hotel company.

The taxi-cab service aggregator Uber, founded in 2009, has been such a spectacular success that it has birthed a neo-euphemism 'Uberization' that refers to the use of under-utilized capacity or skills through tele-networks to provide highly economical and efficient services. The major market drivers of the industry are technological innovations including inventory-aware automation, warehouse execution systems (an evolution of warehouse management systems), IoT platforms, improved transport management systems and data analytics, and digitization of supply chain among many others.

Sustained growth in capacity and emerging solutions for cross-supply-chain visibility of shipments have also birthed successful logistics e-commerce startups such as Freightos and Saloodo, and several on-demand warehousing companies such as Flexe, Warehouse Exchange and Flowspace.

Online marketplaces for logistics services are well on their way to fulfilling a long-held promise – uberization of global transportation and warehousing networks by utilizing unused capacity instead of building capacity for peak demand, and all of this at unheard of, highly economical spend. The success of online marketplaces for products and services will drive the adoption of blockchain with integrated technologies to scale up, improve efficiencies, and reduce operational costs.

Mega cities and the millennial consumer

Mega cities are defined as having very large populations with residence rates of over 10 million people. The USA has 15 emerging mega cities; others are spread throughout the world and they can help us better understand where and why emerging markets are cropping up.

Over the next decade, there will be a significant rise in the number of mega cities worldwide. By 2030, the following 12 cities are expected to enter the ranks of the planet's mega cities:

- Bogota;
- Lahore;
- Lima;
- Luanda;
- Johannesburg;
- Ahmadabad;
- Hyderabad;
- Bangalore;
- Chennai;
- Bangkok;
- Chengdu;
- Ho Chi Minh City.

Notably, these cities are not in the declining markets of the US and Europe, but are spread throughout Asian and South American emerging markets.

The '"millennial generation' is a demographic cohort that emerged into young adulthood at the start of the new millennium. According to Pew Research, a millennial would be someone born between 1981 and 1996. Compared to their predecessors, they are more likely to live within these emerging market mega cities and belong to an expanding middle class with access to global markets through technology, more disposable income, and greater levels of education.

As a result of their educations and technological proficiency, millennial consumers are much more likely to perceive their economic or social situation in a global context – not only local or national. Thus they are driven toward a desire for quick, convenient and accessible retail experiences as well as a preference for retailers who participate in sustainable supply chains and corporate social responsibility. They are even willing to pay more to retailers that meet the latter criterion.

Furthermore, the millennial middle class has become the engine of consumer spending in emerging markets. If we break down the millennial middle class by geography, it becomes clear that most of this generation will be concentrated in the emerging markets. The middle class income group in the ASEAN region will exceed 100 million people by 2020.

Figure 9.3   Post-1990s consumers have different priorities

Post-90s consumers have different priorities

39%	27%	16%	10%	8%
Happiness seekers	Success seekers	Laid back	Spendthrifts	Homebirds

86% Believe success means pursuing a happy life (vs. 43%[1])	**64%** Believe success means being rich (vs. 55%)	**32%** Believe that "as long as you work hard, you can change your life" (vs. 45%)	**48%** Are willing to spend to try new things (vs. 34%)	**96%** Have parents paying for big ticket items (vs.21%)
54% Not concerned about brands, but the actual product (vs. 44%)	**58%** Buy what they like (vs. 41%)	**Less likely** To pay a premium new tecnology (27% vs. 37%)	**38%** Believe expensive products are better (vs. 25%)	**47%** willing to pay for the latest technology (vs. 37%)
53% willing to pay extra for environmentally friendly products (vs. 46%)	**Less likely** To save for rainy days: only 28% believe one should always prepare for uncertainty (vs. 39%)		**42%** Proud to afford small luxury items to show their taste (vs. 33%)	**54%** Seek for and pay a premium for good quality item (vs. 41%)

1 Statistics for the total survey population shown in brackets

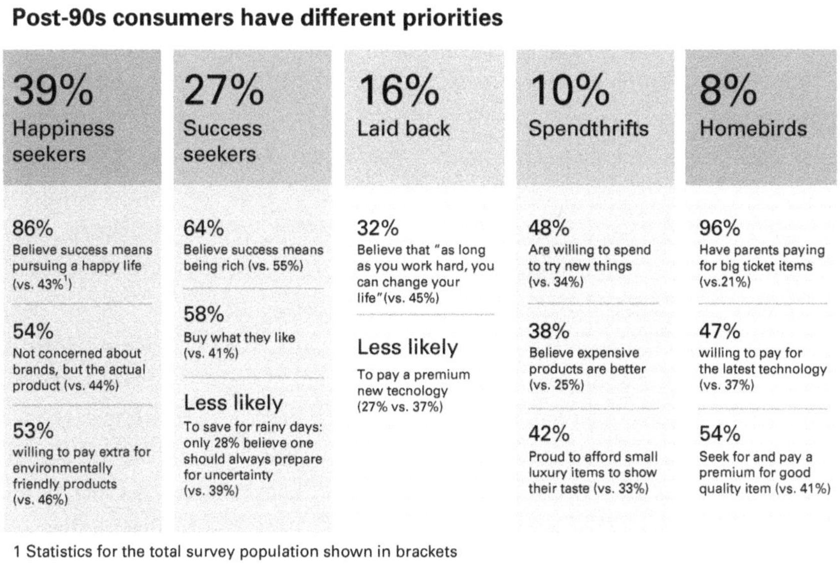

SOURCE McKinsey China, 2017

NOTE Statistics for the total survey population shown in brackets.

A Morgan Stanley report says that, by 2020, India will have 410 millennials, who will spend $330 billion annually. Consulting firm McKinsey and Company found that China's post-1990s generation (see Figure 9.3), which accounts for 16 per cent of its population, will 'help China shift towards a consumption driven economy, given their propensity to spend'.

In Africa, meanwhile, forecasters predict the average middle-class family will earn US $20,000 or more by 2020. The effects on consumption and supply chain will be felt locally and globally, through this population's use of expendable income as well as its cultural philosophies surrounding consumption.

Beyond millennials' personal goals of travel and retail consumption, there continues to be a widespread belief that businesses and retailers should positively affect a range of societal issues, such as resource scarcity, climate change and income inequality. This heavily affects how retailers – and the emerging e-commerce market – will function in the future. Both these trends – the rise of urban centres and the greater say of the millennial consumer – will push companies into leveraging technologies such as robotics, autonomous vehicles, machine learning, and artificial intelligence integrated with blockchain to drive efficiencies.

The growing complexity of industries

Industries such as automotive, consumer durables, pharmaceuticals, food products and shipping have three challenges in common: increasingly complex supply chains, growing market uncertainties and meeting fast-changing customer needs. All these industries have found use cases for blockchain. Car makers have started to develop blockchain-based solutions for all the nodes of supply chain, starting from procurement, to manufacturing, supplier relationship management, insurance, aftermarket sales and services, to innovative services for connected and autonomous cars.

In the shipping industry the biggest company, Maersk, has teamed up with IBM to form TradeLens, a blockchain-based platform to bring together ports and terminal operators and customers to create transparency, reduce complexity and possibly enable sharing of relevant information among all the stakeholders of the container shipping industry. Across sectors, large companies such as Walmart, Unilever, Nestlé, BHP Billiton, Walt Disney, Ford Motor Company, Siemens and scores of others are exploring blockchain for various uses. Recently, *Forbes* magazine reported that around 50 of Forbes Global 200 are doing so.[1]

Standardizing blockchain for ROI[2]

The supply chain industry is a classic example of how collaborative exercises work in the real world. Any ecosystem whose very survival depends on the quality of collaborative relationships between its members takes years of sustained efforts and calibration to achieve functional efficiency. The ecosystem of supply chains, even before it was recognized as one, was riddled with issues of trust between the participants, who continued to show their reluctance to effectively collaborate. Take any industry, examine closely its end-to-end supply chain network, and you are certain to see disparate silos that contribute to, even generate, inefficiencies that slow down the growth of that industry. For example, companies trading abroad from the UK waste about three hours per shipment requesting and funnelling data between trading partners by phone or email, whereas all that can be done digitally. Overall, more than 100 million hours of time are wasted every year in supply chain functions costing business a total $1.98 billion annually, revealed a recent study done by Zencargo, a UK-based digital freight forwarder.[2] In pharma, issues of trust, a lack of transparency, and an unwillingness to share data cause supply-chain inefficiencies that cost manufacturers a total of $25 billion annually, as per a McKinsey estimate.[3]

A critical step towards addressing issues of trust and inefficient functioning is to create standards, which, by definition, all parties are in agreement with.

For a thought experiment, consider the history of railroad infrastructure in the United States. If railroad companies involved in the initial construction of railway lines such as the Grand Trunk Railway and the Southern Pacific Transportation Company would have decided to create tracks of different width and sizes, it would be impossible to scale up and monetize the services that we have today. As a matter of fact, at the turn of the nineteenth century, America's rail companies were more than willing to cooperate to turn the railroads business into an oligopoly,[4] but not so much when it came to agreeing on standard rates to make the services accessible to all the customers. Industrialist and financier JP Morgan, himself a railroad company owner[5] brought together railroad presidents through conferences to agree upon standardized rates for travellers. A takeaway from that example is that standards must be created with the primary aim of improving efficiencies that would benefit the customer. Another is that creating standards would be one way to ensure that large businesses do not collaborate among themselves to keep out competition. A good way to create standards would be to establish a shared platform not owned by one industry or entity or company, but rather is shared by all.

A great example of such a shared platform is Internet Engineering Task Force (IETF), a non-profit organization that determines the standardization of internet protocols. Any entity from any part of the world, having gained the required expertise, can become a member of IETF. In fact, IETF is responsible for development and management of the Internet Protocol Suite (TCP/IP),[6] a set of standards that enabled worldwide proliferation of interconnected networks, or internet in short.

Another stellar example of creating a standard that galvanized supply chains was containerization in shipping. When discussing the IBM–Maersk blockchain platform we looked at how containerization, introduced in 1956, transformed the business of shipping. All it took was the creation of a standard 8 feet wide, 40 feet long, and 8 feet high shipping container to bring down the cost of loading by a factor of 100. That was one of the biggest supply chain innovations, one that fuelled the exponential growth of shipping and accelerated globalization.

There needs to be a similar thought process when we talk about standards for blockchain and integrated technologies and their applications within the supply chain. Blockchain is an emerging technology. Therefore it's understandable that presently there are no established standards without which users cannot access blockchain, in the same way that devices (and therefore people) cannot access the internet without performing the TCP handshake, and transporters cannot move goods by sea without putting them into standard-size containers.

There are several organizations that are working on the creation and establishment of standards for blockchain. The problem is, none of their standards are universally followed. In the UK, the British Standards Institution (BSI) has commissioned RAND Europe to carry out a study to understand some of the areas related to blockchain that could use standardization from the perspective of a UK stakeholder.[7] BSI is a historic institution that created the earliest standard for locomotive, machinery and BS 5750 for quality management, the ancestor of ISO 9000. BSI's standard for blockchain is called Publicly Available Specification (PAS) 19688.

In the USA, the given job is being done by IEEE Standards Association (IEEE-SA), a standards-setting body within the Institute of Electrical and Electronics Engineers (IEEE). The IEEE, which was formed in the 19th century, is known worldwide for creating WiFi standards such as IEEE 802.11. IEEE has always worked at the forefront of technological development.[8] For example, currently IEEE is working to create standards for connected and autonomous cars. It has also developed a standard for blockchain called IEEE 2418.3, to be used for the application of blockchain in agriculture.[9]

In Australia, Standards Australia submitted a New Field of Technical Activity proposal for the ISO to consider developing standards to support blockchain.[10] ISO is popularly known for its quality management standards such as ISO 9000.[11] Since September 2016, ISO along with Standard Australia has created an initiative termed ISO/TC 307 for making new international standards on blockchain.

ISO/TC 307 has currently 33 member nations, including Germany, the United Kingdom, Japan, Russia, France, Singapore, China and the USA. It has eleven ISO blockchain standards under development.

Likewise, each industry is developing one or more collaborative platform to advance the adoption of blockchain. For example, Everledger is a provenance-tracking blockchain application for the diamond industry. Hyperledger is an open source collaborative effort hosted by the Linux Foundation, used by major tech companies such as IBM and SAP to advance cross-industry blockchain technologies. Then there is TradeLens, an IBM–Maersk driven permissioned blockchain that promises to transform the shipping industry.

We need bigger and bolder efforts to bring together all supply chain stakeholders from all industries to form global standards.

The centres of excellence within the universities can play an important role in creating such a shared platform that has participation from the government and the industry. Such a shared platform will give everyone an equal opportunity to not only trade but also take advantage of RoI^2.

At USC Marshall Centre for Global Supply Chain Management, we have taken the strategic initiative of launching the Institute of Blockchain in Supply Chain (IBISC), to put forth such an initiative. The objective of IBISC is to facilitate collaborative efforts between industry stakeholders and different government departments that we work with, such as the United States Department of Commerce, to drive standardization and implementation of blockchain within supply chain.

The future belongs to organizations that reach out upstream and downstream to find synergistic opportunities to partner with other players. This can only be made possible through a shared platform that integrates technologies for transparency and collaboration. Such a shared platform will create rapid transformation and high yield on ROI^2.

Re-imagining the future with blockchain

Organizations that approach the standard-driven adoption of blockchain will be able to create a future vastly different than how we imagine it today.

Imagine a future where you will be able to see the carbon footprint of a food product from farm to plate. Where you scan the tag on a McDonald's burger to see the end-to-end supply chain of each of its five SKUs. You can see the location of the farm where the particular crop of wheat was grown, the quality of the soil content of the farm, the number of employees working on the farm, their wages, check the names of transporters that moved the wheat to the warehouse, the place where it was milled into flour and see when was the last time the mill had done a pest control programme. And you can check the carbon footprint of ingredients at every node upstream all the way to the neatly packaged burger that sits on your plate, waiting to be consumed. Imagine the level of credibility, trust and authenticity that organizations will have to build in order to be a part of a supply chain network.

The year 2018 witnessed an increase in food recalls in the USA following reports of contamination and disease outbreak. Companies such as Kellogg's and Cargill had to recall thousands of food items. In September retail major Walmart swung into action and asked all suppliers of leafy green vegetables to upload their data to the blockchain within a year.[12] Walmart's blockchain solution, jointly developed with IBM, will not only help the retailer to improve supply chain transparency, it will also help it reduce costs in case of future food recalls. By tying incidences of outbreaks to the sources, retailers can identify the source and discard the food before it is put on shelves.

Inspired, Starbucks has also announced it is launching a pilot programme to incorporate blockchain into its coffee supply chain.[13] The programme will have the participation of select producers in Costa Rica, Colombia and Rwanda over an initial two-year period, according to an announcement issued just before the company's 2018 annual meeting of shareholders in Seattle.

Similarly, the palm oil industry's SUSTAIN blockchain platform will provide open access to palm oil industry stakeholders such as dealers and smallholders, who could use downloadable tools to establish traceability, monitor policy compliance, efficiently trade fresh fruit bunches, obtain best practice guides, and find out about available micro-financing.

Blockchain will help multinational companies ensure fair practices at contractor locations based in developing companies. A company headquartered in New York can check workers' biometric data such as fingerprints, facial recognition, age, etc. That will allow companies to prevent unfair practices like child labour.

Reflection

One may like it or not, but globalization is here to stay. It's unstoppable. Despite the current political climate where ideologies fly thick and fast and new points of contention and friction are discovered every day, despite Brexit and trade wars, the growth of the global economy and therefore the need for economic collaborations will continue to accelerate. Thanks to all the technology advancements, the world is becoming much more integrated. 5G, which made its debut in 2019, is up to 100 times faster than 4G.[14] The rapid increase in computing power will soon make artificial intelligence ubiquitous. 3D printing now makes parts for rockets, and wrist watches monitor our heart. All of these developments present immense opportunities for blockchain and integrated technologies.

The true opportunity for a global citizen will be that of supporting a circular economy and sustainability. Most relevant here, however, is the current inability of supply chain actors to track the provenance of materials, components and products throughout the chain so that anyone along the way can assert their circularity – from the moment they were first extracted or created, all the way through their (many) life cycles.

There are several blockchain-based solutions that are already doing that. For example, a blockchain software called Bext360, launched by US-based entrepreneur Daniel Jones, uses IoT, blockchain, and artificial intelligence to track commodities across coffee, seafood, timber, minerals, cotton and palm oil supply chains. Bext360 recently partnered with a Uganda-based coffee exporter, Great Lakes Coffee, and Denver, Colarado-based Coda Coffee to trace coffee beans through their journey from farm to espresso machine.[15]

At the end of the day, the biggest peril that we face is the continued loss of critical resources – water, air and top soil. The use of integrated blockchain technologies can help not only preserve but also protect our critical resources for centuries to come, by being responsible and holding accountability and visibility end-to-end for future generations.

Notes

1 https://www.forbes.com/sites/michaeldelcastillo/2018/07/03/big-blockchain-the-50-largest-public-companies-exploring-blockchain/
2 https://www.supplychaindive.com/news/digital-freight-forwarding-supply-chain-inefficiency/527945/
3 http://www.pharmtech.com/digital-supply-chain-seizing-pharma-s-untapped-opportunity
4 https://books.google.co.in/books?id=R4vjgmic44QC&redir_esc=y
5 http://www.hup.harvard.edu/catalog.php?isbn=9780674587298
6 https://www.ripe.net/participate/internet-governance/internet-technical-community/ietf
7 https://www.rand.org/randeurope/research/projects/blockchain-standards.html
8 https://www.ieee.org/about/ieee-history.html
9 http://standards.ieee.org/develop/project/2418.3.html
10 https://www.standards.org.au/engagement-events/flagship-projects/blockchain
11 https://www.iso.org/committee/6266604.html
12 https://www.forbes.com/sites/andrewrossow/2018/09/25/why-walmarts-move-to-the-blockchain-could-do-more-than-cure-e-coli-outbreaks/

13 https://www.platinumtradinginstitute.com/crypto/a-newly-found-interest-in-blockchain-technology

14 https://www.cnet.com/news/5g-is-finally-starting-to-feel-real/

15 https://www.ibtimes.co.uk/blockchain-traceable-coffee-bext360-partners-africa-europe-north-america-1645350

ACKNOWLEDGEMENTS

Nick Vyas

I want to first thank my incredible wife Hemali for continuing to encourage me to pursue my dreams and stretch my boundaries. From helping me contextualize early drafts, to editing the final book – you are a blessing in my life. To my children Siddhartha and Pooja who have been incredibly supportive. Your passion for life and social consciousness inspires me to focus on what excites me more than words can describe. I also want to thank my late parents for their unconditional love and nurturing, which has shaped me into who I am today. And I also want to thank my sisters Anju and Uma, and my brothers-in-law Rohan and Rakesh, for their selfless gestures of support throughout the writing process.

I would like to thank my co-authors and remarkable friends Bhaskar Krishnamachari and Aljosja Beije for your countless insights and for bringing your unique perspectives on IOT, AI, ML and blockchain. It's amazing what we've been able to put together through our combined efforts. You are amazing teammates to work with, and I hope that this is one of many books we write together.

Thank you to my friends Jonathan Rosenthal, Gene Seroka, Rob Allan, Maureen Smith, Randy Kendrick, Noel Hacegaba, Rick Blasgen, Patrick Burnson and others who fostered conversations on blockchain when no one else was discussing blockchain in the supply chain.

Thank you to Nenah and Hemali for looking over the chapters and helping the book to realize its final form.

Thank you to Julia and Ro'isin at Kogan Page. From our initial meeting in Amsterdam, to updating multiple versions of the text, to the book's final publishing – you have been a joy to work with.

Gratitude goes out to my team at USC Marshall School of Business – Marvi, Cindy, Katy, and Darcie. Your continued support running MS in GSCM and Center of GSCM is greatly appreciated.

Special thanks to my contributors Aanand, Soumyo, Riddhi, and Dilmini for supplying various ideas for the book.

I want to thank my colleagues at USC Marshall Business School, Data Science & Operations (DSO) – especially Yehuda, Raj, Raman, Kimon, Vishal, Abbass, Omar and others for encouraging me and accepting me into the department.

Thank you to my students – past, current, and future. It is because of you that I do what I do in higher education.

I am blessed to have so many friends, followers and supporters that I cannot name here – thank you for your continued support throughout my journey leading the global supply chain.

Lastly, I'd like to send sincere appreciation to my mentor and friend, Dr Ravi Kumar, for believing and trusting in my ability to enter into the higher education space.

Aljosja Beije

The point of a journey is not to arrive. And yet, here we are; a finished book. With all the i's dotted and t's crossed, now is the time for reflection and thanking those that have accompanied us on this journey. Nick, Bhaskar, most of our communication was 'cold binary' as a result of the physical distance between Rotterdam and Los Angeles, but this somehow became a 'warm analogue' friendship; therefore great thanks to the both of you! You are at the top of your respective fields and it is a privilege to be mentioned in the same breath as co-author of this book. Already looking forward to our next venture. Also, thank you Hemali, Siddhartha and Pooja for making me feel part of the family during my stay in your home; I already look forward to our kitchen table talks this year!

This book is as much about blockchain and supply chain management as it is about Deliver and Blocklab. Deliver gave me the opportunity to learn and was a continuous source of inspiration when writing the book. Therefore a big thanks to the Deliver core-team members: Alfred, Bas, Bob, Elric and Mikhail from ABN-AMRO Bank, Eric-Jan, Lars, Robert, Simon and Ward from Samsung SDS and Maarten and Martijn from Port of Rotterdam. We have only just begun!

Blocklab started out just like this book, as a clean piece of paper. Fast forward to March 2019 and we find ourselves working on some of the most exciting blockchain projects in energy and eogistics. Thank you Janjoost, with whom I share the love for uphill battles. Thank you Ilhan, Jan-Gerrit, Jorik and Max; you guys are the best! A double thank you to Max, who helped with proofreading. A big thanks also to Blocklab's board members Emile Hoogsteden and Tim de Knegt from the Port of Rotterdam and Menno Huijs from the Municipality of Rotterdam, who all three manage to combine vision with the typical Rotterdam 'can do' attitude.

A big thanks to Paul Walter from the Port of Rotterdam and Staszek Chlapowski from Hoogwegt Group who provided detailed feedback on some of the draft chapters. Also thanks to all those people I have met at conferences, worked with in projects etc. You have all been a great source of inspiration. What may have looked like absenteeism to you, was actually my mind wondering off how something you said could be incorporated into the book.

Thank you amazingly efficient team at Kogan Page. Your guidance and attention to detail has been extremely helpful for this author newbie.

Thank you family and friends for quietly accepting my absence from birthday parties, cancelling dinner appointments and other anti-social behavior. I'll do my best to make up for it! Thank you mum, for making sure 'giving up' isn't part of my vocabulary.

Last but not least a big thank you to my girl, Madelief. When we met, you thought it was cool that I was out of bed at 8 o'clock on Saturday to work on a book and despite all the hours I had to put in during weekends and holidays, you still think the same way.

Dedicated in loving memory of Albert Beije, my dad and best friend.

Bhaskar Krishnamachari

I would like to dedicate my efforts in this project to the memory of my mother, Vijayalakshmi Krishnamachari, who has been an inspiration and source of immeasurable support all my life.

My deep thanks to my wife, Zhen, and my dear children Shriram, Anuj and little Lila for all their loving support and encouragement, and my father, T R Krishnamachari, whose background in economics and government audit has played a huge role in expanding my interests beyond pure technology to considering its impact on business and society, the very theme of this book.

I would like to express my gratitude to my colleagues, students, staff and leadership at the USC Viterbi School of Engineering for all their support, particularly as I undertook my explorations of Blockchain technology through the auspices of our relatively new Centre for Cyber-Physical Systems and the Internet of Things. I would like to particularly thank Dr Gowri Sankar Ramachandran for working with me intensely on relevant topics in the past two years, Ms Brienne Moore, our centre coordinator for helping to organize many interdisciplinary events that have grown my own understanding of this emerging space, and Dean Yannis Yortsos for his steadfast encouragement and support for interdisciplinary initiatives. I would like to thank the many industry leaders that have been kind enough to share their insights about the implications of this emerging technology with me.

I took on this writing project only because of the trust I had in my colleague Nick Vyas that he could help me understand the implications of this technology in the business context of supply chain, and it has been an extremely enriching and rewarding experience to learn from him. I am just as grateful to Aljosja Beije for the rich conversations we have had and his generous sharing of lessons he has learned himself as a pioneering practitioner in this area. It was so rewarding to work together as a team, and I look forward to continued interactions with both my co-authors.

INDEX

CPSIA information can be obtained
at www.ICGtesting.com
Printed in the USA
JSHW022146010820
7058JS00001B/1

9 780749 484026